CONTRIBUTORY NEGLIGENCE

Justin Levinson

of Middle Temple, Barrister

© Justin Levinson 2002

Published by
EMIS Professional Publishing Ltd
31–33 Stonehills House
Welwyn Garden City
Hertfordshire
AL8 6PU

ISBN 1 85811 292 3

Typeset by Tracey Dabell.

Cover design by Jane Conway.

Printed and bound in the UK by
Creative Print and Design (Wales), Ebbw Vale.

CONTENTS

FOREWORD

This book is intended as a practical guide to the workings of the Law Reform (Contributory Negligence) Act 1945. This apparently straightforward Act is frequently encountered in personal injury and, increasingly, other areas of practice and has given rise to some complicated problems.

The book is divided into two parts. Part One considers the principles of the defence of contributory negligence, its application to different areas of practice and related matters.

Part Two is arranged by category and contains examples of cases involving allegations of contributory negligence. The emphasis is on situations which are likely to recur and be encountered by practitioners.

Contributory negligence is a commonly raised defence and one of the difficulties facing practitioners in making accurate predictions as to the likely outcome of litigation is that, whilst there are many good sources available enabling an estimate to be made as to the appropriate level of damages, one is frequently left to resort to intuition when it comes to estimating the likely extent of any finding of contributory negligence. As such a large proportion of claims are resolved by settlement, practitioners rarely have the opportunity to compare their predictions with judicial decisions.

It is self evident that the margin of error can become unsatisfactory when a confident estimate of the level of damages is multiplied by an uncertain percentage to take account of contributory negligence.

It is hoped that the collection of cases in Part Two of this book will help to remove some of the uncertainty. The decisions, of course, all turn on their own facts, but it will be seen that there are some discernible patterns and tariffs have developed in some frequently recurring situations.

I have used the descriptions claimant and defendant throughout for ease of reading. I have done so both where the litigation pre-dates the coming into force of the Civil Procedure Rules 1998 and where the litigation was conducted outside of England and Wales.

The law is stated as it is thought to be on 7 February 2002.

Justin Levinson
Temple.
February 2002

Publisher's Note

EMIS Professional Publishing welcome the submission of case reports that will enhance this title in future editions and in any electronic version which EMIS produces. Any such submissions should be made to the Editor, *Contributory Negligence* at the publisher's address on page (ii). They will be acknowledged and, if published, qualify the submissor for a voucher redeemable against EMIS Professional Publishing products and services.

The author may be contacted through the publisher most effectively through editorial@emispp.com.

TABLE OF CASES

TABLE OF STATUTES

TABLE OF ABBREVIATIONS

CA ....Court of Appeal
CC..County Court
Ch D....................................Chancery Division of the High Court of Justice
CPR ....Civil Procedure Rules 1998 as amended
HL ....House of Lords (England & Wales)
HLS ....House of Lords (Scotland)
IH ....Inner House of the Court of Session
KBD ....King's Bench Division of the High Court of Justice
LR(CN)A 1945 ....Law Reform (Contributory Negligence) Act 1945
NICA ....Court of Appeal in N Ireland
NIQB ....Queen's Bench Division of the High Court of Justice in N Ireland
OH ....Outer House of the Court of Session
OR ....Official Referee's Court / Technology and Construction Court
PC ....Privy Council
QBD ....Queen's Bench Division of the High Court of Justice
SH..Sheriff Court
SP..Sheriff Principal

PART ONE
GENERAL PRINCIPLES

CHAPTER ONE
INTRODUCTION

At common law, prior to the coming into force of the Law Reform (Contributory Negligence) Act 1945,[1] contributory negligence was a complete defence to a claim.[2] Accordingly, where both parties were at fault, there was no scope for apportioning the loss between them and the court had to consider "whose negligence was the real or substantial cause of the accident."[3] If the fault was the claimant's, the claim failed and no compensation was payable.

The position was fundamentally altered by the LR(CN)A 1945, which removed the common law obstacle faced by careless claimants.

> "The legal effect of the Act of 1945 is simple enough. If the [claimant's] negligence was one of the causes of his damage, he is no longer defeated altogether. He gets reduced damages."[4]

In order to make out the defence of contributory negligence, it is not necessary to show that the claimant's conduct amounted to a breach of some duty owed to the defendant; it is sufficient to show a lack of reasonable care by the claimant for his own safety.[5]

Accordingly, in the normal personal injuries case the defence of contributory negligence can arise where the claimant's fault contributes to cause the accident, or where the claimant exposes himself to a risk of being involved

---

1. Royal Assent was given on 15 June 1945.
2. *Butterfield* v *Forrester* (1809) 11 East 60.
3. *Swadling* v *Cooper* [1931] AC 1 (HL).
4. *Davies* v *Swan Motor Co (Swansea) Ltd* [1949] 2 KB 291 per Denning LJ at 322, [1949] 1 All ER 620 (CA).
5. *Davies* v *Swan Motor Co (Swansea) Ltd* [1949] 2 KB 291, [1949] 1 All ER 620 (CA).

in an accident, or where the claimant fails to take reasonable precautions to minimise his injuries should an accident occur.

The Act applies where damage is caused partly as the result of the claimant's fault and partly as the result of the defendant's fault and enables a court to reduce the claimant's damages to the extent thought just and equitable having regard to the extent to which the claimant was himself to blame for his loss.

> "The principle involved is that where a man is part author of his own injury, he cannot call on the other party to compensate him in full."[6]

Accordingly, unlike other defences, contributory negligence will generally only be a partial defence to a claim.

The court must consider whether the damage sustained was caused:

(a) wholly by the fault of the claimant: in which case the claim fails and the Act does not apply;

(b) wholly by the fault of the defendant: in which case the claim succeeds entirely and the Act again does not apply; or

(c) partly by the claimant's fault and partly by the defendant's fault: in which case the Act does apply.

In the last of these scenarios the court must assess the damages to which the claimant would have been entitled had it not been for any contributory negligence and thereafter the extent to which it is appropriate to reduce the claimant's damages to reflect his responsibility for the damage.

Accordingly, if the court finds that the claimant's contributory negligence amounts to 25% and that he would otherwise have been entitled to an award of damages of £10,000, the court will award the claimant £7,500.

Whilst the Act does not apply to claims brought under all causes of action, its scope is not confined to claims brought in negligence.[7]

---

6. *Nance* v *British Columbia Electric Railway Co Ltd* [1951] AC 601 per Viscount Simon at 611, [1951] 2 All ER 448 (PC).

7. For consideration of the types of claim in which contributory negligence may be raised, reference should be made to Chapter 6 below.

The Act applies to Scotland as well as England and Wales, but not to Northern Ireland.[8] The position in Northern Ireland is governed by the Law Reform (Miscellaneous Provisions) Act (Northern Ireland) 1948.[9] There is also similar legislation in the Isle of Man,[10] Jersey[11] and Guernsey.[12]

Most common law jurisdictions have a similar doctrine. However, in the United States of America contributory negligence remains a complete bar to recovery in some states. In other states there will be a proportionate reduction provided that the claimant's share of the responsibility is less than 50% and in other states liability will be apportioned equally. Finally, there are a number of states that have the doctrine of comparative negligence and allow apportionment in line with principles similar to those applicable in the UK.

---

8. Section 6(2) LR(CN)A 1945.
9. Section 2(1), which is identically worded to section 1(1) LR(CN)A 1945.
10. Law Reform (Contributory Negligence) Act 1946.
11. Article 6 of the Law Reform (Miscellaneous Provisions) (Jersey) Law, 1960.
12. Section 1 of the Law Reform (Tort) (Guernsey) Law, 1979.

CHAPTER TWO
GENERAL PRINCIPLES

The partial defence of contributory negligence is available where some act or omission of the claimant has materially contributed to cause his damage and that act or omission can be described as having been negligent.

Section 1(1) of the LR(CN)A 1945 provides:

> "Where any person suffers damage as the result partly of his own fault and partly of the fault of any other person or persons, a claim in respect of that damage shall not be defeated by reason of the fault of the person suffering the damage, but the damages recoverable in respect thereof shall be reduced to such extent as the court thinks just and equitable having regard to the claimant's share in the responsibility for the damage ..."

The various elements of s 1(1) of the Act will now be considered in turn.

"Where any person..."

This includes a body of persons corporate or unincorporate.[1]

"...suffers damage..."

Damage is defined by s 4 of the Act to "include loss of life and personal injury" and the principles apply equally to damage to property.

The Act applies to the damage suffered by the claimant and the defence is not limited to cases where the claimant's fault has contributed to the event causing that damage. So, for example, the defence is available where the

---

1. Section 5 and Sched 1 Interpretation Act 1978.

claimant suffers injury in a road traffic accident as a result of his failure to wear a seat belt, whether or not the claimant bears any responsibility for the accident itself.

The section does not create a right of action; rather it removes an obstacle that existed at common law. The word "damage" refers to that which is suffered and for which a "claim" may be made and for which "damages" are recoverable. The word "damage" is quite inapt to cover the liability of a defendant who has had a judgment for damages for negligence given against him. Accordingly, a tortfeasor who is partly to blame for an injury cannot avail himself of the provisions of the subsection in order to obtain a contribution from someone else who is also to blame for the injury.[2]

"...as the result..."

"Causation is the decisive factor in determining whether there should be a reduced amount payable to the [claimant]"[3] and only fault which is causative of the damage suffered will be relevant for the purposes of contributory negligence. Causation is considered further in Chapter 4 below.

"...partly..."

It has been held that there is no reason why a claimant's contributory negligence should not be assessed at 100% in appropriate circumstances and further that there comes a stage where the claimant's degree of fault is so great that the court ceases to make fine distinctions and holds that, in practical terms, the fault is entirely that of the claimant.[4] A finding of 100% contributory negligence on the part of the claimant has been made in a number of reported cases.[5]

---

2. *Drinkwater* v *Kimber* [1952] 2 QB 281, [1952] 1 All ER 701 (CA).
3. *Davies* v *Swan Motor Co (Swansea) Ltd* [1949] 2 KB 291 per Denning LJ at 326, [1949] 1 All ER 620 (CA).
4. *Jayes* v *IMI (Kynoch) Ltd* [1985] ICR 155 (CA), see page 113 below. See also *Norris* v *W Moss & Sons Ltd* [1954] 1 WLR 346, [1954] 1 All ER 324 (CA), where the claimant's method of correcting a defect in scaffolding was described as being fantastically wrong and the sole cause of the accident, notwithstanding that his employers were in breach of statutory duty by the scaffolding being incorrectly erected.
5. See e.g. *Cope* v *Nickel Electro* [1980] CLY 1268 (QBD), the facts of which are set out at page 112 below, and *Humphries* v *Silent Channel Products* [1981] CLY 1209 (QBD), the facts of which are set out at page 113 below.

However, in *Pitts* v *Hunt*[6] the Court of Appeal said, obiter, that there could not be a finding of 100% contributory negligence. The wording of s 1 of the LR(CN)A 1945 provides that the defence applies where the claimant suffers damage partly as a result of his own fault and partly as a result of the fault of some other person(s). The effect of a finding of 100% contributory negligence would be that the damage was found to be wholly the fault of the claimant. Accordingly, the Act should not apply. If the damage was not even partly the fault of the defendant, the claim should fail on the basis that there was no breach of duty or causation. Later sub-sections of the Act also presuppose that the claimant will recover some damages.

Accordingly, there are conflicting Court of Appeal decisions on the point and whilst it is submitted that the logic in *Pitts* v *Hunt* is attractive, the point cannot be regarded as having been conclusively determined.[7]

"...of his own..."

Whilst the contributory negligence will generally be that of the claimant, there are certain circumstances where the claimant's damages will be reduced to take account of the negligence of a non-party. The doctrine of identification is considered in Chapter 5 below.

"...fault..."

"Fault" is defined as meaning negligence, breach of statutory duty or other act or omission which gives rise to a liability in tort or would, apart from the LR(CN)A 1945, give rise to the defence of contributory negligence.[8]

---

6. [1991] 1 QB 24 per Beldam LJ at 50, [1990] 3 WLR 542, [1990] 3 All ER 344 (CA), see page 221 below.
7. However, in the speeches of Lord Reid in *Imperial Chemical Industries Ltd* v *Shatwell* [1965] AC 656, [1964] 3 WLR 329, [1964] 2 All ER 999 (HL), and Lord Hoffmann in *Reeves* v *Commissioner of Police of the Metropolis* [2000] 1 AC 360, [1999] 3 WLR 363, [1999] 3 All ER 897 (HL), it was impliedly accepted that a 100% finding is possible, although the remarks were obiter in both cases.
8. Section 4 LR(CN)A 1945. Reference should be made to Chapter 6 below for consideration of the types of claim in which contributory negligence can be raised.

Fault on the part of the claimant for the purposes of the LR(CN)A 1945 means negligence[9] and no reduction should be made on the basis of some fault falling short of negligence, even if causative of the loss.[10]

Similarly, poor conduct on the part of the claimant will not, of itself, reduce the compensatory damages recoverable by him.[11] It has been said:

> "I entirely reject the contention that because [a claimant] who has suffered a civil wrong has behaved badly, this is a matter which the court may take into account when awarding him compensatory damages for physical injuries which he has sustained as the result of the wrong which has been unlawfully inflicted on him ... I cannot see how logically or on any principle of law the fact that [the claimant] has behaved rather badly and is a cantankerous old man can be even material when considering what is the proper compensation for the physical injury which he has suffered."[12]

In order to constitute contributory negligence, it is not necessary that the claimant's conduct amounted to breach of a duty owed to the defendant, although it may well do.[13] It is sufficient to show that the claimant failed to take reasonable care for his own safety and contributed, by that failure, to his injury.[14]

> "It is, perhaps, unfortunate that the phrase 'contributory negligence' uses the word 'negligence' in a sense somewhat different from that which the latter word would bear when negligence is the cause of action."[15]

---

9. Or a breach of statutory duty by the claimant himself. See *Boyle* v *Kodak Ltd* [1969] 1 WLR 661, [1969] 2 All ER 439 (HL), page 132 below.
10. *Jones* v *Price* [1963] CLY 2316 (CA).
11. Although poor conduct might reduce or extinguish any aggravated or exemplary damages. See *Lane* v *Holloway* [1968] 1 QB 379, [1967] 3 WLR 1003, [1967] 3 All ER 129 (CA), the facts of which are set out at page 295 below.
12. *Lane* v *Holloway* [1968] 1 QB 379 per Salmon LJ at 390, a case where the claimant provoked an assault from the defendant, see page 295 below.
13. Where the claimant's breach of duty causes the defendant damage, this will entitle the defendant to counterclaim.
14. *Nance* v *British Columbia Electric Railway Co Ltd* [1951] AC 601, [1951] 2 All ER 448 (PC). See also *Davies* v *Swan Motor Co (Swansea) Ltd* [1949] 2 KB 291, [1949] 1 All ER 620 (CA).
15. *Nance* v *British Columbia Electric Railway Co Ltd*, supra, per Viscount Simon at 612.

Accordingly, the defence might be better described by the title "contributory fault".

> "Although contributory negligence does not depend on a duty of care, it does depend on foreseeability. Just as actionable negligence requires the foreseeability of harm to others, so contributory negligence requires the foreseeability of harm to oneself. A person is guilty of contributory negligence if he ought reasonably to have foreseen that, if he did not act as a reasonable, prudent man, he might hurt himself; and in his reckonings he must take into account the possibility of others being careless."[16]

There is plainly a distinction between deliberate or reckless conduct and conduct which is merely negligent. However, there is no valid distinction between negligence in not noticing a danger and negligence after noticing it. So, if a motorist notices an obstruction and deliberately or recklessly runs into it, he will not be permitted to recover as the accident will have been his fault.[17] However, if he is simply negligent in not taking steps to avoid the obstruction, then he could recover subject to his contributory negligence.[18]

Where the claimant's actions constitute a common law crime (e.g. escaping from custody), which does not give rise to tortious liability, the LR(CN)A 1945 will not apply.[19]

The standard of care required of the claimant is considered in Chapter 3 below.

---

16. *Jones* v *Livox Quarries Ltd* [1952] 2 QB 608 (CA) per Denning LJ at 615. However, in relation to this passage it was said by Lord Kilbrandon in *Westwood* v *Post Office* [1974] AC 1 at 17, [1973] 3 WLR 287, [1973] 3 All ER 184 (HL), "the closing words of the passage from Denning LJ's judgment ... while appropriate to a common law claim, which was there being considered, may be inapplicable in a case of statutory liability".
17. However, a deliberate act can constitute "fault" for the purposes of contributory negligence as in *Reeves* v *Commissioner of Police of the Metropolis* [2000] 1 AC 360, [1999] 3 WLR 363, [1999] 3 All ER 897 (HL), where a suicide was held to amount to contributory negligence in circumstances where the defendant's breach of duty was the failure to prevent the suicide in the context of it being a known risk. See page 256 below.
18. *Davies* v *Swan Motor Co (Swansea) Ltd*, supra, *Harvey* v *Road Haulage Executive* [1952] 1 KB 120, (1952) 95 SJ 759 (CA).
19. *Vellino* v *Chief Constable of Greater Manchester Police* [2002] 1 WLR 218 (CA), but see *Revill* v *Newberry* [1996] QB 567, [1996] 2 WLR 239, [1996] 1 All ER 291 (CA), the facts of which are set out at page 292 below.

"...and partly of the fault of any other person or persons..."

The LR(CN)A 1945:

> "applies only in a case where the accident is caused partly by the
> fault of the [claimant] and partly by the fault of somebody else ... the
> common law principle is still valid to this extent, that, if the accident
> is wholly caused by the [claimant's] own fault he is disentitled to
> recover."[20]

Where both an employer and an employee are in breach of statutory duty,
there will be no liability on the part of the employer where the accident was
the fault of the employee and there is no fault on the part of the employer,
which goes beyond or is independent of the employee's fault.[21] Accordingly,
where an employer has properly delegated the performance of a statutory
duty to an employee who is injured by reason of his failure to comply with
that duty, the employee will be unable to argue that his injuries are
attributable to the employer's breach of statutory duty as opposed to his own
act or omission.[22]

It has been said:

> "In each case it is a question of fact whether or not a breach of
> [statutory duty] by an employer through the fault of an employee
> gives rise to any claim by that employee. An employer can defeat
> such claim if he can say:
>
> > 'I am in breach of the regulations because of, and only because
> > of, your default. I, myself, have not failed in any respect (apart
> > from my vicarious default through your wrongful act) and my
> > breach is co-terminous with yours.'"[23]

---

20. *Ginty* v *Belmont Building Supplies Ltd* [1959] 1 All ER 414 per Pearson J at 424
    (QBD).
21. *Ginty* v *Belmont Building Supplies Ltd*, supra.
22. *Gallagher* v *Dorman, Long & Co Ltd* [1947] 2 All ER 38 (CA). See also *Manwaring* v
    Billington [1952] 2 All ER 747 (CA), where there was no formal delegation, but
    nonetheless the accident only occurred by reason of the claimant's failure to carry
    out his instructions. See page 99 below for the facts.
23. *Jenner* v *Allen West & Co Ltd* [1959] 1 WLR 554 per Pearce LJ at 561, [1959] 2 All
    ER 115 (CA).

However, when there has been a breach of statutory duty by both the claimant and the defendant, then "however venial the fault of each of them they must share between them the responsibility for the whole of the damage".[24]

The provisions of the LR(CN)A 1945 bind the Crown.[25]

The various causes of action to which the defence can be raised are considered in Chapter 6.

"...the damages recoverable in respect thereof shall be reduced..."

It is clear that the correct approach is to first calculate the damages to which the claimant would have been entitled, disregarding any contributory negligence. The extent of any reduction for contributory negligence should then be assessed in accordance with the principles set out below and that reduction should then be applied to the sum to which the claimant would otherwise have been entitled.

Similarly, when apportioning liability between a claimant and several defendants, the claimant's damages should first be calculated. Those damages should then be reduced as appropriate to take account of any contributory negligence on the claimant's part. Thereafter, the liability of the defendants *inter se* should be considered pursuant to the Civil Liability (Contribution) Act 1978.[26] It is wrong to deal with the second and third issues simultaneously. The assessment of the claimant's share in the responsibility for the damage suffered does not involve a determination of each defendant's culpability, but rather the totality of the defendants' negligence. Accordingly, the claimant's damages will be reduced by the same percentage against each defendant.

It has been held by the EFTA Court of Justice[27] that as third party motor insurance enabling an injured third party to obtain compensation is

---

24. *Boyle* v *Kodak Ltd* [1969] 1 WLR 661 per Lord Diplock at 674, [1969] 2 All ER 439 (HL), see page 132 below.
25. Section 4 Crown Proceedings Act 1947 as amended.
26. *Fitzgerald* v *Lane* [1989] AC 328, [1988] 3 WLR 356, [1988] 2 All ER 961 (HL), see page 234 below.
27. *Storebrand Skadeforsikring AS* v *Finanger* [2000] Lloyd's Rep IR 462, [1999] 3 CMLR 863 (EFTA Court of Justice), see page 230 below.

compulsory throughout the EEA, a national law[28] denying compensation to a passenger in a motor vehicle who knew the driver to be unfit to drive is incompatible with European law. Whilst a reduction for contributory negligence is permissible in exceptional circumstances, a disproportionate reduction would be incompatible with the Motor Vehicle Insurance Directives.[29]

In *South Australia Asset Management Corporation* v *York Montague Ltd*[30] it was held that where a professional adviser has provided negligent information (as opposed to advice), his liability will be restricted to the specific consequences of that information being inaccurate. Accordingly, where a valuer instructed by a lender has negligently overvalued a property, the valuer's liability will generally be "capped" at the difference between the negligent valuation and a correct valuation. It will not, therefore, include all of the consequences flowing from the transaction, such as a fall in the property market, where these exceed the extent of the overvaluation.

The interaction between this principle and contributory negligence was considered in *Platform Home Loans Ltd* v *Oyston Shipways Ltd*.[31] It was held that where only part of the overall loss is recoverable in damages on the principles set out in the *South Australia Asset Management Corporation* case, the damages should not be reduced twice (once to take account of the "cap" and then again for contributory negligence). Rather, the total amount of the loss should be reduced to take account of any contributory negligence and the claimant awarded that reduced figure or the damages recoverable on *South Australia Asset Management Corporation* principles, whichever is the lower.

"...the court..."

The "court" means in relation to any claim, the court or arbitrator by or before whom the claim falls to be determined.[32]

---

28. Such as existed in Norway. In the United Kingdom s 149 of the Road Traffic Act 1988 precludes the defence of *volenti non fit injuria* in cases arising out of road traffic accidents where insurance is compulsory.
29. First Council Directive 72/166, Second Council Directive 84/5 and Third Council Directive 90/232.
30. [1997] AC 191, [1996] 3 WLR 87, [1996] 3 All ER 365 (HL).
31. [2000] 2 AC 190, [1999] 2 WLR 518, [1999] 1 All ER 833 (HL), see page 197 below.
32. Section 4 LR(CN)A 1945.

"...thinks just and equitable..."

Whilst the Act provides for the damages to be reduced to the extent the court thinks "just and equitable" having regard to the claimant's share in the responsibility for the damage, once a court has found contributory negligence, it may not disregard that negligence when awarding damages on the ground that it would not be just and equitable to reduce the claimant's damages.[33]

"...having regard to the claimant's share in the responsibility for the damage..."

"Whilst causation is the decisive factor in determining whether there should be a reduced amount payable to the [claimant], nevertheless, the amount of the reduction does not depend solely on the degree of causation. The amount of the reduction is such an amount as may be found by the court to be 'just and equitable', having regard to the claimant's share in the 'responsibility' for the damage. This involves a consideration, not only of the causative potency of a particular factor, but also of its blameworthiness. The fact of standing on the steps of [a dustcart which is involved in an collision] is just as potent a factor in causing the damage, whether the person standing there be a servant acting negligently in the course of his employment or a boy in play or a youth doing it for a 'lark', but the degree of blameworthiness may be very different."[34]

In other words, "the decision ... must turn not simply on causation, but on responsibility".[35]

Accordingly, in *Cullip* v *Horsham DC*[36] a motorcyclist was found to have been negligent in coming round a blind bend so as to collide with a stationary

---

33. *Boothman* v *British Northrop Ltd* (1972) 13 KIR 112 (CA), disapproving the obiter remarks to the contrary of Fisher J in *Hawkins* v *Ian Ross (Castings) Ltd* [1970] 1 All ER 180 at 188 (QBD).
34. *Davies* v *Swan Motor Co (Swansea) Ltd* [1949] 2 KB 291 per Denning LJ at 326, [1949] 1 All ER 620 (CA). See also *Brown* v *Thompson* [1968] 1 WLR 1003, [1968] 2 All ER 708 (CA) where it was stressed that the emphasis was on fault and not solely on the causative potency of the acts or omissions.
35. *M'Lean* v *Bell* 1932 SC (HL) 21 per Lord Wright at 29 (HLS).
36. Unreported, 1981 (CA).

dust lorry. However, his fault was so small in comparison to that of the driver of the dust lorry in parking where he did, that the claimant motorcyclist's share of the responsibility for the accident was assessed at nil.

Further, in *C v Imperial Design Ltd*,[37] C, aged 13, was playing with some friends on an open area of land close to ID's factory. He came across a container that had a residue of waste solvent in it, which had been negligently discarded by ID. C set fire to the solvent, which exploded causing him to suffer severe burns. C knew that setting fire to the container was dangerous, but did not expect there to be an explosion. It was said:

> "the question ... is, [did C take] such care of his own safety as it is reasonable to expect of a 13-year-old child? In this case the answer is obviously that he [did] not ... The issue is one of apportionment ... there are two matters to be taken into account: the relative causative potency of what each of the parties did and their respective blameworthiness."[38]

On the former issue, C was indeed more responsible than ID. On the latter issue, however, C was simply too young and inexperienced to recognise the real risk of explosion. Overall, C's contributory negligence was assessed at 50%.

> "Section 1 [of the LR(CN)A 1945] requires the court to apportion ... not merely degrees of carelessness but 'responsibility', and ... an assessment of responsibility must take into account the policy of the rule, such as the Factories Acts, by which liability is imposed. A person may be responsible although he has not been careless at all, as in the case of breach of an absolute statutory duty. And he may have been careless without being responsible, as in the case of 'acts of inattention' by workmen."[39]

However, that is not to say that causation is not an important factor in determining the correct apportionment:

---

37. [2001] Env LR 593 (CA).
38. [2001] Env LR 593 per Hale LJ at 603.
39. *Reeves v Commissioner of Police of the Metropolis* [2000] 1 AC 360 per Lord Hoffmann at 371, [1999] 3 WLR 363, [1999] 3 All ER 897 (HL).

"A court must deal broadly with the problem of apportionment and in considering what is just and equitable must have regard to the blameworthiness of each party, but 'the claimant's share in the responsibility for the damage' cannot ... be assessed without considering the relative importance of his acts in causing the damage apart from his blameworthiness."[40]

"The words 'have regard to' call for the exercise of a broad judgment and any arithmetical conclusion is qualified by what is deemed to be fair and reasonable."[41]

Particularly in road traffic accidents, the respective faults of the parties are not to be calculated by assessing percentages attributable to different aspects of negligence in a mathematical computation, but rather by looking at the matter generally and doing justice in sharing out the blame.[42] However, the probabilities of damage can be a useful starting point where such data is available.[43]

Where both parties have been negligent, but there is no preponderance of culpability or causative potency, liability should be shared equally and contributory negligence should, therefore, be assessed at 50%.[44] Similarly, where both parties are to blame and there is no means of distinguishing between them, the blame should be cast equally on each.[45]

For example, in *Jenkins* v Holt[46] J drove his car into collision with H, who had commenced a U turn into the path of J's car. It was found that both parties would have seen each other if they had been exercising reasonable care.

---

40. *Stapley* v *Gypsum Mines Ltd* [1953] AC 663 per Lord Reid at 682, [1953] 3 WLR 279, [1953] 2 All ER 478 (HL).
41. *Palser* v *Grinling* [1948] AC 291 per Lord Simon at 315, [1948] 1 All ER 1 (HL).
42. *Gregory* v *Kelly* [1978] RTR 426 (QBD), see page 222 below.
43. See e.g. *Froom* v *Butcher* [1976] QB 286, [1975] 3 WLR 379, [1975] 3 All ER 520 (CA), where it was said that the damages for injuries caused in a road traffic accident by a failure to wear a seat belt should normally be reduced by 25% as the chances of injury are four times as great when a seat belt is not worn. See further page 246 below.
44. *McMath* v *Rimmer Brothers (Liverpool) Ltd* [1962] 1 WLR 1, [1961] 3 All ER 1154 (CA). See page 132 below for the facts.
45. *Baker* v *Market Harborough Industrial Co-Operative Society Ltd* [1953] 1 WLR 1472 (CA), a case where both drivers involved in a collision died. See page 215 below for the facts.
46. [1999] RTR 411 (CA).

Blame was apportioned equally on the basis that J neglected to avoid the danger created by H. It was said:

> "put in terms of negligence, the defendant created the danger of a collision and the [claimant] failed to avoid it. In these circumstances it seems to me that blame falls equally on both parties."[47]

Small percentages of apportionment ought not to be made and any contributory negligence will be disregarded unless the extent of the responsibility falling on one of the parties is at least 10%.[48]

Whilst the appropriate apportionment will vary from case to case, some guidance has been given. In the context of accidents at work it has been said that where an employer:

1.   fails to give instructions to an employee;

2.   fails to have in place a proper system of work; and

3.   is able to easily recognise that these failures are likely to result in serious injury;

he must be more at fault than the employee who is ultimately injured as a result of the failures of both of them to take reasonable care.[49]

Further, in cases concerning a breach of statutory duty:

> "the more culpable and continuing the breach of the regulation, the higher the percentage of blame that must fall on the defendant."[50]

Likewise, in *Quintas* v *National Smelting Co Ltd* it was said:

---

47. [1999] RTR 411 per Sedley LJ at 416.
48. *Johnson* v *Tennant Bros Ltd*, unreported, 1954 (CA). See also *Rushton* v *Turner Brothers Asbestos Co Ltd* [1960] 1 WLR 96 per Ashworth J at 102, [1959] 3 All ER 517 (QBD). Although see e.g. *Laszczyk* v *National Coal Board* [1954] 1 WLR 1426, [1954] 3 All ER 205 (QBD) where a 5% reduction was made, and *Johnson* v *Croggan & Co Ltd* [1954] 1 WLR 195, [1954] 1 All ER 121 (QBD), where a 99% reduction would have been made had liability been established.
49. *Evans* v *National Coal Board*, unreported, 1982 (CA).
50. *Mullard* v *Ben Line Steamers Ltd* [1970] 1 WLR 1414 per Sachs LJ at 1418, [1971] 2 All ER 424 (CA), see page 136 below.

"The nature and extent of the defendant's duty is, in my view, highly important in assessing the effect of the breach or failure of duty on the happening of the accident giving rise to the [claimant's] claim and on the conduct of the [claimant]. There is an interaction of factors, acts and omissions to be considered."[51]

In a case concerning a collision between a pedestrian and a motorist, the House of Lords found the motorist to be more blameworthy and Lord Reid said:

"A pedestrian has to look to both sides as well as forwards. He is going at perhaps 3 mph and at that speed he is rarely a danger to anyone else. The motorist has not got to look sideways though he may have to observe over a wide angle ahead: and if he is going at a considerable speed he must not relax his observation, for the consequences may be disastrous."[52]

---

51. [1961] 1 WLR 401 per Sellers LJ at 408, [1961] 1 All ER 630 (CA).
52. *Baker* v *Willoughby* [1970] AC 467 at 490, [1970] 2 WLR 50, [1969] 3 All ER 1528 (HL). See page 239 below for the facts.

CHAPTER THREE
STANDARD OF CARE

GENERALLY

The standard of care in contributory negligence is generally the same as that in negligence.[1] In other words, the standard is normally objective and the claimant is to be measured against the reasonable man in the circumstances.

The standard of care applicable will not necessarily be the same for all those involved in an accident.[2]

The standard of care to be expected may be enhanced by the claimant's knowledge of the risks involved[3] or lessened where the claimant has been thrown off guard by the defendant's conduct and reasonably induced to believe that he may proceed with safety.[4]

Subject to the situations discussed below, the standard is objective and no account will be taken of the particular characteristics of the claimant. In *Kelly v McElligott*[5] K fell through a skylight, which she could see, whilst trying to escape from a fire. As the standard of care to be applied was that of a person of reasonable prudence and fortitude, evidence of K's previous experience of fires was inadmissible.

Whilst there is no rule that inadvertence cannot amount to contributory negligence,[6] the standard required is only that of the reasonable man in the circumstances.

> "It is not every mistake or inadvertence that amounts to contributory negligence."[7]

> "[One] has no right to complain if in the agony of the collision the [other party] fails to take some step which might have prevented a collision unless that step is one which a reasonably careful man would fairly be expected to take in the circumstances."[8]

---

1. Accordingly, the apportionment will not be affected by which of the parties is the claimant. See *Henley* v *Cameron* (1949) 65 TLR 17 (CA).
2. See e.g. *Dawrant* v *Nutt* [1961] 1 WLR 253, [1960] 3 All ER 681 (QBD), the facts of which are set out at page 216 below.
3. *Hicks* v *British Transport Commission* [1958] 1 WLR 493, [1958] 2 All ER 39 (CA).
4. *North Eastern Railway* v *Wanless* (1874) LR 7 HL 12, 6 QB 481 (HL).
5. *Current Law* 47–51/6632 (Eire).
6. *Hicks* v *British Transport Commission* [1958] 1 WLR 493, [1958] 2 All ER 39 (CA).
7. *Gallagher* v *Dorman, Long & Co Ltd* [1947] 2 All ER 38 per Wrottesley LJ at 42 (CA).
8. *Swadling* v *Cooper* [1931] AC 1 per Lord Hailsham at 9 (HL).

Similarly, the taking of a reasonable risk by the claimant will not amount to contributory negligence, even if the risk could have been avoided:

> "There may be many cases where a [claimant] is 'free' in one sense to avoid the risk altogether but where it would be reasonable to run the risk. When the [claimant] has full or partial knowledge of the danger the question must always be: was the injury, in all the circumstances, including the [claimant's] knowledge, due solely to his own negligence or was it due solely to the negligence of the defendant or was it due to the negligence of each?"[9]

Accordingly, there was no contributory negligence on the part of a police officer whose car was damaged when he positioned it as a roadblock to obstruct the path of an escaping suspect, who drove into the police car at speed.[10] There was also no bar to recovery by the occupier of a requisitioned house who had reported a crack in the kitchen ceiling to the local authority, but continued using the kitchen until it fell and injured her as:

> "She was not free to avoid the danger. She had to stay there and live in her kitchen. Although she had notice of the danger, it does not disentitle her from recovering for the negligence of the defendants."[11]

The claimant will be guilty of contributory negligence if he ought reasonably to have foreseen that if he did not act as a reasonable, prudent man, he might hurt himself. In his reckonings he must take into account the possibility that others might be careless[12] as "a prudent man will guard against the possible negligence of others, when experience shows such negligence to be common".[13] However, it has been doubted whether one must reckon on others being careless in cases concerning a breach of statutory duty.[14]

---

9. *A C Billings & Sons v Riden* [1958] AC 240 per Lord Somervell at 266, [1957] 3 WLR 496, [1957] 3 All ER 1 (HL). See page 272 below for the facts.
10. *Hambley v Shepley* (1967) 63 DLR (2d) 94 (Canada).
11. *Greene v Chelsea Borough Council* [1954] 2 QB 127 per Denning LJ at 140, [1954] 3 WLR 12, [1954] 2 All ER 318 (CA). See also *Porter v Jones* [1942] 2 All ER 570 (CA).
12. See *Jones v Livox Quarries Ltd* [1952] 2 QB 608 (CA). See page 106 below.
13. *Grant v Sun Shipping Co Ltd* [1948] AC 549 per Lord Du Parcq at 567, [1948] 2 All ER 238 (HLS).
14. *Westwood v Post Office* [1974] AC 1, [1973] 3 WLR 287, [1973] 3 All ER 184 (HL).

Whilst a driver of a motor vehicle need not anticipate folly in all its forms, he is not "entitled to put out of consideration the teachings of experience as to the form these follies commonly take".[15]

CHILDREN

Infancy is not a status conferring rights[16] and whilst children can be found guilty of contributory negligence, a lower standard of care is usually expected of children than adults. Indeed, the Occupiers' Liability Act 1957[17] specifically provides that an occupier must be prepared for children to be less careful than adults.

The standard of care expected of a child claimant will be proportionate to the age of the child, so as to take account of his or her particular level of understanding.[18] Accordingly, it has been held that a child's actions will not amount to contributory negligence where they are only that which is to be expected of a child of that age.[19]

Further:

> "When it comes to taking care of themselves, there is a greater difference between big and little children than there is between big children and adults ... Adults and big children can be guilty of contributory negligence; a little child cannot."[20]

The position has been summarised as follows:

> "A very young child cannot be guilty of contributory negligence. An older child may be. But it depends on the circumstances. A judge should only find a child guilty of contributory negligence if he or she

15. *London Passenger Transport Board* v *Upson* [1949] AC 155 per Lord Uthwatt at 173, [1949] 1 All ER 60 (HL).
16. *Glasgow Corp* v *Taylor* [1922] 1 AC 44 per Lord Sumner at 67 (HLS).
17. Section 2(3)(a).
18. *Minter* v *D A H Contractors (Cambridge) Ltd* [1983] CLY 2544 (CA).
19. *Jones* v *Lawrence* [1969] 3 All ER 267 (QBD), see page 172 below.
20. *Phipps* v *Rochester Corporation* [1955] 1 QB 450 per Devlin J at 458, [1955] 2 WLR 23, [1955] 1 All ER 129 (QBD).

is of such an age as to be expected to take precautions for his or her own safety: and then he or she is only to be found guilty if blame should be attached to him or her."[21]

However, the test is not wholly subjective as the applicable standard is that of an ordinary child of the claimant's age and an ordinary child is neither scatterbrained nor a paragon of prudence.[22]

In *Lynch* v *Nurdin*[23] N negligently left his horse and cart unattended in the street. L, aged 7, climbed onto the cart and was thrown down and injured when another child led the horse on. It was argued that L had been contributorily negligent in failing to exercise ordinary care. It was said:

> "Ordinary care must mean that degree of care which may reasonably be expected from a person in the [claimant's] situation; and this would evidently be very small indeed in so young a child."[24]

Further:

> "The most blameable carelessness of this servant having tempted the child, he ought not to reproach the child for yielding to that temptation. He has been the real and only cause of the mischief. He has been deficient in ordinary care; the child, acting without prudence or thought, has, however, shown these qualities in as great a degree as he could be expected to possess them."[25]

As a matter of law, there is no minimum age at which a child can be found guilty of contributory negligence[26] and it is difficult to ascertain a particular age below which, for practical purposes, contributory negligence will not be found. Certainly, the Scottish courts have been more willing to find contributory negligence against very young children than the English courts

---

21. *Gough* v *Thorne* [1966] 1 WLR 1387 per Lord Denning MR at 1390, [1966] 3 All ER 398 (CA). See page 170 below for the facts.
22. *Gough* v *Thorne* [1966] 1 WLR 1387 per Salmon LJ at 1391, [1966] 3 All ER 398 (CA). See also *Mullin* v *Richards* [1998] 1 WLR 1304, [1998] 1 All ER 920 (CA).
23. (1841) 1 QB 29.
24. Per Lord Denman CJ at 36.
25. Per Lord Denman CJ at 38.
26. The Royal Commission on Civil Liability and Compensation for Personal Injury, Cmnd. 7054–I (1978) recommended that children below the age of twelve should not be found guilty of contributory negligence in cases of injury caused by motor vehicles.

have been. For example, the Scottish Outer House[27] has found a five-year-old boy guilty of contributory negligence in running across a road, whereas the English Court of Appeal[28] has been unwilling to find contributory negligence even on the part of an eight-year-old girl who stepped out into the path of a moving car, saying:

> "The little girl was only eight years of age, and … it would not be right to count as negligence on her part such a momentary, though fatal, act of inattention or carelessness."[29]

In *Ducharme* v *Davies*[30] it was held that a three-year-old child was incapable of contributory negligence and that the negligence of a parent in failing to ensure that a child is restrained by a seat belt cannot be imputed to the child.

Reference should be made to Chapter 10 below for a selection of cases involving allegations of contributory negligence against children. Through examination of these, it is evident that no clear correlation exists between the ages of the children and the extent of the findings of contributory negligence. This can only partly be explained by the causative potency of their fault.

DILEMMA

The taking of a reasonable risk by the claimant will not amount to contributory negligence where the need to take that risk only arose by reason of the negligence or breach of statutory duty on the part of the defendant and the risk was one that a reasonable person in the claimant's position would have taken.

Accordingly, it will not necessarily be contributorily negligent where a person, who is placed in a position of danger or inconvenience by another's negligence, is forced to make a quick decision and chooses a course of action which turns out not to have been the best way out of the difficulty.[31]

---

27. *McKinnell* v *White* 1971 SLT 61 (OH), see page 169 below.
28. *Andrews* v *Freeborough* [1967] 1 QB 1, [1966] 3 WLR 342, [1966] 2 All ER 721 (CA), see page 171 below.
29. [1967] 1 QB 1 per Davies LJ at 16.
30. [1984] 1 WWR 699 (Canada), see also *Prudence* v *Lewis* (1966) *The Times*, May 21 (QBD).
31. *Swadling* v *Cooper* [1931] AC 1 (HL).

"When one man by his negligence puts another in a position of difficulty the court ought to be slow to find that other man negligent merely because he may have failed to do something which, looking back on it afterwards, might possibly have reduced the amount of damage. The question is whether at the time he ought to have done it and was negligent not to do it."[32]

So, in *Jones* v *Boyce*[33] when the horses of the defendant's stage coach bolted, the claimant was entitled to recover in respect of the injuries he sustained when, in the agony of the moment, he jumped from the stage coach, even though he would not have been injured had he remained in the stage coach as it did not, in fact, overturn.

However, the reasonable man should remain calm and take reasonable precautions for his own safety, even in a crisis; "it will not do to equate the reasonable man to the young man in a hurry".[34] In each case the court will determine the reasonableness of the claimant's actions by balancing the consequences of the defendant's negligence or breach of statutory duty against the risk taken by the claimant to extricate himself from the situation.

In *Sayers* v *Harlow UDC*[35] S found herself locked in a toilet cubicle as a result of a defective lock. She tried to escape by climbing over the door and placed a foot on a revolving toilet roll. She realised that she was not going to be able to escape this way and tried to climb down. In so doing, she put weight on the toilet roll, which revolved and she fell. It was held that it was reasonable in the circumstances for S to have explored the possibility of escaping in the way that she did. However, S was careless in allowing her balance to depend upon the toilet roll. Her contributory negligence was assessed at 25%.

Further, it has been held in an Australian case[36] that where the defendant's negligence puts the claimant in a position whereby he can only escape inconvenience by taking a risk, the claimant's reasonableness can only be assessed by weighing that risk against the inconvenience.

---

32. *The Older* (1949) 66 TLR 105 per Bucknill LJ at 109 (CA).
33. (1816) 1 Stark 493.
34. *Ghannan* v *Glasgow Corp* 1950 SC 23 per Lord Cooper at 28, 1950 SLT 2.
35. [1958] 1 WLR 623, [1958] 2 All ER 342 (CA).
36. *Caterson* v *Commissioner for Railways (NSW)* (1973) 47 ALJR 249 (Australia), see page 288 below.

EMPLOYEES

Whilst the standard of care in contributory negligence is generally the same as in negligence, this rule is modified in the case of employees injured as a result of their employer's breach of statutory duty. Accordingly, the result can differ according to whether the claim succeeds upon a breach of statutory duty or negligence.[37]

In *Caswell* v *Powell Duffryn Associated Collieries Ltd*[38] it was said that the courts should give:

> "due regard to the actual conditions under which men work in a factory or mine, to the long hours and the fatigue, to the slackening of attention which naturally comes from constant repetition of the same operation, to the noise and confusion in which the man works, to his preoccupation in what he is actually doing at the cost perhaps of some inattention to his own safety."[39]

In *Staveley Iron & Chemical Co Ltd* v *Jones*[40] J was employed at SIC's factory. He was preparing a load to be lifted in a pan by an overhead crane. Attached to the crane was a main hook, from which hung four chains with smaller hooks on the end. J and another employee attached the four hooks to the pan, but they failed to check that the main hook was over the centre of the pan. The crane driver lifted the pan without warning and did not pause after taking the strain to ensure that the weight would be taken evenly. The pan was raised and swung out, injuring J. It was argued that if the crane driver's error would not amount to contributory negligence in a claim brought by her, then it should not amount to negligence on the part of her employers in respect of a claim brought by another workman (J).

It was held that SIC were liable for the crane driver's negligence in failing to pause after taking the strain. There was insufficient evidence to find that J was contributorily negligent in not ensuring that the hook was centred. It was said by Lord Tucker:

---

37. For example, in *Westwood* v *Post Office* [1974] AC 1, [1973] 3 WLR 287, [1973] 3 All ER 184 (HL) there was no reduction for contributory negligence in a claim based upon a breach of statutory duty, but had the claim been decided in negligence, there may have been such a reduction.
38. [1940] AC 152, [1939] 3 All ER 722 (HL).
39. [1940] AC 152 per Lord Wright at 178.
40. [1956] AC 627, [1956] 2 WLR 479, [1956] 1 All ER 403 (HL).

"While accepting ... in relation to cases under the Factories Acts and other statutes imposing absolute obligations on employers or occupiers of premises [that it is not for every risky thing which a workman in a factory may do in his familiarity with the machinery that he ought to be held guilty of contributory negligence], I doubt very much whether [that principle was] intended or could properly be applied to a simple case of common law negligence ... where there was no evidence of work-people performing repetitive work under strain or for long hours at dangerous machines ...

I do not consider that [the LR(CN)A 1945] has in any way altered the standard of care which is required from workmen or employers ...

It is true that, in accordance with what was said in this House in *Caswell* v *Powell Duffryn Associated Collieries Ltd*[41] there may be cases, such as those involving breach of statutory duty, where an employer who is in breach of his duty cannot be heard, as against his own servant who has been injured thereby, to say that some risky act due to familiarity with the work or some inattention resulting from noise or strain amounts to contributory negligence. In this respect, it is possible the same act may have different consequences when the injured man is the [claimant] suing his employers, and where the employer is being sued by a third party (including another employee) in respect of the same act or omission. This is not so illogical as may appear at first sight when it is remembered that contributory negligence is not founded on breach of duty, although it generally involves a breach of duty, and that, in cases under the Factories Act, the purpose of imposing the absolute obligation is to protect the workmen against those very acts of inattention which are sometimes relied upon as constituting contributory negligence, so that too strict a standard would defeat the object of the statute. [The doctrine of contributory negligence] cannot be used so as to require any modification in the standard of care required from a workman in relation to his fellow servants or other third parties or the resulting liability of his employers."

In cases concerning an employer's breach of statutory duty, the court will be mindful of the purpose of that statutory duty. In *Mullard* v *Ben Line Steamers Ltd* it was said:

---

41. [1940] AC 152, [1939] 3 All ER 722 (HL), see above.

"What has happened was indeed exactly of the nature intended to be guarded against by the precautions prescribed by the regulations; and when a defendant's liability stems from such a breach the courts must be careful not to emasculate those regulations by the sidewind of apportionment. Moreover, the more culpable and continuing the breach of the regulation, the higher the percentage of blame that must fall on the defendant."[42]

Further:

"It has often been held that there is a high responsibility on a defendant who fails to comply with his statutory duty, which is absolute and has penal sanctions. A workman is not to be judged so severely."[43]

In *Grant* v *Sun Shipping Co Ltd* it was said:

"Almost every workman constantly, and justifiably, takes risks in the sense that he relies on others to do their duty, and trusts that they have done it. I am far from saying that everyone is entitled to assume, in all circumstances, that other persons will be careful. On the contrary, a prudent man will guard against the possible negligence of others, when experience shows such negligence to be common. Where, however, the negligence is a breach of regulations, made to secure the safety of workmen, which may be presumed to be strictly enforced in the ordinary course of a ship's discipline, I am not prepared to say that a workman is careless if he assumes that there has been compliance with the law."[44]

Where the employer has generated conditions in the employee, such as tiredness, which cause him to be careless, the courts will be reluctant to find contributory negligence on the part of the employee:

---

42. [1970] 1 WLR 1414 per Sachs LJ at 1418, [1971] 2 All ER 424 (CA), see page 136 below.
43. *Quintas* v *National Smelting Co Ltd* [1961] 1 WLR 401 per Sellers LJ at 408, [1961] 1 All ER 630 (CA).
44. [1948] AC 549 per Lord Du Parcq at 567, [1948] 2 All ER 238 (HLS), a case concerning a fall through an open and unlit hatch on a ship. The accident occurred before the coming into force of the LR(CN)A 1945 and so had contributory negligence been found, it would have afforded a complete defence. See page 143 below for the facts.

> "I decline to condemn a man as negligent of his own safety when the charge is made against him by employers who themselves produced the conditions which deprived him of the capacity to care properly for his own safety."[45]

Where a practice of ignoring an obvious danger has grown up, it will not generally be reasonable to expect an individual workman to take the initiative in devising and using precautions.[46]

The standard of care expected of an employee can also be affected by the manner in which he is paid:

> "Common sense entitles the court to assume that if [an employee] is working on piece-work [he] cannot be expected to take quite so much care for [his] own safety as if [he was] not."[47]

Reference should be made to Chapter 9 below for a selection of cases involving accidents at work and allegations of contributory negligence.

INFIRM PEOPLE

Where it is known or anticipated that a person may suffer from a disability, the extent of the duty of care owed to him will be adjusted in the light of that knowledge.[48] However, the position is different when it comes to considering contributory negligence and a distinction can be drawn between situations where the contributory negligence amounts to a breach of duty and situations where it simply amounts to a failure to take reasonable care for oneself.

---

45. *Smith* v *Stages* [1988] ICR 201 per Glidewell LJ at 213 (CA), approving the trial judge's observations. The point was not considered by the House of Lords at [1989] AC 928, [1989] 2 WLR 529, [1989] 1 All ER 833. See page 229 below for the facts. See also *Holmes* v *T & J Harrison Ltd* [1962] 1 Lloyd's Rep 455 (CA).
46. *General Cleaning Contractors Ltd* v *Christmas* [1953] AC 180, [1953] 2 WLR 6, [1952] 2 All ER 1110 (HL). See page 142 below for the facts.
47. *Boothman* v *British Northrop Ltd* (1972) 13 KIR 112 per Stephenson LJ at 119 (CA), see page 129 below.
48. *Paris* v *Stepney Borough Council* [1951] AC 367, [1951] 1 All ER 42 (HL), *Haley* v *London Electricity Board* [1965] AC 778, [1964] 3 WLR 479, [1964] 3 All ER 185 (HL).

In cases where the contributory negligence alleged amounts to a breach of duty, a person with special characteristics will owe the same duty of care to others as anyone else. The relevant standard of care will be the normal objective standard and no allowance will be made for any disabilities. If the position were otherwise, the person suffering from a disability would be in a better position as a claimant than he would be as a defendant.

For example, in the case of a collision between motor vehicles, the same standard will apply to both drivers and it is not open to one of the drivers to argue that for one reason or another he was unable to drive as skilfully as the other driver. Further, the standard remains unaltered even where one party knows of the other's lack of skill or disability.[49]

However, where the contributory negligence alleged is that the claimant failed to take reasonable care for his own safety, account can be taken of the limitations which the claimant's disability imposes. A defendant must take his victim as he finds him.[50]

> "On a question of contributory negligence, you are entitled to take into account the defective eyesight or other infirmity of a person who meets with an accident."[51]

More recently it has been said that "a mentally ill patient could only be held to the degree of care permitted by his diminished capacity".[52]

For example, in *Daly* v *Liverpool Corp*[53] a 69-year-old woman was run over by a bus. The bus driver saw the claimant crossing the road, but assumed that she would be able to get out of the way. However, the claimant was unable

---

49. *Nettleship* v *Weston* [1971] 2 QB 691, [1971] 3 WLR 370, [1971] 3 All ER 581 (CA), a case concerning a learner driver and her instructor. See page 222 below.
50. *Widdowson* v *Newgate Meat Corporation* [1998] PIQR P138 (CA), see page 235 below.
51. *M'Kibbin* v *Glasgow Corp* 1920 SC 590 per Lord Salvensen at 597 (IH), see also *Paul (R & W) Ltd* v *G E Railway* (1920) 36 TLR 344.
52. *Reeves* v *Commissioner of Police of the Metropolis* [2000] 1 AC 360 per Lord Hope at 385, [1999] 3 WLR 363, [1999] 3 All ER 897 (HL), approving the approach taken by the Supreme Court of North Dakota in *Champagne* v *USA* (1994) 513 NW 2d 75. See page 256 below for the facts of *Reeves* v *Commissioner of Police of the Metropolis*.
53. [1939] 2 All ER 142 (KBD).

to avoid the accident due to her advanced age. There was no finding of contributory negligence, as a tortfeasor must take his victim as he finds him.

However, people with disabilities are nonetheless expected to take reasonable precautions for their own safety and what is reasonable will be considered in the light of their characteristics. In *Haley* v *London Electricity Board*[54] it was held that those conducting excavations in a city pavement should anticipate the infirmities of those likely to be present, such as blind people. But equally, it was to be expected that a blind person would himself exercise reasonable care, which would involve him in taking the special precautions necessary for his safety. It was said:

> "Blind persons as well as other infirm persons cannot complain of a breach of duty if they do not themselves take great care and use such means of vigilance as are available to them."[55]

The taking of reasonable care might involve seeking available assistance in appropriate cases.[56]

In *Reeves* v *Commissioner of Police of the Metropolis*[57] it was held that a deliberate decision taken by someone of sound mind to commit suicide whilst in police custody amounted to contributory negligence. However, it was said that if the deceased had been of unsound mind, there may have been no such finding on the ground that it would not be just and equitable to attribute responsibility to someone who did not have a full understanding of the danger he was running, as in the cases involving young children.[58]

However, in *Baxter* v *Woolcombers Ltd*[59] B, a man of low intelligence, injured his hand on a machine whilst working for W as a result of W's failure to

---

54. [1965] AC 778, [1964] 3 WLR 479, [1964] 3 All ER 185 (HL).
55. [1965] AC 778 per Lord Hodson at 806.
56. *A C Billings & Sons* v *Riden* [1958] AC 240, [1957] 3 WLR 496, [1957] 3 All ER 1 (HL). See page 272 below for the facts.
57. [2000] 1 AC 360, [1999] 3 WLR 363, [1999] 3 All ER 897 (HL), see page 256 below.
58. See the speech of Lord Hoffmann at [2000] 1 AC 360, 372. See also *Kirkham* v *Chief Constable of Greater Manchester Police* [1989] 3 All ER 882 (QBD), where the trial judge found that no share of responsibility should be attributed under the LR(CN)A 1945 to a clinically depressed prisoner who committed suicide. That finding was not considered on the appeal reported at [1990] 2 QB 283, [1990] 2 WLR 987, [1990] 3 All ER 246 (CA).
59. (1963) 107 SJ 553 (CA).

provide a safe system of work and breach of statutory duty in failing to fence the machine. B's contributory negligence was assessed at two thirds. It was said that the accident could only have happened if B had been in direct disobedience of orders and it could not be said that such an act could not be regarded as contributory negligence. In connection with the conduct found to be negligent, the intelligence of B was irrelevant. The standard was that of a reasonable man and B had to be judged accordingly.[60] However, B's intelligence level was relevant to the standard of duty owed to him by his employers.

INTOXICATION

It is no defence to an allegation of contributory negligence to argue that the claimant was unable to take reasonable care for his own safety by reason of his self induced drunken state.[61] Accordingly, a passenger in a car who was too drunk to realise that the driver was unfit to drive through drink, was nonetheless guilty of contributory negligence when the car was negligently driven into a collision injuring the passenger.[62]

However, in cases where a duty of care has arisen precisely because the defendant should have anticipated that the claimant might get drunk and thereby not be in a position to be as careful as he might otherwise have been, findings of contributory negligence will reflect the relative blameworthiness of the parties.[63]

Examples of cases concerning drunkenness and contributory negligence can be found in Chapters 13 and 14 below.

---

60. Per Wilmer LJ
61. *M'Cormick* v *Caledonian Railway* (1903) 5 F 362.
62. *Owens* v *Brimmell* [1977] QB 859, [1977] 2 WLR 943, [1976] 3 All ER 765 (QBD), see page 225 below.
63. See e.g. *Jebson* v *Ministry of Defence* [2000] 1 WLR 2055, [2001] RTR 22, [2000] PIQR P201 (CA) and *Brannan* v *Airtours Plc* [1999] CLY 3945 (CA). See pages 254 and 257 below for the facts of both cases.

RESCUERS

When considering the conduct of a rescuer, allowance will be made for the amount of time available for the decision as to the manner of the rescue to be made, but a rescuer will not escape a finding of contributory negligence where he has acted unreasonably in the circumstances.

In *O'Keefe* v *John Stewart & Co Shipping Ltd*[64] the claimant was the boatswain on a cargo ship. He was footing a ladder for a seaman who, whilst working up the ladder, appeared to get himself into difficulty and seemed to be in imminent danger of falling. The claimant went up the ladder to assist the seaman without getting someone else to foot the ladder for him. The ladder slipped and the claimant was injured. There was found to have been no contributory negligence. The risk to the seaman far outweighed the slight risk of the ladder slipping.

> "In deciding whether ... a rescuer is justified in putting himself into a position of such great peril, the law has to measure the interests which he sought to protect and the other interests involved. We have all heard of the reasonable man who the law postulates in certain circumstances; the reasonable man here must be endowed with qualities of energy and courage, and he is not to be deprived of a remedy because he has in a marked degree a desire to save human life when in peril. So regarded, [the claimant] was not acting unreasonably in the risks he took."[65]

However,

> "If a rescuer acts with a wanton disregard of his own safety it might be that in some circumstances it might be held that any injury to him was not the result of the negligence that caused the situation of danger."[66]

---

64. [1979] 1 Lloyd's Rep 182 (QBD).
65. *Haynes* v *Harwood* [1935] 1 KB 146 per Maugham LJ at 162 (CA), where a policeman was injured in attempting to stop bolting horses, fearing that they might injure children on the highway.
66. *Baker* v *T E Hopkins & Son Ltd* [1959] 1 WLR 966 per Morris LJ at 977, [1959] 3 All ER 225 (CA).

In *Ogwo* v *Taylor*,[67] a case concerning the liability of someone who negligently started a fire to firemen injured tackling the fire and questions of remoteness, it was said:

> "The chain of causation between the negligence and the injury must be established by the [claimant] and may be broken in a number of ways. The most obvious would be where the [claimant's] injuries were sustained by his foolhardy exposure to an unnecessary risk either of his own volition or acting under the orders of a senior fire officer."[68]

Similarly, a rescuer must take reasonable steps so as to minimise the danger. In *Harrison* v *British Railways Board*[69] H was the guard on a train, which D attempted to board whilst it was moving. In those circumstances the system was that H was required to signal the driver to stop and/or apply the emergency brakes. H gave the wrong signal to the driver and the train continued. H then tried to grab hold of D, who fell off the train injuring H.

It was held that a person being rescued, who has not taken reasonable care for his own safety, owes a duty of care to someone whom he ought reasonably to foresee might try to assist him. It was said:

> "[There] is a feeling of distaste about finding a rescuer guilty of contributory negligence. It can rarely be appropriate to do so ... Here, however, the contributory negligence which is alleged does not relate to anything done in the course of the actual rescue. What is alleged is the failure by [H] to reduce the danger by doing what he was duty bound to do."[70]

As H had not applied the emergency brakes as required, his contributory negligence in failing to reduce the danger to himself was assessed at 20%.

A rescuer's right to claim is an independent right and is not derived from that of the victim. Accordingly, the rescuer will not be tainted by any negligence of the victim in getting himself into the position of peril.[71]

---

67. [1988] AC 431, [1987] 3 WLR 1145, [1987] 3 All ER 961 (HL).
68. [1988] AC 431 per Lord Bridge at 446.
69. [1981] 3 All ER 679 (QBD).
70. [1981] 3 All ER 679 per Boreham J at 686.
71. *Videan* v *British Transport Commission* [1963] 2 QB 650, [1963] 3 WLR 374, [1963] 2 All ER 860 (CA).

CHAPTER FOUR
CAUSATION

It is impossible to separate any theory of contributory negligence from the concept of causation. The defence is concerned with negligence which contributes to cause the injury[1] and the word "contributory" means "something which is a direct cause of the accident."[2]

At common law, prior to the passing of the LR(CN)A 1945, contributory negligence constituted a complete defence. This tended to produce unjust results in some cases as a claimant who had been careless, even if to a much lesser extent than the defendant, was precluded from recovering altogether.

The court had to determine "whose negligence was the real or substantial cause of the accident".[3] Rules of causation developed to avoid harsh outcomes and prime amongst these was the "last opportunity" test.[4] This dictated that where both parties had been careless, the party who had the last opportunity of avoiding the accident was solely liable for the consequences. For example, where the claimant tethered his donkey so as to obstruct a highway and the defendant carelessly drove his wagon into the donkey killing it, the defendant alone was held liable for the accident as he could have avoided the consequences of the claimant's earlier negligence.

The provisions of the LR(CN)A 1945 rendered such a test unnecessary and enabled the courts to do justice by apportioning the responsibility between

---

1. *Caswell v Powell Duffryn Associated Collieries Ltd* [1940] AC 152 per Lord Atkin at 165, [1939] 3 All ER 722 (HL).
2. *Caswell v Powell Duffryn Associated Collieries* Ltd, supra, per Lord Porter at 186.
3. *Swadling v Cooper* [1931] AC 1 (HL).
4. *Davies v Mann* (1842) 10 M & W 546, although some reported decisions treat the "last opportunity" rule as being distinct to the rule in *Davies v Mann*. See e.g. the judgment of Evershed LJ in *Davies v Swan Motor Co (Swansea) Ltd* [1949] 2 KB 291, [1949] 1 All ER 620 (CA). Cf the judgment of Denning LJ in the same case.

the parties. The last opportunity rule is no longer part of the law,[5] although the sequence of the parties' negligence may be relevant when it comes to determining their respective culpability.

> "The legal effect of the Act of 1945 is simple enough. If the [claimant's] negligence was one of the causes of his damage, he is no longer defeated altogether. He gets reduced damages. The practical effect of the Act is, however, wider than its legal effect. Previously, to mitigate the harshness of the doctrine of contributory negligence, the courts in practice sought to select, from a number of competing causes, which was *the* cause – the effective or predominant cause – of the damage and to reject the rest. Now the courts have regard to all the causes and apportion the damages accordingly. This is not a change in the law as to what constitutes contributory negligence – the search, in theory, was always for all the causes – but it is a change in the practical application of it."[6]

When determining whether contributory negligence is made out, the correct question is what was the cause of the damage, not who or what caused the accident.[7] It is perfectly possible for the claimant's negligence to have been in no way causative of the accident, but to have been causative of the damage suffered.

For example, in *Davies v Swan Motor Co (Swansea) Ltd*[8] the claimant's husband was riding on the steps of a dustcart, which was forbidden by his employers. He was crushed in an accident between the dustcart and a bus. The accident was caused by the negligence of both drivers. Although the claimant's husband's negligence in riding on the steps did not cause or contribute to the accident, it did contribute to his injuries. His contributory negligence was assessed at 20%.

A similar situation arises in cases where drivers or passengers who fail to wear seat belts are injured in collisions caused by the fault of someone else. The failure to wear a seat belt cannot be said to have been a cause of the accident, but it will often have contributed to the injuries sustained and a finding of

---

5. *Davies v Swan Motor Co (Swansea) Ltd* [1949] 2 KB 291, [1949] 1 All ER 620 (CA).
6. *Davies v Swan Motor Co (Swansea) Ltd* [1949] 2 KB 291 per Denning LJ at 322, [1949] 1 All ER 620 (CA).
7. See e.g. *Capps v Miller* [1989] 1 WLR 839, [1989] 2 All ER 333 (CA), see page 251 below.
8. [1949] 2 KB 291, [1949] 1 All ER 620 (CA).

contributory negligence will generally be appropriate in such cases.[9] However, where the claimant's negligence in not wearing a seat belt has not contributed to his damage, for example because a seat belt would not have lessened his injuries, no reduction will be made.[10]

Similarly, consideration should be given to the question of whether or not the contributory negligence has caused or contributed to all of the damage or only part of it. In the case of a car driver who failed to wear a seat belt, the damages in respect of his personal injuries and consequential losses may well fall to be reduced on account of his contributory negligence. However, it might not be appropriate to reduce the part of his damages relating to the damage to his vehicle, as this is unlikely to have been affected by the failure to wear a seat belt. Nonetheless, this may be taken into account when determining the appropriate level of the reduction, so that the reduction can then be applied to the totality of the damages.

The rules governing causation in contributory negligence are the same as those applicable when determining primary liability[11] and it does not matter whether the claimant's negligence occurs before, after or at the same time as the defendant's wrongdoing.

A common sense approach to the question is to be adopted and "causation is to be understood as the man in the street, and not as either the scientist or the metaphysician would understand it".[12]

> "One may find that as a matter of history several people have been at fault and that if any one of them had acted properly the accident would not have happened, but that does not mean that the accident must be regarded as having been caused by the faults of all of them. One must discriminate between those faults which must be discarded as being too remote and those which must not. Sometimes it is proper to discard all but one and to regard that as the sole cause, but in other cases it is proper to regard two or more as having jointly

---

9. *Froom* v *Butcher* [1976] QB 286, [1975] 3 WLR 379, [1975] 3 All ER 520 (CA). See page 246 below.
10. See, for example, *Neill* v *Doherty & Akram* [1997] CLY 3772 (QBD). See page 248 below.
11. For the details of which, see e.g. *Clerk & Lindsell on Torts*, 18th edn.
12. *Yorkshire Dale S S Co* v *Minister of War Transport* [1942] AC 691 per Lord Wright at 706, [1942] 2 All ER 6 (HL).

caused the accident. I doubt whether any test can be applied generally."[13]

"Although contributory negligence does not depend on a duty of care, it does depend on foreseeability. Just as actionable negligence requires the foreseeability of harm to others, so contributory negligence requires the foreseeability of harm to oneself. A person is guilty of contributory negligence if he ought reasonably to have foreseen that, if he did not act as a reasonable, prudent man, he might hurt himself; and in his reckonings he must take into account the possibility of others being careless."[14]

Therefore, the harm sustained by the claimant must belong to the general class of perils to which he exposed himself by his negligence, although foreseeability of the precise nature of the injury is not required.[15] Accordingly, if a man sits on an unsafe wall, he would not be held to have been contributorily negligent if he suffered injuries when a careless motorist drove his car into the wall.[16] However, once negligence on the part of the claimant has been established, the consequences do not depend on foreseeability, but causation.[17]

A good example of the fundamental importance of causation in questions of contributory negligence is provided by *Neill* v *Doherty & Akram*.[18] In that case N was a passenger in the rear of a taxi that was involved in a collision with another vehicle. The force of the accident was very severe and N was ejected from the vehicle. N, who was found to have failed to take reasonable care by not wearing a seat belt, was paralysed. However, as it was found that N's paralysing spinal injury occurred on the initial impact and before N was

---

13. *Stapley* v *Gypsum Mines Ltd* [1953] AC 663 per Lord Reid at 681, [1953] 3 WLR 279, [1953] 2 All ER 478 (HL). See page 101 below.
14. *Jones* v *Livox Quarries Ltd* [1952] 2 QB 608 per Denning LJ at 615, (CA). However, in relation to this passage it was said by Lord Kilbrandon in *Westwood* v *Post Office* [1974] AC 1 at 17, [1973] 3 WLR 287, [1973] 3 All ER 184 (HL) "the closing words of the passage from Denning LJ's judgment ... while appropriate to a common law claim, which was there being considered, may be inapplicable in a case of statutory liability".
15. *Jones* v *Livox Quarries Ltd* [1952] 2 QB 608 (CA).
16. See the judgment of Singleton LJ in *Jones* v *Livox Quarries Ltd* [1952] 2 QB 608 at 612.
17. See *Jones* v *Livox Quarries Ltd* [1952] 2 QB 608 (CA) – page 106 below.
18. [1997] CLY 3772 (QBD).

ejected from the vehicle, no reduction was made for contributory negligence as N's negligence had no causative effect.

Whilst causation is fundamental in deciding whether or not there should be a reduction, when deciding upon the appropriate level of the reduction, consideration should be given "not only to the causative potency of a particular factor, but also its blameworthiness".[19]

---

19. *Davies* v *Swan Motor Co (Swansea) Ltd* [1949] 2 KB 291 per Denning LJ at 326, [1949] 1 All ER 620 (CA). See further Chapter 2 above.

CHAPTER FIVE

IDENTIFICATION

In some circumstances the claimant will be identified with the negligence of another person and have his damages reduced as if he had been contributorily negligent himself.

Apart from particular instances where the negligence of certain individuals will be attributed to the claimant pursuant to statute, the test to be applied when considering whether the claimant should be identified with the negligence of another is the "both ways" test.[1] In other words, the fault of a connected person should be attributed to the claimant as contributory negligence where, and only where, the relationship between them is such that the claimant would be liable to a third party because of the errors of the connected person.

However, where the entire purpose of the defendant's duty is to protect the claimant against the activities of certain of its staff, the courts have been reluctant to identify claimants with the fault of those members of its staff.[2]

BAILMENT

The bailor of a chattel is not identified with the negligence of his bailee so as to affect his remedy against a third party who has damaged the chattel.[3] In *France* v *Parkinson*[4] F hired out his car to Fitzgerald, who drove it into collision with P's car. It was held that even if Fitzgerald had been negligent, F was entitled to recover his full damages from P, provided that he could establish some negligence on P's part.

CARRIERS

A passenger in a vehicle will not be identified with the negligence of the driver.[5] Accordingly, if an accident is caused by the combined negligence of

---

1. See Bartlett, "Attribution of Contributory Negligence" (1998) 114 LQR 460. See also *AWA Ltd* v *Daniels t/a Deloitte Haskins & Sells* (1995) 16 ACSR 607 (Australia).
2. See e.g. *Henderson* v *Merrett Syndicates Ltd (No. 2)* [1996] 1 PNLR 32 (QBD), the facts of which are set out at page 187 below. See also the other claims against auditors set out in Chapter 12 below.
3. *Wellwood* v *A King Ltd* [1921] 2 IR 274.
4. [1954] 1 WLR 581, [1954] 1 All ER 739 (CA).
5. *Mills & Ors* v *Armstrong & Ors, The "Bernina"* (1888) 13 App Cas 1 (HL).

the drivers of two cars, passengers in either car will not, absent negligence on their own part, have their damages reduced in line with those of the driver of their car.[6]

FATAL ACCIDENTS

A dependant's damages under the Fatal Accidents Act 1976 will be reduced not only where his own negligence contributed towards the death, but also to take account of any negligence on the part of the deceased.[7] Similarly, the contributory negligence of the deceased will reduce the estate's claim under the Law Reform (Miscellaneous Provisions) Act 1934. Contributory negligence in the case of fatal accidents is considered further in Chapter 6 below.

PARENTS

Under section 1(7) of the Congenital Disabilities (Civil Liability) Act 1976, where a child is born disabled by reason of his or her parent's carelessness, the child's damages will be reduced by an amount the court considers appropriate having regard to the extent of the parent's responsibility. However, a refusal to have a pregnancy terminated will not be regarded as unreasonable conduct on the mother's part save in the most exceptional circumstances.[8]

The doctrine of identification will not apply to a parent's negligence once the child has been born. The old rule whereby a child was unable to claim damages if he was injured whilst in the care of an adult is no longer relevant.[9]

---

6. Assuming they would otherwise have no vicarious liability for the driver's negligence. However, passengers have been identified with the negligence of drivers where the passenger was the owner of the car and the driver was driving it for the passenger's purposes. See *Lampert* v *Eastern National Omnibus Co Ltd* [1954] 1 WLR 1047, [1954] 2 All ER 719 (QBD), a case concerning a husband and wife going on holiday together in the wife's car.
7. Section 5 Fatal Accidents Act 1976.
8. *Emeh* v *Kensington, Chelsea and Westminster Area Health Authority* [1985] QB 1012, [1985] 2 WLR 233, [1984] 3 All ER 1044 (CA).
9. *Oliver* v *Birmingham and Midland Omnibus Co Ltd* [1933] 1 KB 35, where a child in the care of his grandfather was run over whilst crossing a road.

So, for example, in a Canadian case[10] it has been held that the negligence of a parent in failing to ensure that a three-year-old child was restrained by a seat belt could not be imputed to the child and the child was entitled to recover in full. However, in such circumstances it may be possible for the defendant to achieve a reduction in the damages ultimately payable by him to the child by the more circuitous route of seeking a contribution from the parents[11] on the basis that they were joint tortfeasors.[12]

RESCUERS

A rescuer's right to claim is an independent right and is not derived from that of the victim. Accordingly, the rescuer will not be tainted by any negligence of the victim in getting himself into the position of peril.[13]

SPOUSES

The claimant will not be identified with the negligence of his or her spouse. In *Mallett & another* v *Dunn*[14] M's wife was injured in a road traffic accident as a result partly of D's negligence and partly as a result of her own negligence. The wife's damages were reduced to take account of her contributory negligence. However, M's claim in respect of medical and household expenses incurred by him was not subject to a reduction; he had not suffered damage "as the result partly of his own fault".[15]

---

10. *Ducharme* v *Davies* [1984] 1 WWR 699 (Canada), see page 179 below.
11. Such a claim was made in *Jones* v *Wilkins* [2001] PIQR P179, [2001] RTR 283 (CA), where the child's mother's responsibility (together with the child's aunt who was driving) was assessed at 25% under the Civil Liability (Contribution) Act 1978. See page 247 below for the facts.
12. Or, more likely, several tortfeasors.
13. *Videan* v *British Transport Commission* [1963] 2 QB 650, [1963] 3 WLR 374, [1963] 2 All ER 860 (CA).
14. [1949] 2 KB 180, [1949] 1 All ER 973 (KBD).
15. See section 1(1) LR(CN)A 1945.

VICARIOUS RESPONSIBILITY

Where an employee of the claimant has been negligent, the claimant will be vicariously responsible for his actions on normal principles and his damages will be reduced according to the extent of the employee's fault.[16] Accordingly:

> "If the owner of a motorcar sends it out with a driver and, while he is driving in the course of his employment, the car is damaged in a collision by the faults of both drivers, the owner must take responsibility for his own driver's negligence. He only gets reduced damages. But if the driver takes the car out on a frolic of his own, outside the course of his employment, the owner recovers full damages for the car because he is then not responsible for the driver's negligence."[17]

An employer will not normally be identified with the negligence of an independent contractor.[18]

COMPANIES

A related question is whether the contributory negligence of a company can only be that of its directors. It has been held in an Australian case[19] that the fault to be imputed to a company could be that of a member of its senior management as well as its directors. The reasoning was that many companies are today too large to be supervised and administered by a board of directors except in matters of high policy; necessarily senior management exercise the powers of decision and management.

---

16. See e.g. *Carberry* v *Davies* [1968] 1 WLR 1103, [1968] 2 All ER 817 (CA). The vicarious responsibility of a principal for his agent's negligence will also be determined on normal principles of vicarious liability.
17. *Inland Revenue Commissioners* v *Hambrook* [1956] 2 QB 641 per Denning LJ at 660, [1956] 3 WLR 643, [1956] 3 All ER 338 (CA).
18. *Burrows* v *March Gas and Coke Co* (1872) LR 7 Exch 96.
19. *AWA Ltd* v *Daniels t/a Deloitte Haskins & Sells* (1995) 16 ACSR 607, see also the first instance decisions at (1992) 7 ACSR 759 and (1992) 9 ACSR 383. See page 186 below for the facts.

However, the fault of directors will not always be attributed to the company. In *British Racing Drivers' Club Ltd* v *Hextall Erskine & Co*[20] the company's directors exercised poor judgement in entering into a transaction, which adversely affected the value of its shares. There was no contributory negligence on the part of the company in a claim against its solicitors for failing to advise that the venture required the approval of the members of the company.[21] It was said that it would be wholly inconsistent with the statutory scheme to attribute the undoubted negligence of the directors to the company.

The activities of fraudulent employees will generally not be attributed to claimant companies. It has been said:

> "The interests of the fraudsters in concealing the fraud and the interests of the company were antithetical in the extreme. It would be inappropriate to hold the company responsible pursuant to either the principle of corporate identification, the doctrine of imputed negligence or the concept of vicarious liability."[22]

However, there may be contributory negligence on the part of the claimant company in failing to notice the fraudulent activities of its employees.[23]

---

20. [1996] 3 All ER 667 (Ch D).
21. Pursuant to section 320 Companies Act 1985.
22. *Dairy Containers Ltd* v *NZI Bank Ltd* [1995] 2 NZLR 30 per Thomas J at 30 (New Zealand).
23. *Dairy Containers Ltd* v *NZI Bank Ltd* [1995] 2 NZLR 30 (New Zealand).

CHAPTER SIX
CAUSES OF ACTION OTHER THAN NEGLIGENCE

The defence of contributory negligence is plainly applicable to claims brought in the tort of negligence. This chapter considers the availability of the defence in other types of claims.

ADMIRALTY

The LR(CN)A 1945 does not apply to any claims to which s 1 of the Maritime Conventions Act 1911 applies,[1] which has now been repealed by the Merchant Shipping Act 1995. Section 187 of the 1995 Act in essence provides that where, by the fault of two or more ships, damage is caused to one or more of the ships or to any property on board, liability in respect of that damage shall be borne in proportion to the degree in which each ship was at fault. If it is not possible to establish different degrees of fault, liability is to be apportioned equally.

ANIMALS

A breach of ss 2–4 of the Animals Act 1971 (liability of keepers for damage caused by animals) can constitute fault for the purposes of the LR(CN)A 1945 and so the defence of contributory negligence is available.[2] However, examples of successful pleas of contributory negligence are scarce and the courts have been readier to find claimants to have voluntarily accepted the risk of injury[3] than to have been contributorily negligent.[4] In *Gordon* v *MacKenzie*[5] an allegation of contributory negligence failed in circumstances

---

1. Section 3(1) LR(CN)A 1945.
2. Section 10 Animals Act 1971.
3. Which amounts to a complete defence pursuant to s 5(2) Animals Act 1971.
4. See e.g. *Cummings* v *Grainger* [1976] QB 397, [1976] 3 WLR 842, [1977] 1 All ER 104 (CA), where the trial judge found the claimant to have been 50% to blame for her injuries when she trespassed at a scrap yard where she knew there to be a ferocious dog and was attacked by the dog. However, the Court of Appeal found the claimant to have voluntarily accepted the risk in addition to finding the defendant not to have been unreasonable in having the dog guard his scrap yard. The first instance decision is reported at [1975] 1 WLR 1330, [1975] 2 All ER 1129 (QBD).
5. 1913 SC 109 (IH), a case decided before the Animals Act 1971 and the LR(CN)A 1945.

where the claimant in a negligence action had been bitten whilst patting a dog, which was unknown to him.

BAILMENT

The bailor of a chattel is not identified with the negligence of his bailee so as to affect his remedy against a third party who has damaged the chattel.[6] So, in *France v Parkinson*[7] F hired his car to Fitzgerald, who drove it into collision with P's car. It was held that even if Fitzgerald had been negligent, F was entitled to recover his full damages from P, provided that he could establish some negligence on P's part.

BRIBERY

In an action founded on the bribery of the claimant's employee, the defendant was unable to rely on the partial defence of contributory negligence to reduce his liability on the basis that the claimant could have intervened in the situation, but had not done so.[8]

CONTRACT

Three categories are to be distinguished between:[9]

1. Where the defendant's liability arises from a contractual provision which does not depend upon negligence on the part of the defendant, contributory negligence is not available as a defence.

---

6. *Wellwood v A King Ltd* [1921] 2 IR 274.
7. [1954] 1 WLR 581, [1954] 1 All ER 739 (CA).
8. *Corporacion Nacional del Cobre de Chile v Sogemin Metals Ltd* [1997] 1 WLR 1396, [1997] 2 All ER 917 (Ch D).
9. *Forsikringsaktieselskapet Vesta v Butcher* [1986] 2 All ER 488 (QBD), affirmed by the Court of Appeal at [1988] 3 WLR 565, [1988] 2 All ER 43. The issue was not considered on the subsequent appeal to the House of Lords reported at [1989] AC 852, [1989] 2 WLR 290, [1989] 1 All ER 402. The High Court of Australia has not followed this approach in respect of a statute similarly worded to the LR(CN)A 1945 and has held that the defence of contributory negligence is not available in contractual claims, see *Astley v Austrust Ltd* [1999] Lloyd's Rep PN 758 (Australia).

2.   Where the defendant's liability arises from a contractual obligation
     which is expressed in terms of taking care (or its equivalent) but does
     not correspond to a common law duty of care which would exist in the
     given case independently of contract, contributory negligence is not
     available as a defence.

3.   Where the defendant's liability in contract is the same as his liability in
     the tort of negligence independently of the existence of any contract,
     contributory negligence is available as a defence unless the contract
     specifically provides otherwise.

Accordingly, contributory negligence is not available as a defence to a claim
founded on a breach of a strict contractual obligation, i.e. an obligation other
than one to take reasonable care.[10]

In *Bristol and West Building Society* v *A Kramer & Co*[11] solicitors were in breach
of an express instruction from a mortgagee requiring that "any matters
which might prejudice the society's security or which are at variance with the
offer of advance should be notified to the society immediately they become
known". It was held that the defence of contributory negligence was not
available, as the term of the retainer did not depend upon the use of
reasonable care. It was said:

> "The obligation [in the retainer was] dependant on the knowledge of
> the matters in question and [was] not in any way dependant upon
> negligence on the part of the defendant firm. The fact that [the
> solicitors were] negligent (as distinct from deliberate) in overlooking

---

10. *Barclays Bank Plc* v *Fairclough Building Ltd* [1995] QB 214, [1994] 3 WLR 1057,
     [1995] 1 All ER 289 (CA). In that case contractors had been engaged to clean
     asbestos roofs. They failed to take any precautions and the premises became
     contaminated. The contractors were unable to rely on the employer's architectural
     department's failure to supervise as they were in breach of a strict contractual
     duty. But see also *Barclays Bank Plc* v *Fairclough Building Ltd (No. 2)* [1995] IRLR
     605, [1995] PIQR P152 (CA), a case involving the sub-contractors. C had been sub-
     contracted to clean the asbestos roof and further sub-contracted the work to T.
     The work was done badly and dangerously by T. T's liability to C was reduced to
     take account of 50% contributory negligence. An apportionment was possible as,
     due to the close relationship between the parties, T owed C a concurrent duty in
     tort to avoid causing economic loss by failing to exercise reasonable care and skill.
11. [1995] NPC 14, (1995) *The Times*, February 6, 1995 (Ch D). Cf *Mortgage Express Ltd*
     v *Newman* [1996] PNLR 603 (Ch D).

[their] obligation to inform the society of what [they] knew does not convert [their] obligation into one that is dependant on negligence."[12]

The unavailability of the defence in cases concerning a breach of a strict contractual duty can produce some curious results. Where the court considers that the circumstances warrant the recognition of a duty of care in the tort of negligence in addition to and concurrent with a contractual obligation, this can have the effect of reducing the claimant's damages on the grounds of contributory negligence. However, a refusal to recognise a concurrent duty in tort would rule out such a reduction.

Further:

"The warranty given by a man employed to do work which requires skill is that he undertakes to possess and exercise reasonable skill in the art he professes. A person employing such a skilled man is entitled to rely on the warranty and, if it turns out that the man is incompetent, to determine his engagement ... It is at least arguable that the present state of the law produces the anomalous result that if in breach of the warranty to exercise his skill the contractor can rely on contributory negligence, but if he has misrepresented that he possesses the necessary skill he cannot."[13]

Accordingly, it may be that a negligent professional will be in a worse position where it is shown that he did not possess the requisite skill (a breach of a strict contractual obligation), than he would be where it is shown that he failed to exercise such skill (where his liability would be the same in contract and negligence).

This can lead to unsatisfactory distinctions and results. For example, where a solicitor allows a client's claim to become time barred, the defence of contributory negligence would be available on the basis of the above if the solicitor simply forgot about the claim, but it might not be available if he did not know that there was a time limit for the bringing of the claim. In either case the client's loss is the same, but if he was also at fault, the damages recoverable by him may differ. The distinction can be difficult to apply in

---

12. [1995] NPC 14 per Blackburne J (Ch D).
13. *Barclays Bank Plc* v *Fairclough Building Ltd* [1995] QB 214 per Beldam LJ at 222–223, [1994] 3 WLR 1057, [1995] 1 All ER 289 (CA).

practice. For example, in cases where the loss is caused by poor advice, did the advisor have bad judgement or did he negligently fail to exercise his good judgement?

The principles of contributory negligence do not operate to defeat any defence arising under a contract.[14] However, this relates only to an express clause in a contract governing the liability of the parties in the event of one of them being at fault.[15]

Where a claim is brought in tort and a counterclaim made in contract, both claims being attributable to two concurrent causes acting contemporaneously, liability cannot be apportioned under the LR(CN)A 1945.[16] However, by assessing the damages recoverable under each claim on the basis of causation, a similar result may be reached.

In *Tennant Radiant Heat Ltd* v *Warrington Development Corporation*[17] TRH rented a unit in a warehouse from WDC. Most of the remainder of the units at the warehouse were unlet. TRH's unit became flooded due to the roof collapsing when 20 rainwater outlets on the roof became blocked and the rainwater was unable to drain away. WDC had been warned of the danger of the rainwater outlets becoming blocked by their architects and yet had not attended to them. Nineteen of the blockages were held to have been the fault of WDC. However, one of the rainwater outlets was blocked as a result of TRH's breach of its repairing covenant with WDC to keep the rainwater outlet in the roof above its unit clear.

It was found that WDC's failure to keep the outlets under its control clear was the major cause of the collapse of the roof above TRH's unit, but that TRH's fault in failing to keep their outlet clear was a contributory cause of the damage to the entire building. TRH's claim against WDC in negligence and

---

14. Section 1(1)(a) LR(CN)A 1945.
15. *Quinn* v *Burch Bros (Builders) Ltd* [1966] 2 WLR 430, [1965] 3 All ER 801 (QBD), affirmed by the Court of Appeal at [1966] 2 QB 370, [1966] 2 WLR 1017, [1966] 2 All ER 283.
16. *Tennant Radiant Heat Ltd* v *Warrington Development Corporation* [1988] 1 EGLR 41 (CA).
17. [1988] 1 EGLR 41 (CA). This decision was inferentially doubted in *Bank of Nova Scotia* v *Hellenic Mutual War Risks Association (Bermuda) Ltd, "The Good Luck"* [1990] 1 QB 818 per May LJ at 904, [1990] 2 WLR 547, [1989] 3 All ER 628 (CA). The decision was not considered on the appeal to the House of Lords reported at [1992] 1 AC 233, [1991] 2 WLR 1279, [1991] 3 All ER 1.

nuisance succeeded, as did WDC's cross claim against TRH in respect of the breach of their repairing covenant. As the claim was based in tort and the counterclaim was in contract it was not possible to apportion liability under the LR(CN)A 1945. However, an apportionment could be made at common law on principles of causation and TRH were held to be entitled to recover 90% of their losses and WDC, 10%. This apportionment was arrived at on the basis that WDC were responsible for nine of the ten rainwater outlets on the material half of the roof and TRH was responsible for the remaining one.

However, a claimant's fault following the defendant's breach of a strict contractual term will usually have the effect of the claim failing entirely on principles of causation. For example, in *Lambert* v *Lewis*[18] a retailer sold a defective towing hitch. Despite it being obviously defective, the claimant continued to use it, which resulted in a trailer becoming loose and causing an accident. It was held that the accident was caused by the claimant's carelessness in using the towing hitch, which he knew to be defective, and not the breach of contract. Accordingly, the retailer was not liable for the subsequent damage.

Similarly, in *Quinn* v *Burch Bros (Builders) Ltd*[19] the claimant, an independent sub-contractor, was carrying out building work for the defendant, who was the main contractor on a project. The claimant requested a stepladder to attend to a ceiling, but the defendant failed, in breach of contract, to supply one. Accordingly, the claimant propped a folded trestle against the wall and used that as a ladder. The trestle was not footed and slipped, causing the claimant to fall and suffer injuries. As the claimant was an independent contractor, the defendant was under no duty to take reasonable care to ensure that reasonable and safe equipment was provided. Its obligation was purely contractual, to provide a ladder. It was held that the defendant's breach of contract did not cause the accident, but simply gave the claimant the opportunity to injure himself by using unsuitable equipment. The sole cause of the accident was the claimant's choice to use the unsuitable equipment.

---

18. [1982] AC 225, [1981] 2 WLR 713, [1981] 1 All ER 1185 (HL).
19. [1966] 2 QB 370, [1966] 2 WLR 1017, [1966] 2 All ER 283 (CA). See also the first instance decision at [1966] 2 WLR 430, [1965] 3 All ER 801.

CONVERSION

After some early cases holding that contributory negligence could be raised as a defence, it is now clear that it cannot be raised in proceedings founded on conversion or on intentional trespass to goods.[20] Accordingly, there may be a benefit to a claimant who has carelessly lent property to a defendant who negligently destroys it, in suing in conversion as opposed to negligence. Contributory negligence by a drawer can be raised in a claim against a bank for conversion of a cheque.[21]

CRIMINAL INJURIES COMPENSATION

The Criminal Injuries Compensation Authority may withhold or reduce an award, *inter alia*, where the conduct of the applicant before, during or after the incident giving rise to the application makes it inappropriate that a full award or any award at all be made.[22]

DECEIT

The defence of contributory negligence is not available in relation to claims for fraud and so a defendant who is found liable in deceit will be unable to establish a defence based upon the contributory fault of the claimant. Deceitful conduct does not fall within the definition of "fault" under the LR(CN)A 1945.[23] Similarly, there is no defence of contributory deceit.[24]

---

20. Section 11(1) Torts (Interference with Goods) Act 1977, although the defence is available to claims brought under ss 1(c) or (d) of the 1977 Act.
21. Section 47 Banking Act 1979.
22. Paragraph 13(d) of the Criminal Injuries Compensation Scheme (1995).
23. *Nationwide Building Society* v *Thimbleby & Co* [1999] Lloyd's Rep PN 359, [1999] PNLR 733 (Ch D), *Alliance and Leicester Building Society* v *Edgestop Ltd* [1993] 1 WLR 1462, [1994] 2 All ER 38 (Ch D).
24. *Standard Chartered Bank* v *Pakistan National Shipping Corp* [2001] QB 167, [2000] 3 WLR 1692, [2000] 2 All ER (Comm) 929 (CA).

DISREPAIR

A claim arising out of a breach of a repairing covenant under a lease, being an absolute contractual obligation, cannot be defended by an allegation of contributory negligence.[25] However, contributory negligence can be raised in answer to a claim brought under s 4 of the Defective Premises Act 1972 in respect of a landlord's liability for defects in premises.[26]

FATAL ACCIDENTS

The defence of contributory negligence on the part of the deceased is available in respect of both the dependants' claims under the Fatal Accidents Act 1976[27] and the estate's claim under the Law Reform (Miscellaneous Provisions) Act 1934.

Section 5 of the Fatal Accidents Act 1976[28] provides:

> "Where any person dies as the result partly of his own fault and partly of the fault of any other person or persons, and accordingly if an action were brought for the benefit of the estate under the Law Reform (Miscellaneous Provisions) Act 1934 the damages recoverable would be reduced under s 1(1) of the Law Reform (Contributory Negligence) Act 1945, any damages recoverable in an action brought for the benefit of the dependants of that person under this Act shall be reduced to a proportionate extent."

Similarly, a dependant's damages will also be reduced where his own negligence contributed towards the death of the deceased. However, the defence may well not be applicable to the claims under both Acts, as there may have been contributory negligence on the part of the dependant, but not the deceased.

---

25. *Tennant Radiant Heat Ltd* v *Warrington Development Corporation* [1988] 1 EGLR 41 (CA). See page 59 above for the facts and the section above on contractual claims generally.
26. *Sykes* v *Harry* [2001] QB 1014, [2001] 3 WLR 62 (CA). See page 301 below for the facts.
27. Section 5.
28. As amended by the Administration of Justice Act 1982.

In *Mulholland* v *McCrea*[29] the claimant's wife was a passenger in a vehicle driven by the claimant. She died in a collision, which was partly the fault of the claimant and partly the fault of the other driver. It was held that:

1. the claimant's damages under the Fatal Accidents Act should be reduced to take account of his contributory negligence;

2. the claim under the Law Reform Act, being on behalf of the wife's estate, should not be reduced to take account of the husband's contributory negligence; and

3. as the funeral expenses were claimed under the Law Reform Act, they were recoverable in full.

Similarly, it may be that the defence of contributory negligence should not be applied to all of the claimants' claims under the Fatal Accidents Act as the remedy under the Act is given to the dependants individually and not as a group. So, in *Dodds* v *Dodds*[30] a man was killed in a road traffic accident as a result of his wife's negligence. The deceased's wife was unable to bring a claim under the Fatal Accidents Act (as a result of her own fault), but the deceased's child could claim in respect of his loss of dependence and there was no reduction of his award.

FIDUCIARY DUTY

It has been held at first instance that contributory negligence cannot be raised as a defence to an action based upon a breach of a fiduciary duty, although the claimant's conduct may be relevant to questions as to the remoteness of any loss.[31]

---

29. [1961] NI 135 (NICA).
30. [1978] QB 543, [1978] 2 WLR 434, [1978] 2 All ER 539 (QBD).
31. *Nationwide Building Society* v *Richard Grosse & Co* [1999] Lloyd's Rep PN 348 (Ch D), *Nationwide Building Society* v *Goodwin Harte* [1999] Lloyd's Rep PN 338 (Ch D). The New Zealand Court of Appeal held that the defence was available on the basis that "he who seeks equity must do equity" in *Day* v *Mead* [1987] 2 NZLR 433. This was followed by the Supreme Court of Canada in *Canson Enterprises Ltd* v *Broughton & Co* (1991) 85 DLR (4th) 129. However, in New Zealand and Canada a breach of a fiduciary duty can be committed innocently, whereas in the *Nationwide Building Society* cases it was found that a deliberate betrayal of trust was required for there to have been a breach of the fiduciary duties owed.

"In English law contributory negligence has never been a defence to an intentional tort: in such cases the 1945 Act has no application. By parity of approach I can see no good reason why equity ... should adopt a less rigorous approach. I therefore take the view that where, in order to establish a breach of fiduciary duty, it is necessary to find that the fiduciary was consciously disloyal to the person to whom his duty was owed, the fiduciary is disabled from asserting that the other contributed, by his own want of care for his own interests, to the loss which he suffered flowing from the breach. To do otherwise ... risks subverting the fundamental principle of undivided and unremitting loyalty which is at the core of the fiduciary's obligation ... This does not mean that the conduct of the person to whom the fiduciary duty is owed is irrelevant. There comes a point, following breach of the fiduciary duty, where the loss is too remote for the breach to be said to be a loss flowing from it ... or where the claimant's own conduct comes into play as a factor determining the loss for which he can recover."[32]

MISREPRESENTATION

Contributory negligence cannot be raised as a defence to a claim based upon a fraudulent misrepresentation.[33]

Contributory negligence can be raised in response to a claim for misrepresentation under s 2(1) of the Misrepresentation Act 1967 where there would be concurrent liability in negligence.[34] However, it has been found not to be just and equitable to order apportionment in a case where the claimant suffered loss by relying on a misrepresentation, which the defendant had intended him to regard as accurate, as carelessness in not making other inquiries provides no answer to a claim when the claimant has done that which the representor intended he should do.[35]

---

32. *Nationwide Building Society* v *Balmer Radmore* [1999] Lloyd's Rep PN 241 per Blackburne J at 281 (Ch D).
33. See page 61 above.
34. *Gran Gelato Ltd* v *Richcliff (Group) Ltd* [1992] Ch 560, [1992] 2 WLR 867, [1992] 1 All ER 865 (Ch D).
35. *Gran Gelato Ltd* v *Richcliff (Group) Ltd* [1992] Ch 560, [1992] 2 WLR 867, [1992] 1 All ER 865 (Ch D).

A reduction for contributory negligence will not be possible where the misrepresentation has been made innocently, as there will be no concurrent liability in tort for a misrepresentation that is not negligent.

NEGLIGENT MISSTATEMENT

Where the claim is based upon negligent misstatement under the principles set out in *Hedley Byrne & Co Ltd* v *Heller and Partners Ltd*,[36] the defence of contributory negligence will be available in principle in common with other claims in negligence. However, the essence of the defendant's duty in such cases is the assumption of responsibility together with reasonable reliance by the claimant on the defendant's statement. Accordingly, in line with the approach taken in *Gran Gelato Ltd* v *Richcliff (Group) Ltd*,[37] it is difficult to envisage circumstances arising in practice where the claimant would be found to have been at fault in relying on the defendant's statement.

NUISANCE

Whilst the defence may, in theory, be available in claims based on private nuisance, there is a lack of authority in this area and the relevance of the defence is limited by the rule that it is no answer to a claim for nuisance to argue that the claimant came to the nuisance.[38]

However, there is no doubt that the defence applies to actions arising out of a nuisance on the highway.

In *Trevett* v *Lee*,[39] a case concerning the obstruction of a highway by the laying of a hosepipe across it, it was said:

> "Having regard to the language of ss 1 and 4 of the Law Reform (Contributory Negligence) Act 1945, it is not open to doubt that in a claim for damages based on nuisance the defendant may set up and rely upon a fault consisting of what is commonly called contributory

---

36. [1964] AC 465, [1963] 3 WLR 101, [1963] 2 All ER 575 (HL).
37. [1992] Ch 560, [1992] 2 WLR 867, [1992] 1 All ER 865 (Ch D), see above.
38. See e.g. *Miller* v *Jackson* [1977] QB 966, [1977] 3 WLR 20, [1977] 3 All ER 338 (CA).
39. [1955] 1 WLR 113, [1955] 1 All ER 406 (CA).

negligence, so as to reduce or extinguish his own liability. But because the judge held on the negligence claim that any liability of the defendants in negligence was wholly extinguished by the conduct or fault of [the claimant], it does not, I think, necessarily follow that, in so far as the claim is based on nuisance, there would be a similar extinguishment of the [claimant's] claim ... I do not express any conclusion on the question whether the standard of fault in the two kinds of claim is the same or similar ..."[40]

There is no clear authority on whether or not the defence can be raised against claims based on the rule in *Rylands* v *Fletcher*, although it is thought that it can be as it has been said that the defendant "can excuse himself by showing that the escape was due to the [claimant's] default".[41]

OCCUPIERS' LIABILITY

The defence is available to claims based on a breach of the common duty of care under the Occupiers' Liability Act 1957.[42] Contributory negligence can also be raised in defence of claims brought under the Occupiers' Liability Act 1984,[43] although the standard of care expected of the trespasser may well be higher than would be expected of a visitor.

PRODUCT LIABILITY

Section 6(4) of the Consumer Protection Act 1987 provides that where any damage is caused partly by a defect in a product and partly by the fault of the person suffering the damage, then, in order to give effect to the law relating to contributory negligence, the defect shall be treated as if it were the fault of every person who would be liable for it under the provisions of the Consumer Protection Act 1987.

---

40. [1955] 1 WLR 113 per Lord Evershed MR at 122.
41. *Rylands* v *Fletcher* (1868) 1 LR Ex 265 per Blackburn J at 279.
42. See e.g. *Wheat* v *E Lacon & Co Ltd* [1966] AC 552, [1966] 2 WLR 581, [1966] 1 All ER 582 (HL).
43. *Revill* v *Newberry* [1996] QB 567, [1996] 2 WLR 239, [1996] 1 All ER 291 (CA). See also *Ratcliff* v *McConnell* [1999] 1 WLR 670, [1999] PIQR P170 (CA), where the trial judge found contributory negligence, but the Court of Appeal reversed the decision as to liability.

As the 1987 Act provides for liability to attach to a producer without fault, any apportionment will be based upon the relative causal responsibility of the parties' actions and should not, it is submitted, take account of their respective blameworthiness.[44]

The defence of contributory negligence is also available in common law claims against manufacturers. However, the claimant will generally be entitled to assume that a manufacturer has complied with his duties.[45]

Further reference should be made to Chapter 11 of this book for a selection of cases on this topic.

STATUTORY DUTY

Contributory negligence can be raised in defence of a claim arising out of a breach of statutory duty.[46] Even where the intention of a statute is to protect against folly on the part of a workman, in a claim based upon a breach of that statutory duty there could still be a finding of 100% contributory negligence on the part of the workman.[47]

When there has been a breach of statutory duty by both the claimant and the defendant, then "however venial the fault of each of them they must share between them the responsibility for the whole of the damage".[48]

Several statutes expressly provide that contributory negligence (or a similar defence) may be raised as a defence to claims made pursuant to their provisions. These include: the Animals Act 1971,[49] the Banking Act 1979,[50]

---

44. However, there is no authority on the approach to be adopted.
45. See e.g. *Mason v Williams & Williams Ltd* [1955] 1 WLR 549, [1955] 1 All ER 808 (QBD), where it was held that an employer was entitled to assume that tools supplied by a reputable manufacturer were free from defects.
46. Section 4 LR(CN)A 1945, *Caswell v Powell Duffryn Associated Collieries Ltd* [1940] AC 152, [1939] 3 All ER 722 (HL).
47. *Jayes v IMI (Kynoch)* [1985] ICR 155 (CA), see page 113 below. Cf *Pitts v Hunt* [1991] 1 QB 24, [1990] 3 WLR 542, [1990] 3 All ER 344 (CA), see page 9 above.
48. *Boyle v Kodak Ltd* [1969] 1 WLR 661 per Lord Diplock at 674, [1969] 2 All ER 439 (HL), see page 132 below.
49. Section 10.
50. Section 47.

the Carriage by Air Act 1961,[51] the Civil Aviation Act 1982,[52] the Congenital Disabilities (Civil Liability) Act 1976,[53] the Consumer Protection Act 1987,[54] the Control of Pollution Act 1974,[55] the Employer's Liability (Defective Equipment) Act 1969,[56] the Employment Rights Act 1996,[57] the Environmental Protection Act 1990,[58] the Fatal Accidents Act 1976,[59] the Financial Services Act 1986,[60] the Financial Services and Markets Act 2000,[61] the Gas Act 1965,[62] the Merchant Shipping Act 1995,[63] the Nuclear Installations Act 1965,[64] the Housing Act 1988,[65] the Water Industry Act 1991[66] and the Water Resources Act 1991.[67]

Reference should be made to Chapter 3 above for consideration of the standard of care applicable to the claimant in cases concerning accidents at work caused by an employer's breach of statutory duty. The situation where an employee's default places an employer in breach of statutory duty is considered in Chapter 2.

---

51. Section 6 and Article 21 of Schedule 1. See also Article 21 of Schedule 1 to the Carriage by Air and Road Act 1979 (not yet in force).
52. Section 76.
53. Section 1(7).
54. Section 6(4).
55. Section 88.
56. Section 1(1).
57. Sections 122 & 123.
58. Section 73(9).
59. Section 5.
60. Section 62.
61. Section 150.
62. Section 14.
63. Sections 153 and 154, which concern pollution from tankers and other ships. For the provisions relating to collisions between ships see s 187 of the 1995 Act and page 55 above.
64. Section 13(6), although the test is different to that under the LR(CN)A 1945 and a higher degree of culpability is required.
65. Section 27(7).
66. Section 209.
67. Section 208.

TRESPASS TO THE PERSON

Contributory negligence can be raised in response to a claim for intentional trespass to the person.[68] However, the argument that provocation by the victim constituted contributory negligence has been rejected.[69] Whilst provocation in such cases would not reduce the claimant's compensatory damages, it may reduce or extinguish any exemplary damages.[70]

For examples of cases involving trespass to the person and allegations of contributory negligence, reference should be made to Chapter 18 below.

UNFAIR DISMISSAL

Section 123(6) of the Employment Rights Act 1996 provides that where the tribunal finds that the dismissal was to any extent caused or contributed to by any action of the complainant, it shall reduce the amount of the compensatory award by such proportion as it considers just and equitable having regard to that finding. In respect of the basic award, the tribunal may make a reduction by reason of any conduct of the complainant before the dismissal.[71]

Accordingly, there need be no causal connection between the conduct and the dismissal for a reduction in the basic award, although there must be such a connection for a reduction in the compensatory award.[72]

---

68. *Murphy* v *Culhane* [1977] QB 94, [1976] 3 WLR 458, [1976] 3 All ER 533 (CA), see page 294 below.
69. *Lane* v *Holloway* [1968] 1 QB 379, [1967] 3 WLR 1003, [1967] 3 All ER 129 (CA), see page 295 below.
70. *Barnes* v *Nayer*, (1986) *The Times*, December 19 (CA). See page 294 below.
71. Section 122 of the Employment Rights Act 1996.
72. However, where facts emerge which would have justified a procedurally unfair dismissal had they been known at the time, nothing may be awarded on the grounds that this is just and equitable pursuant to s 123(1) of the Employment Rights Act 1996, see *W Devis & Sons Ltd* v *Atkins* [1977] AC 931, [1977] 3 WLR 214 (HL).

UNLAWFUL EVICTION

Section 27(1) of the Housing Act 1988 gives an entitlement to damages, *inter alia*, to residential occupiers who have been unlawfully evicted or who have had their peace and comfort interfered with by their landlord in an attempt to cause them to give up possession.

Section 27(7)(a) provides that if it appears to the Court that prior to the event which gave rise to the liability, the conduct of the former residential occupier or any person living with him in the premises concerned was such that it is reasonable to mitigate the damages for which the landlord in default would otherwise be liable the court may reduce the amount of damages which would otherwise be payable by such amount as it thinks appropriate.

UTMOST GOOD FAITH

Contributory negligence cannot be raised in defence of an allegation of a breach of a duty of utmost good faith, such as arises in insurance contracts.[73]

WARRANTY OF AUTHORITY

The defence is not available to a claim brought in respect of a solicitor's breach of his warranty of authority.[74]

---

73. *Banque Keyser Ullmann S A* v *Skandia (UK) Insurance Co Ltd* [1987] 2 WLR 1300, [1987] 2 All ER 923 (QBD). The question was not considered by the Court of Appeal at [1990] 1 QB 665, [1989] 3 WLR 25, [1989] 2 All ER 952 or the House of Lords at [1991] 2 AC 249, [1990] 3 WLR 364, [1990] 2 All ER 947.
74. *Zwebner* v *The Mortgage Corporation Ltd* [1997] PNLR 504 (Ch D). The point was not considered by the Court of Appeal at [1998] PNLR 769.

CHAPTER SEVEN
CONTRIBUTORY NEGLIGENCE AND
RELATED DOCTRINES

There are a number of doctrines besides contributory negligence which can have the effect of reducing the claimant's damages by preventing him from recovering some or any of his losses, and which are or can be based upon the claimant's conduct. The distinction between these concepts is not always easy to apply in practice and a detailed consideration of the niceties of the various doctrines is beyond the scope of this book.[1]

VOLENTI NON FIT INJURIA

The maxim arose as a principle of estoppel applicable to a Roman citizen who consented to being sold as a slave. It operates as a complete defence on the basis that the claimant has either waived any right to make a claim or that his consent negates any duty that would otherwise have been owed to him by the defendant.

> "If the defendant desires to succeed on the ground that the maxim *volenti non fit injuria* is applicable, he must obtain a finding that the claimant freely and voluntarily, with full knowledge of the nature and extent of the risk he ran, impliedly agreed to incur it."[2]

Notwithstanding the basis of the defence, *volenti non fit injuria* can be raised against a minor.[3]

Where the claimant has simply been careless, contributory negligence is the more likely defence, whereas the defence of *volenti non fit injuria* tends to be based on more deliberate acts.

In *Stermer* v *Lawson*[4] the defendant loaned his motorcycle to the claimant and gave him only brief instructions as to how to use it. The claimant was injured in an accident caused by his inexperience. As the claimant was not aware of the precise dangers of the machine, merely that he was embarking on a risky exercise, the defence of *volenti non fit injuria* did not apply and his damages were reduced by 50% on account of his contributory negligence.

---

1. For a more detailed consideration of these topics and the distinctions between them, reference should be made to *McGregor on Damages*, 16th edn or *Clerk & Lindsell on Torts*, 18th edn.
2. *Letang* v *Ottawa Electric Railway Co* [1926] AC 725 per Lord Shaw at 731 (PC).
3. *Buckpitt* v *Oates* [1968] 1 All ER 1145 (QBD).
4. [1977] 5 WWR 628 (Canada).

Volenti non fit injuria is not generally available as a defence to a claim for breach of a statutory duty imposed on the defendant.[5] However, in *Imperial Chemical Industries Ltd* v *Shatwell*[6] S and his brother were employed as shot firers at ICI's quarry. They deliberately tested explosive charges in a dangerous manner, which was in breach of their instructions and the applicable regulations, injuring S. The Court of Appeal found S to have been contributorily negligent to the extent of 50%, enabling both brothers to recover.

The House of Lords reversed this decision and held that the complete defence of *volenti non fit injuria* applied to S's conduct. There was found to have been an implied agreement that the brothers would not sue each other and ICI were vicariously entitled to the benefit of that agreement. ICI were not themselves in breach of statutory duty and S had deliberately breached the statutory duties imposed upon him. Lord Reid observed that in such cases the difference between a finding of 100% contributory negligence and one of *volenti non fit injuria* mattered and explained the difference between the two defences:

> "There is a world of difference between two fellow-servants collaborating carelessly, so that the acts of both contribute to cause injury to one of them, and two fellow-servants combining to disobey an order deliberately, though they know the risk involved. It seems reasonable that the injured man should recover some compensation in the former case, but not in the latter ... In the first case only the partial defence of contributory negligence is available. In the second volenti non fit injuria is a complete defence, if the employer is not himself at fault and is only liable vicariously for the acts of the fellow-servant. If the [claimant] invited or freely aided and abetted his fellow-servant's disobedience, then he had volens in the fullest sense. He cannot complain of the resulting injury either against the fellow-servant or against the master on the ground of his vicarious responsibility for his fellow-servant's conduct."[7]

The complete defence of *volenti non fit injuria* has been successful less frequently since the enactment of the LR(CN)A 1945, as a finding of

---

5.   *Wheeler* v *New Merton Board Mills Ltd* [1933] 2 KB 669 (CA).
6.   [1965] AC 656, [1964] 3 WLR 329, [1964] 2 All ER 999 (HL).
7.   [1965] AC 656 at 672.

contributory negligence allows the court to apportion liability in appropriate cases and reach a fairer conclusion. It has been said:

> "Now that contributory negligence is not a complete defence, but only a ground for reducing the damages, the defence of *volenti non fit injuria* has been closely considered and in consequence, it has been severely limited. Knowledge of the risk of injury is not enough. Nor is a willingness to take the risk of injury. Nothing will suffice short of an agreement to waive any claim for negligence. The [claimant] must agree, expressly or impliedly to waive any claim for any injury that may befall him due to the lack of reasonable care by the defendant."[8]

In *Morris* v *Murray*[9] it was held that a passenger who knowingly and willingly embarked on a flight in a light aircraft with a pilot, whom he knew to be very drunk, was prevented by the defence of *volenti non fit injuria* from claiming damages against the pilot when the plane crashed. However, there are many examples of only contributory negligence being found in cases where passengers have accepted lifts from drivers they knew to be drunk.[10]

The mere fact of the claimant's knowledge that a driver has been drinking will not absolve the driver from a duty of care. However, the position is plainly different where the claimant undertakes an inherently risky exercise with a pilot who is so drunk that there is no possibility of him taking reasonable care. Further, s 149 of the Road Traffic Act 1988 precludes the defence of *volenti non fit injuria* in cases arising out of road traffic accidents where insurance is compulsory.

EX TURPI CAUSA NON ORITUR ACTIO

The defence of *ex turpi causa* or illegality operates as a complete defence and arises where the claimant has to rely on illegality to assert his claim.[11] The defence is not limited to criminal conduct on the part of the claimant, but

---

8. *Nettleship* v *Weston* [1971] 2 QB 691 per Lord Denning MR at 701, [1971] 3 WLR 370, [1971] 3 All ER 581 (CA). See page 222 below for the facts.
9. [1991] 2 QB 6, [1991] 2 WLR 195, [1990] 3 All ER 801 (CA).
10. See e.g. *Owens* v *Brimmell* [1977] QB 859, [1977] 2 WLR 943, [1976] 3 All ER 765 (QBD) and the other cases in Chapter 13.
11. *Tinsley* v *Milligan* [1994] 1 AC 340, [1993] 3 WLR 126, [1993] 3 All ER 65 (HL).

will also apply where the conduct was so reprehensible or grossly immoral that it would not be proper for the law to provide a remedy.[12]

The distinction between *ex turpi causa* and contributory negligence is effectively one of proportionality. The more serious the claimant's conduct in relation to that of the defendant, the more likely the defence of *ex turpi causa* is to apply.

In *Pitts* v *Hunt*[13] the claimant, a motorcycle pillion passenger, was injured in a collision. He had encouraged the intoxicated, uninsured and unlicensed rider to ride in a reckless manner. It was held that the action arose directly *ex turpi causa* and the claimant was precluded from recovering. The court would have also upheld a plea of *volenti non fit injuria*, were this not precluded by the Road Traffic Act.[14]

However, participation by the claimant in even a serious crime will not give rise to the defence of *ex turpi causa* where the defendant is significantly more culpable. For example, in *Revill* v *Newberry*[15] the conduct of a burglar who was shot by the premises' occupier amounted to contributory negligence and his claim was not barred as being *ex turpi causa*. The occupier had used excessive force, which was out of all proportion to the claimant burglar's conduct.[16]

In *Evans* v *Souls Garages Ltd*[17] E and his friend, both aged 13, purchased some petrol from SG's garage. They inhaled the petrol and some of it spilled onto E's trousers. E's friend then threw a match and the petrol ignited causing E to suffer extensive burns. SG was held to have been negligent in supplying the petrol to E. It was not clear that E had done anything illegal in purchasing and sniffing the petrol, although E thought it was wrong and possibly dangerous. Whilst the public would have found E's conduct blameworthy, his conduct, when balanced against SG's misconduct in selling the petrol and in the light of the damage suffered, did not deprive E of a right of action and the defence of *ex turpi causa* failed. Similarly, the defence of *volenti non fit injuria* did not apply as by assenting to sniffing petrol, E was not assenting to

---

12. *Kirkham* v *Chief Constable of Greater Manchester Police* [1990] 2 QB 283, [1990] 2 WLR 987, [1990] 3 All ER 246 (CA).
13. [1991] 1 QB 24, [1990] 3 WLR 542, [1990] 3 All ER 344 (CA).
14. See page 75 above.
15. [1996] QB 567, [1996] 2 WLR 239, [1996] 1 All ER 291 (CA). See page 292 below for the facts.
16. See also the cases in Chapter 18.
17. [2001] TLR 51 (QBD).

all the foolish behaviour which his friend might have indulged in as a result of the solvent abuse. However, the defence of contributory negligence did apply and E's contributory negligence was assessed at one third. E was at fault in acquiring the petrol, which he knew to be inflammable, and although he might not have known of its volatility or that someone sniffing it would do something dangerous, by sniffing the petrol in a joint venture with B, the boys became less responsible and that played some part in the accident.

NOVUS ACTUS INTERVENIENS

A *novus actus interveniens* is some intervening event that is so significant that it has the effect of breaking the chain of causation between the defendant's wrong and the claimant's loss. A *novus actus interveniens* may arise out of an act or omission of a third party or be a natural event. However, it is perfectly possible for the claimant's own conduct to constitute a *novus actus interveniens*.

Where the claimant's conduct increases his losses, this will generally be held to be a failure to mitigate or contributory negligence. In either case, the claimant's damages will be reduced.[18] However, the claimant's subsequent conduct may either be so unreasonable or have such a significant impact on his losses, that it will be held to have broken the chain of causation altogether and constitute a *novus actus interveniens*. In other words, the claimant's conduct will be found to have been the sole effective cause of his loss.

If the defendant's act or omission would not have resulted in the damage alleged had it not been for the claimant's unreasonable intervening act, the defendant will not be liable for that damage. It will be for the claimant to show that the loss for which he seeks to recover is not too remote.

Generally, damage will be found to be too remote where the claimant's conduct subsequent to the defendant's wrong separately increases the original damage. Where the claimant's conduct fails to reduce the future loss that would flow from the original damage, this will be regarded as a failure to mitigate.

---

18. In the case of a failure to mitigate by disallowing the increased loss, whereas in the case of contributory negligence by apportioning the loss.

For example, in *McKew* v *Holland & Hannen & Cubbitts (Scotland) Ltd*[19] M suffered injuries as a result of HHC's negligence. One of the effects of the injuries was that his leg gave way beneath him from time to time. As M was descending a steep flight of stairs, without a handrail or assistance, his leg gave way and he fell and sustained further injuries. It was held that as M knew of the weakness of his leg, he was obliged to act reasonably and carefully. His act in attempting to descend the stairs was to take an unreasonable risk and constituted a *novus actus interveniens* so as to break the chain of causation between HHC's negligence and the later injuries. However, the issue of contributory negligence was not raised.[20]

As a general rule, where the claimant's subsequent conduct is reckless, it will be regarded as constituting a *novus actus interveniens*.[21] Where the conduct is merely unreasonable, it will be viewed as contributory negligence. However, the distinction is essentially one of degree and is somewhat blurred in the cases where the claimant has been held to have been contributorily negligent to the extent of 100%.[22]

In *Sayers* v *Harlow UDC*[23] the claimant found herself locked in a toilet cubicle as a result of a defective lock. She tried to escape by climbing over the door and placed a foot on a revolving toilet roll. She realised that she was not going to be able to escape this way and tried to climb down. In so doing, she put weight on the toilet roll, which revolved and she fell. It was held that it was reasonable in the circumstances for the claimant to have explored the possibility of escaping in the way that she did. However, whilst the damage

---

19. [1969] 3 All ER 1621 (HLS).
20. Cf *Wieland* v *Cyril Lord Carpets Ltd* [1969] 3 All ER 1006 (QBD), where the issue of contributory negligence was also not raised and *Pyne* v *Wilkenfeld* (1981) 26 SASR 441 (Australia), where it was. See page 267 for the facts. See also *Carlsholm (owners)* v *Calliope (owners), "The Calliope"* [1970] 2 WLR 991, [1970] 1 All ER 624 (QBD), where the doctrine of contributory negligence and not remoteness was applied to a subsequent injury, allowing some recovery.
21. However, in *Reeves* v *Commissioner of Police of the Metropolis* [2000] 1 AC 360, [1999] 3 WLR 363, [1999] 3 All ER 897 (HL) a deliberate act of suicide was held to amount to contributory negligence and not a *novus actus interveniens*. In circumstances where the defendant's duty was to prevent the deceased from committing suicide, it would have rendered that duty meaningless to hold the suicide to be a novus actus interveniens. See further page 34 above and 256 below.
22. See page 8 above.
23. [1958] 1 WLR 623, [1958] 2 All ER 342 (CA).

was not too remote, the claimant was careless in allowing her balance to depend upon the toilet roll. Accordingly, she was found to have been contributorily negligence to the extent of 25%.

However, in *Sabri-Tabrizi* v *Lothian Health Board*[24] the claimant had unprotected sexual intercourse following a sterilisation operation, which she knew had failed. She had already fallen pregnant once before following the operation and had had that pregnancy terminated. Her actions in again having unprotected sexual intercourse constituted a *novus actus interveniens* and so broke the chain of causation between the negligent sterilisation operation and her subsequent pregnancy. The claimant's conduct went beyond that which could be described as negligent. It was found to have been unreasonable of her to expose herself to the risk of becoming pregnant, which she knew existed.[25] Whilst it may be correct to say that the claimant consented to the risk of becoming pregnant, the maxim of *volenti non fit injuria* did not apply as the claimant's acceptance of the risk did not occur either before or contemporaneously with the defendant's negligence.

MITIGATION

The claimant's damages will be limited to the losses actually sustained and will be reduced where he has failed to take reasonable steps either to reduce his original loss or to avert further loss. In other words, the claimant is not entitled to sit back and suffer loss, which could have been avoided by reasonable efforts.

The doctrine:

> "imposes on a [claimant] the duty of taking all reasonable steps to mitigate the loss consequent on the breach, and debars him from claiming any part of the damage which is due to his neglect to take such steps."[26]

---

24 1998 SLT 607 (OH).

25. However, a refusal to have a pregnancy terminated will not be regarded as an unreasonable act on the mother's part save in the most exceptional circumstances. See *Emeh* v *Kensington, Chelsea and Westminster Area Health Authority* [1985] QB 1012, [1985] 2 WLR 233, [1984] 3 All ER 1044 (CA).

26. *British Westinghouse Co* v *Underground Electric Railways* [1912] AC 673 per Viscount Haldane at 689 (HL).

Talk of a "duty" to mitigate can be misleading; the claimant is entitled to do as he pleases. However, he will not be entitled to recover for those losses, which he could reasonably have avoided.

For example, in *McAuley* v *London Transport Executive*[27] the injured claimant unreasonably refused to undergo an operation. The defendant was only held liable for the claimant's loss of earnings up to the time when he would have returned to work had he had the operation. However, it will not be unreasonable to refuse to undergo an operation with evenly balanced prospects of success[28] or one that is risky.[29]

Essentially, the doctrine of mitigation is concerned with the reasonableness of the claimant's conduct in taking action to minimise his loss resulting from the defendant's wrong. Where the doctrine applies to a particular category of loss, the whole of that category will be disallowed. Contributory negligence, on the other hand, is concerned with blameworthy conduct that is a contributory cause of the loss. Where contributory negligence is found, the loss caused thereby will be apportioned between the parties.

The onus of establishing a failure to mitigate will be on the defendant.[30] Whilst the claimant will be expected to act reasonably, the standard required of him will not be especially high as it is only by reason of the defendant's wrong that he finds himself in that position at all.

> "It is often easy after an emergency has passed to criticise the steps which have been taken to meet it, but such criticism does not come well from those who have themselves created the emergency."[31]

Further:

> "A court of justice ought to be very slow in countenancing any attempt by a wrong-doer to make captious objections to the methods by which those whom he has injured have sought to repair the injury ... In judging whether they have acted reasonably, I think a

27. [1957] 2 Lloyd's Rep 500 (CA).
28. *Savage* v *Wallis* [1966] 1 Lloyd's Rep 357 (CA).
29. *Richardson* v *Redpath Brown & Co Ltd* [1944] AC 62, [1944] 1 All ER 110 (HL).
30. *British Westinghouse Co* v *Underground Electric Railways* [1912] AC 673 (HL).
31. *Banco de Portugal* v *Waterlow & Sons* [1932] AC 452 per Lord Macmillan at 506 (HL).

court should be very indulgent and always bear in mind who was to blame."[32]

The claimant will not be expected to take steps to mitigate his position until he becomes aware that a wrong has been committed against him.[33] A step taken by the claimant before the defendant's tortious conduct to offset the loss, for example by taking out an insurance policy, will generally be considered to be a benefit which is collateral to the defendant's liability and so will not reduce it. However, where the claimant fails to take a precautionary step to reduce the risk of injury before the defendant's tortious conduct, for example by not wearing a seat belt, this may amount to contributory negligence.

SUMMARY OF THE DOCTRINES

The distinctions between the above doctrines are not always easy to apply in practice and this position has not been helped by some of the authorities using unhelpful descriptions for the claimant's conduct.

When considering the conduct of the claimant in a particular case, it is suggested that the questions of:

1. *volenti non fit injuria,*

2. *ex turpi causa,*

3. *novus actus interveniens,*

4. contributory negligence, and

5. mitigation

should be considered in that order. Once the claimant's conduct has been found to be covered by one of the doctrines, the remaining ones in the list will generally not apply.

Whilst it is perfectly possible for more than one of the above doctrines to apply in a single case, for example where the claimant has been

---

32. *Lodge Holes Colliery Company Limited* v *Wednesbury Corporation* [1908] AC 323 per Lord Loreburn at 325 (HL).
33. *County Ltd* v *Girozentrale Securities* [1996] 3 All ER 834 (CA).

contributorily negligent and has then to failed to mitigate his loss, the contributory negligence and the failure to mitigate will then be attributable to different acts or omissions on the claimant's part.

An example of a claimant stepping out into the road in front of the defendant's moving car and breaking his leg in the ensuing collision illustrates the difference between the doctrines:

1. If the claimant deliberately, carelessly or blamelessly stepped out in front of the car, giving the defendant car driver no opportunity to avoid him, the claim will fail as there will have been no negligence on the defendant's part. Accordingly, the stage of considering the claimant's conduct will not even be reached.

2. If the claimant agreed to play "dodge the car" with the defendant, the claim will fail on the grounds of *volenti non fit injuria*. The claimant agreed to run the risk of being struck by the defendant's car.

3. If the claimant stepped out in front of the car in an attempt to cause the defendant to stop so that he could steal the defendant's car, the claim will fail on the grounds of *ex turpi causa*.

4. If the claimant carelessly stepped out ahead of the defendant's car in circumstances where the defendant could have avoided him if he had been paying attention, the claim will succeed subject to the claimant's damages being reduced for contributory negligence.

5. If having broken his leg in the accident, the claimant unreasonably failed to attend his physiotherapy appointments and thereby made a more protracted recovery and was off work for an extra month, there will have been a failure to mitigate and the claimant will not recover in respect of his avoidable losses.

6. If having broken his leg in the accident, the claimant decided to take up kick-boxing and due to the weakness in his leg fell and broke his arm, the claimant's conduct will have amounted to a *novus actus interveniens* and he will not be entitled to recover in respect of his additional injuries.

In some instances there will be little practical difference to the claimant consequent upon which doctrine his conduct is found to fall within. However, it is important to maintain the distinctions as the examples above show that in many cases the amount recoverable will differ.

Applying the correct label to the claimant's conduct will also be relevant when it comes to considering the defendant's counterclaim in respect of the damage caused to his car in the collision. In the above examples, the defendant would be entitled to recover in full in every case except for (2) where the defence of *volenti non fit injuria* would apply equally to him and (4) where he would recover reduced damages on account of his own contributory negligence.

Further, the onus of proving negligence on the defendant's part and that the loss suffered is not too remote is on the claimant, whereas the burden in respect of the other doctrines will be on the defendant.

CONTRIBUTION/INDEMNITY

A claim to a contribution or an indemnity differs from contributory negligence and the other doctrines discussed in this chapter in that it is not a defence and does not impact upon the level of damages awarded to the claimant.

Section 1(1) of the Civil Liability (Contribution) Act 1978 provides that, subject to qualifications, any person liable in respect of any damage suffered by another person may recover contribution from any other person liable in respect of the same damage (whether jointly with him or otherwise).

When apportioning liability between a claimant and several defendants, the claimant's damages should first be calculated. Those damages should then be reduced as appropriate to take account of any contributory negligence on the claimant's part. Thereafter, the liability of the defendants *inter se* should be considered pursuant to the Civil Liability (Contribution) Act 1978.[34] The assessment of the claimant's share in the responsibility for the damage suffered does not involve a determination of each defendant's culpability, but rather the totality of the defendants' negligence.

---

34. *Fitzgerald* v *Lane* [1989] AC 328, [1988] 3 WLR 356, [1988] 2 All ER 961 (HL), see page 234 below.

The amount of the contribution recoverable will take account of any deduction from the damages payable to the claimant on account of contributory negligence[35] and will be such sum as may be found by the court to be just and equitable having regard to the extent of the parties' responsibility for the damage in question.[36]

In *Pride Valley Foods Ltd* v *Hall & Partners (Contract Management) Ltd*[37] it was said that the approach to the apportionment of liability between defendants differed from the approach to be adopted when considering questions of contributory negligence. Whilst the principles for assessing contributory negligence could in some cases form the basis for the apportionment of liability between defendants, it did not follow that the reverse was true. The difference arose because a reduction for contributory negligence would not be made where the damage caused by the claimant's negligence was the same damage as it was the defendant's duty to guard him against:

> "While the principles for gauging contributory negligence can ... furnish a template for the apportionment of liability between joint tortfeasors, it does not follow that the converse will be the case. This is because the starting point of the two exercises is different. Contribution starts from a point at which two or more defendants have been held to have contributed by their own fault to the claimant's injury. The remaining task is then to measure their contributions by gauging the relative causative potency of their respective faults and their comparative blameworthiness. Contributory negligence, by contrast, starts from a point at which the defendant alone has been held to have caused the claimant's injury by his fault. Not one but three questions then arise. The first is whether the claimant too was materially at fault. The second, if he was, is whether his fault lay within the very risk which it was the defendant's duty to guard him against. It is only if his fault was not, or not wholly, within the causative reach of the defendant's own neglect that the question of relative culpability enters the picture. Here, no doubt, the similarities with the principles applicable under the 1978 Act will be considerable; but here too it may be relevant that the claimant's neglect was linked to the unfulfilled duty owed to him by the defendant."[38]

---

35. Section 2(3)(b) Civil Liability (Contribution) Act 1978.
36. Section 2(1) Civil Liability (Contribution) Act 1978.
37. (2001) 76 Con LR 1 (CA).
38. (2001) 76 Con LR 1 per Sedley LJ at 59.

In *Jones* v *Wilkins*[39] J, aged two, was sitting on her mother's knee in the front passenger's seat of a car being driven by J's aunt. She was restrained only by the lap belt part of her mother's seat belt. The car was involved in a collision caused by W's negligence, in which J was seriously injured. It was found that if J had been wearing an approved child restraint, the risk of injury would have been practically eliminated. Liability was apportioned under the Civil Liability (Contribution) Act 1978 so that W bore 75% of the responsibility and J's mother and aunt were 25% to blame for J's injuries. The basis for assessing fault under the Civil Liability (Contribution) Act 1978 was held to be similar to the approach to be adopted under the LR(CN)A 1945 and the judge was entitled to rely on the guidelines set out in *Froom* v *Butcher*.[40]

The LR(CN)A 1945 does not create a right to contribution between tortfeasors. Section 1(1) provides, in part:

> "... where any person suffers damage as the result partly of his own fault and partly of the fault of any other person or persons, a claim in respect of that damage shall not be defeated by reason of the fault of the person suffering the damage, but the damages recoverable in respect thereof shall be reduced ..."

That section does not create a right of action, it removes an obstacle. The word "damage" refers to that which is suffered and for which a "claim" may be made and for which "damages" are recoverable. The word "damage" is quite inapt to cover the liability of a defendant who has had a judgment for damages for negligence given against him. Accordingly, a tortfeasor who is partly to blame for an injury cannot avail himself of the provisions of that subsection in order to obtain a contribution from someone else who is also to blame for the injury.[41]

In *Wall* v *Radford*[42] W brought proceedings against R arising out of a road traffic accident in which W and R had been the drivers. In earlier contribution proceedings ancillary to a claim brought against both drivers by W's passenger, it was held that both drivers were equally to blame. It was held that W could not re-open the question of liability or apportionment; her contributory negligence had been determined in the earlier contribution

---

39. [2001] PIQR P179, [2001] RTR 283 (CA).
40. [1976] QB 286, [1975] 3 WLR 379, [1975] 3 All ER 520 (CA), see page 246 below.
41. *Drinkwater* v *Kimber* [1952] 2 QB 281, [1952] 1 All ER 701 (CA).
42. [1991] 2 All ER 741, [1992] RTR 109 (QBD).

proceedings. Similarly, the question of contributory negligence and apportionment between parties could not be re-opened in subsequent proceedings between those same parties.[43]

It has been held in an Australian case[44] that where the claimant company's damages are reduced on account of its contributory negligence and in particular that of its chief executive, a claim for a contribution against the chief executive should fail. To require him to make a contribution would mean that the defendant unjustly receives double compensation.

---

43. *Clyne* v *Yardley* [1959] NZLR 617 (New Zealand), see also *Henderson* v *Henderson* (1843) 3 Hare 100.
44. *AWA Ltd* v *Daniels t/a Deloitte Haskins & Sells* (1995) 16 ACSR 607 (Australia), see also the first instance decisions at (1992) 7 ACSR 759 and (1992) 9 ACSR 383. See page 186 below for the facts.

CHAPTER EIGHT
PRACTICE & PROCEDURE

JURISDICTION

The defence of contributory negligence can be raised in arbitration proceedings as well as those before a court.[1] Where the action is tried by a jury, it is for the jury to determine the extent to which the claimant's damages should be reduced to take account of any contributory negligence.[2]

Where a court has a limited jurisdiction in terms of value, that limit applies to the damages assessed by the court before they are reduced to take account of contributory negligence. So, for example, if a court's jurisdiction is limited to £300 and the claimant's contributory negligence is assessed at one third, the maximum recoverable by the claimant would be £200.[3]

PLEADING

Contributory negligence should be expressly pleaded and particularised in the Defence.[4] Where it has not been pleaded by the defendant, the court should not make such a finding of its own volition.[5] The same principle applies where the defence is pleaded, but not pursued at trial.[6]

CPR 16.5(2) now provides that where the defendant denies an allegation:

(a) he must state his reasons for doing so; and

(b) if he intends to put forward a different version of events from that given by the claimant, he must state his own version.

The effect of this rule is to still require contributory negligence to be pleaded, as a defendant wishing to rely on the defence of contributory negligence will be disputing the causation of the claimant's damage as alleged in the

---

1.   Section 4 LR(CN)A 1945.
2.   Section 1(6) LR(CN)A 1945.
3.   *Kelly* v *Stockport Corpn* [1949] 1 All ER 893 (CA), a case decided under the County Courts Act 1934, which limited the County Courts' jurisdiction over claims based in tort to £200.
4.   *Atkinson* v *Stewart & Partners Ltd* [1954] NILR 146 (NICA), where Lord MacDermott said at 154 "If the defendants ... intend to make a substantive case under the plea they should state the material facts on which they rely".
5.   *Fookes* v *Slaytor* [1978] 1 WLR 1293, [1979] 1 All ER 137 (CA).
6.   *Taylor* v *Simon Carves* 1958 SLT (Sh Ct) 23 (SH).

Particulars of Claim and will often be advancing a different factual basis for the loss.

Where contributory negligence has been raised in the Defence, it is not obligatory to serve a Reply denying the allegations.[7] However, it may be useful to do so where the claimant wishes to allege facts not already set out in the Particulars of Claim in answer to the allegations made in the Defence.

The possibility of a finding of contributory negligence being made against the claimant should be disregarded when quantifying the claim for the purposes of the statement of value to be included in the Claim Form.[8]

EFFECT ON APPLICATIONS FOR SUMMARY JUDGMENT

There is no reason why a plea of contributory negligence should necessarily defeat a claimant's application for summary judgment, especially where the defendant's case, taken at its highest, would not lead to a finding of contributory negligence.[9]

RES JUDICATA

"Where a given matter becomes the subject of litigation in, and of adjudication by, a court of competent jurisdiction, the court requires the parties to that litigation to bring forward their whole case, and will not (except under special circumstances) permit the same parties to open the same subject of litigation in respect of matters which might have been brought forward as part of the subject in contest but which was not brought forward ... the plea of res judicata applies, except in special cases."[10]

---

7. CPR 16.7.
8. CPR 16.3(6)(b).
9. See e.g. Barnes v Nayer (1986) The Times, December 19 (CA). See page 294 below.
10. Henderson v Henderson (1843) 3 Hare 100 per Sir James Wigram VC at 115.

In *Wall* v *Radford*[11] W brought proceedings against R arising out of a road traffic accident in which W and R had been the drivers. In earlier contribution proceedings ancillary to a claim brought against both drivers by W's passenger, it was held that both drivers were equally to blame. It was held that W could not re-open the question of liability or apportionment; her contributory negligence had been determined in the earlier contribution proceedings. Similarly, the question of contributory negligence and apportionment between parties could not be re-opened in subsequent proceedings between those same parties.[12]

Provided that a judgment on liability does not settle the issue, there is no reason why a pleaded allegation of contributory negligence cannot be argued at the assessment of damages stage.[13]

BURDEN OF PROOF

The burden of proving contributory negligence is on the defendant and the standard of proof is the usual balance of probabilities.

> "In order to establish the defence of contributory negligence, the defendant must prove, first, that the [claimant] failed to take ordinary care of himself, or, in other words, such care as a reasonable man would take for his own safety, and, secondly, that his failure to take care was a contributory cause of the accident."[14]

However, it is not necessary for the defendant to adduce evidence to establish contributory negligence, as it may be inferred from the claimant's evidence.[15] Once an allegation of contributory negligence has been pleaded, the court

---

11. [1991] 2 All ER 741, [1992] RTR 109 (QBD), see also *Talbot* v *Berkshire County Council* [1994] QB 290, [1993] 3 WLR 708, [1993] 4 All ER 9 (CA).
12. *Clyne* v *Yardley* [1959] NZLR 617 (New Zealand), see also *Henderson* v *Henderson* (1843) 3 Hare 100.
13. *Maes Finance Ltd* v *A L Phillips & Co (A Firm)* (1997) *The Times*, March 25 (Ch D).
14. *Lewis* v *Denye* [1939] 1 KB 540 per Du Parcq LJ at 554, [1939] 1 All ER 310 (CA), affirmed at [1940] AC 921, [1940] 3 All ER 299 (HL). See also the speech of Lord Wright in *Caswell* v *Powell Duffryn Associated Collieries Ltd* [1940] AC 152 at 172, [1939] 3 All ER 722 (HL).
15. *Sharpe* v *Southern Railway* [1925] 2 KB 311 (CA), a case where the claimant was injured stepping off a train that had not stopped fully at a platform.

must consider it even if the defendant does not attend at the trial. However, the question would have to be resolved on the evidence actually before the court.[16]

FORM OF ORDER

The court must record in its order the total damages which would have been recoverable if the claimant had not been at fault.[17]

The reduction of the claimant's damages is made last, i.e. after all other deductions have been made in order to quantify the claimant's award of damages.

RECOUPMENT OF SOCIAL SECURITY BENEFITS

The Social Security (Recovery of Benefits) Act 1997 provides for the recoupment of various state benefits from certain awards of damages. The 1997 Act makes no provision for the recoupment to be reduced to take account of any finding of contributory negligence.

Accordingly, a defendant who is found liable for only 10% of the claimant's damages will, nonetheless, have to pay the Secretary of State 100% of the certified recoverable benefits. This payment to the Secretary of State can be deducted from the appropriate head of damages payable to the claimant, but where the amount payable to the Secretary of State exceeds the damages payable to the claimant under that particular head, the damages payable to the claimant cannot be reduced below nil.[18]

The recovery of benefits recouped bites into the damages that are actually paid and so any reduction for contributory negligence will have been made before the damages are reduced to reflect the amount of benefits recouped.

---

16. *UCB Bank Plc* v *David Pinder Plc* [1998] PNLR 398 (QBD).
17. Section 1(2) LR(CN)A 1945.
18. See in particular ss 1, 6 and 8 of the Social Security (Recovery of Benefits) Act 1997.

COSTS

In cases where contributory negligence is raised as an issue with or without success, the costs of the litigation will be in the discretion of the court in the normal way.[19]

However, the defendant's degree of success on the issue of contributory negligence and the proportion of the costs incurred in dealing with the allegation will be factors which may be taken into consideration by the court in deciding what order should be made in relation to costs and, in particular, whether a partial order for costs should be made.[20]

In cases, such as those following a road traffic accident, where there is a claim and counterclaim alleging negligence and both parties are found equally to blame, the correct order will generally be for judgment on the claim for 50% of the damages proved and judgment on the counterclaim for 50% of the damages proved. The awarding or refusal of costs to both parties might give an undue advantage to one party or the other and whilst there is no absolute rule, it may be that the fairest course would be for there to be no order as to costs.[21]

APPEALS

Generally an appellate body will not interfere with the discretion exercised by the judge who tried the case.[22] The Court of Appeal will only interfere with a trial judge's assessment of the proportions of responsibility for negligence where the judge has erred in principle or has misapprehended the facts or where the Court of Appeal is satisfied that the assessment made by the trial judge was plainly wrong.[23]

---

19. *Howitt* v *Alexander & Sons Ltd* 1948 SC 154 (IH), where it was said that there was no principle requiring the costs of the litigation to be divided up in the same proportions as liability.
20. See generally CPR 44.3.
21. *Smith* v *W H Smith & Sons Ltd* [1952] 1 All ER 528 (CA).
22. *National Coal Board* v *England* [1954] AC 403, [1954] 2 WLR 400, [1954] 1 All ER 546 (HL).
23. *Kerry* v *Carter* [1969] 1 WLR 1372, [1969] 3 All ER 723 (CA), see also *Hannam* v *Mann* [1984] RTR 252 (CA), *Brown* v *Thompson* [1968] 1 WLR 1003, [1968] 2 All ER 708 (CA).

"[The Court of Appeal] adopts in regard to apportionment the same attitude as it does to damages. [It] will interfere if the judge has gone wrong in principle or is shown to have misapprehended the facts; but, even if neither of these is shown, [it] will interfere if [it is] of opinion that the judge was clearly wrong. After all, the function of [the] court is to be a Court of Appeal. [It is there] to put right that which has gone wrong."[24]

24. *Kerry* v *Carter* [1969] 1 WLR 1372 per Lord Denning MR at 1376, [1969] 3 All ER 723 (CA).

PART TWO
PARTICULAR INSTANCES

CHAPTER NINE

ACCIDENTS AT WORK

For consideration of the principles involved in assessing the standard of care required of employees, reference should made to the section on employees in Chapter 3 above.

1. DISOBEDIENCE

100%   **MANWARING v BILLINGTON**

[1952] 2 All ER 747 (CA)

M was employed by B as a builder. He was instructed not to climb any ladder without first putting sacking under it and tying it securely at the top to prevent it slipping. M set up a ladder with the assistance of another employee, who had received similar instructions. M ascended the ladder without placing sacking under it or tying it at the top. The ladder slipped and M fell, sustaining injuries. It was found that B was in breach of the applicable regulations, which placed on employers the duty of ensuring that ladders were footed and securely fixed. It was held that B's statutory duty had not been delegated to M, but that B was only in breach of the regulations because of the failure of M to perform duties, which were properly and reasonably assigned to him. M had failed to carry out his instructions and, with appreciation of his own omissions, had proceeded to climb the ladder, which then slipped. M's injuries were caused solely by his own negligence.

100%   **HEWSON v GRIMSBY FISHMEAL CO**

[1986] CLY 2255 (QBD)

H was an experienced mechanical shovel driver employed by G. He was operating a mechanical system that became jammed. Whilst attempting to clear the blockage with the assistance of G's foreman, H's arm became trapped and he was injured. H was found to have broken all of the relevant rules for the safe clearance of blockages and was contributorily negligent to the extent of 100%.

90%   **HODKINSON v HENRY WALLWORK & CO LTD**

[1955] 1 WLR 1195, [1955] 3 All ER 236 (CA)

H was employed working at a machine, which stopped working when the wire ropes used in the transmission slipped off their pulleys. H knew that the established practice in such circumstances was to summon the maintenance crew to put the matter right. However, rather than waiting for the maintenance crew, he obtained a ladder and climbed up to the pulleys, which were some nine feet above the ground. H had not switched the power to the machine off and as he was replacing the ropes, the machine started operating and his hand was crushed. It was held that even though the pulleys were high above the ground, they should have been fenced and that the absence of fencing was a cause of the accident. However, given that HWC could not have foreseen H's acts, his contributory negligence in acting in defiance of the established practice was assessed at 90%.

80%   **STAPLEY v GYPSUM MINES LTD**

[1953] AC 663, [1953] 3 WLR 279, [1953] 2 All ER 478
(HL)

S was working with another employee, D, in GM's mine.
They approached a roof, which they recognised to be
dangerous. They informed their foreman, who instructed
them not to work under it until they had brought it down.
S and D were unable to get the roof down easily and
decided to press on with their work. D left the area and S
went to work under the roof. D returned after half an hour
to find S dead under the collapsed roof. S's contributory
negligence was assessed at 80%.

75%   **STOREY v NATIONAL COAL BOARD**

[1983] 1 All ER 375 (QBD)

S rode on a conveyor belt in NCB's mine and was carried
into a chute and killed. NCB had rules forbidding
employees from riding on conveyor belts and there were
various warning notices. NCB should have ensured that the
rules were obeyed, but S was an experienced employee and
placed himself in danger. His contributory negligence was
assessed at 75%.

75%   **LEACH v STANDARD TELEPHONES & CABLES LTD**

[1966] 1 WLR 1392, [1966] 2 All ER 523 (QBD)

L used a rotating saw when he had no business to and had
been instructed not to. He set the guard far too high and
injured his thumb. The guard would not have been
effective even had it been set lower. L's contributory
negligence was assessed at 75%.

66.66%   **TROTMAN v BRITISH RAILWAYS BOARD**

[1975] ICR 95 (QBD)

T was struck by a train whilst working on a railway line. BRB's rules required train drivers to sound their whistles when approaching persons near the track. T was warned of the approach of a train and went to a place of safety. BRB's rules further required employees to wait until a train had passed far enough away to have a clear view of the track before returning to work on the track. T moved from his place of safety before he had a clear view of the track and was struck by another train, which had not sounded its whistle. It was found that T's failure to observe the rules was the main cause of his death and his contributory negligence was assessed at two thirds.

66.66%   **BAXTER v WOOLCOMBERS LTD**

(1963) 107 SJ 553 (CA)

B, a man of low intelligence, injured his hand on a machine whilst working for W as a result of W's failure to provide a safe system of work and breach of statutory duty in failing to fence the machine. B's contributory negligence in disobeying orders was assessed at two thirds and it was said that the applicable standard of conduct was that of a reasonable man. Accordingly, B's intelligence level was irrelevant (although it would be relevant to the standard of duty owed to him by his employers).

50%   **DENYER v CHARLES SKIPPER AND EAST LTD**

[1970] 1 WLR 1087, [1970] 2 All ER 382 (CA)

D, aged 17, was injured whilst cleaning the cylinders of a lithographic printing machine. He had been given clear instructions not to touch the cylinders with a rag whilst they were still moving, yet he did so and his hand became caught and injured. CSE were found liable for exposing D to a risk of injury from the moving parts of the machinery. However, D's carelessness and disobedience of the instructions he had received were found to have been a substantial cause of the accident and his contributory negligence was assessed at 50%.

50%   ## CARGILL v P R EXCAVATIONS

[2000] CLY 4228 (QBD)

PRE employed C as a general labourer. He was working with another employee benching the base of a manhole cover in an excavation approximately 1.8 metres deep, 2 metres wide and 2.4 metres long. No steps were taken to shore up the excavation by using wooden batons or compacting the excavated soil. The soil had been extracted from the pit with a mechanical excavator operated by the other employee. C was injured when struck by a large lump of soil, which fell into the excavation. It was found that:

(1) C and the other employee were of similar status and working together in a position of parity;

(2) the other employee (for whom PRE was vicariously liable) was negligent as the spoil was placed close to the excavation and there was no attempt to shore the excavation up or prevent material from falling into it;

(3) C had attended a two day safety awareness course;

(4) C had disregarded oral and written instructions as to a safe system of work; and

(5) C was aware of the proximity of the spoil and the danger that it posed and nonetheless entered the excavation and worked with that knowledge.

C was held to have been contributorily negligent to the extent of 50%.

50%   **WILLIAMS v PORT OF LIVERPOOL STEVEDORING CO LTD**

[1956] 1 WLR 551, [1956] 2 All ER 69 (QBD)

W and five other employees were unloading bags from a
barge. They were instructed to unload according to the
usual safe method, which they did. However, when the
supervisor left they started to unload and stack the bags
using a different and dangerous method. The stack of bags
collapsed and injured W. It was held that W had been
contributorily negligent to the extent of 50% as his consent
to the dangerous and disobedient system had been
essential to the whole gang adopting that method.

40%   **GRAND METROPOLITAN PLC v CLOSED CIRCUIT COOLING LTD**

[1997] CLY 2607 (CA)

CCC employed C at GM's premises. C was injured driving
a forklift truck, which he knew he did not have authority
to do. He had lied about his ability to drive the truck, had
not referred to a supervisor and had driven it badly with his
leg outside the vehicle. However, C was young and
inexperienced, he had attempted to get his employers to
provide a qualified driver, the keys were left in the truck, a
qualified driver was not available and C had used the fork
lift truck to get his work done. C's contributory negligence
was assessed at 40%.

20%   **DAVIES v SWAN MOTOR CO (SWANSEA) LTD**

[1949] 2 KB 291, [1949] 1 All ER 620 (CA)

D, contrary to his employer's regulations, was riding on the side steps of a dustcart when an accident occurred between the dustcart and an overtaking bus, crushing D. The accident was caused by the fault of both the driver of the dustcart and the driver of the bus. It was found that D had taken up a very dangerous and unnecessary position on the dustcart and his contributory negligence was assessed at 20%.

20%   **JONES v LIVOX QUARRIES LTD**

[1952] 2 QB 608 (CA)

Contrary to instructions, J obtained a lift by standing on the back bumper of a moving excavator without the driver's knowledge. A dumper truck drove into the rear of the excavator and J was injured. J's contributory negligence in unreasonably and improperly exposing himself to this risk was assessed at 20%.

0%   **WESTWOOD v POST OFFICE**

[1974] AC 1, [1973] 3 WLR 287, [1973] 3 All ER 184 (HL)

W was injured after entering a room, the door to which bore a notice that "only the authorised attendant is permitted to enter". W was found to have been disobedient, but not negligent.[1]

---

1.   See page 140 below.

2. FAILURE TO USE PROTECTIVE EQUIPMENT

50%   **CROUCH v BRITISH RAIL ENGINEERING LTD**

[1988] IRLR 404 (CA)

C was employed as a skilled mechanical fitter. He was injured when a steel fragment flew into his eye. Goggles had been available to employees who believed that they needed them, but C had not been wearing them. C's contributory negligence was assessed at 50%.

50%   **CLIFFORD v CHARLES H CHALLEN & SON LTD**

[1951] 1 KB 495, [1951] 1 All ER 72 (CA)

C was employed joining pieces of timber with glue. He was aware of the danger of contracting dermatitis through contact with the glue if he did not use barrier cream and wash his hands after using it. There was no barrier cream available in the workshop, but employees could fetch some from a store. However, none did and the foreman did not encourage its use. C contracted dermatitis and his damages were reduced by 50% to take account of his contributory negligence in failing to take the precautions, which he knew ought to have been taken.

50%   **SAMWAYS v WESTGATE ENGINEERS**

(1962) 106 SJ 937 (CA)

S, a dustman, injured his hand when he picked up a cardboard carton from which a piece of glass protruded at WE's premises. S was not wearing the special protective gloves provided to him by his employers, as it was a hot day. S's contributory negligence was held to have been 50% in exposing himself to the risk of accidents of this kind.

40%   BUX v SLOUGH METALS LTD

[1973] 1 WLR 1358, [1974] 1 All ER 262 (CA)

B was employed as a die caster by SM. He had been issued goggles, but told his supervisor that they were useless as they misted up and stopped wearing them. He was not instructed to continue wearing them and was injured when some molten metal splashed into his eye. It was found that B was himself in breach of the applicable regulations in not making full and proper use of the goggles and his contributory negligence was assessed at 40%.

25%   DOWMAN v WOLVERHAMPTON DIE CASTING CO LTD

[1968] 3 All ER 692 (CA)

D worked handling castings, which sometimes had deposits of chromic acid on them. She had been warned of the danger of direct contact with the castings and had been provided with gloves. However, D did not always wear a glove on her left hand as it was a nuisance, that hand being deformed. D contracted dermatitis and her contributory negligence was assessed at 25%.

3. KNOWN VULNERABILITY

60%   COLES v ENGLISH ABRASIVE CO

[1965] CLY 2651 (QBD)

C did not disclose his history of back trouble when he took a job with EAC involving heavy lifting. He suffered a slipped disc whilst lifting heavy rolls of cloth for which EAC was held liable, but C's contributory negligence in failing to disclose his weakness or ask for assistance was assessed at 60%.

50%   **CORK v KIRBY MACLEAN LTD**

[1952] 2 All ER 402 (CA)

C, an epileptic, was working on a high platform painting the ceiling of a factory. In breach of the applicable regulations, there were no guard rails or toe boards on the platform, which was just over 2 feet wide. C had a fit and fell from the platform to his death. C's contributory negligence in failing to inform his employers that he was subject to epileptic fits and had been forbidden by his doctor from working at heights was assessed at 50%, it being impossible to say that the fault was more on one side than the other.

33.33%   **McCAFFERY v DATTA**

[1997] PIQR Q64 (CA)

M, a nurse, injured her back lifting a patient. It was found that her employers had been negligent on the basis that M's assistant was inadequately trained and had not carried her share of the weight. However, M was found to have been contributorily negligent to the extent of one third as she had ignored medical advice not to undertake heavy lifting following a previous back injury and had not arranged the patient's bed for the most efficient lifting.

4. LIFTING

75%   **MEE-BISHOP v COURTAULDS CHEMICALS**

[1997] CLY 2613 (CC)

M was employed by CC as a supervisor. He injured himself manually handling several very heavy rolls of paper. He had felt a twinge after lifting the first roll, but nevertheless continued to lift further rolls. He was unable to use a forklift truck as usual due to a pool of water on the floor. M had received manual handling training and knew it was dangerous to attempt to lift such large rolls. He did not call for assistance to lift the load or have the water cleared up. M's contributory negligence was assessed at 75%.

60%   **COLES v ENGLISH ABRASIVE CO**

[1965] CLY 2651 (QBD)

C did not disclose his history of back trouble when he took a job with EAC involving heavy lifting. He suffered a slipped disc whilst lifting heavy rolls of cloth for which EAC was held liable, but C's contributory negligence in failing to disclose his weakness or ask for assistance was assessed at 60%.

50%   **MEARNS v LOTHIAN RC**

1991 SLT 338 (OH)

M was employed on a ship and was injured carrying a heavy valve up a ladder without assistance. There were no other employees available to assist M, but he had carried out the same task with assistance the day before. He had not been instructed not to attempt the task alone, but his contributory negligence was assessed at 50%.

50%   ## BROWN v ALLIED IRONFOUNDERS LTD

[1974] 1 WLR 527, [1974] 2 All ER 135 (HLS)

B was employed as a welder at AI's factory. However, on the day in question she was instructed to paint some metal cages. In the course of the painting, the cages needed to be turned over. The cages were too heavy to be safely turned over by one woman and whilst B was not expressly instructed to seek assistance in turning the cages over, she was aware that it was the normal (although not invariable) practice to do so and help was available. B did not seek assistance and injured her back in the course of turning a cage over alone. AI were found to have been in breach of their statutory duty in not expressly telling B not to turn the cages over alone. It was held at first instance that B's contributory negligence amounted to 50% and that finding was not challenged on the subsequent appeals.

33.33%   ## McCAFFERY v DATTA

[1997] PIQR Q64 (CA)

M, a nurse, injured her back lifting a patient. It was found that her employers had been negligent on the basis that M's assistant was inadequately trained and had not carried her share of the weight. However, M was found to have been contributorily negligent to the extent of one third as she had ignored medical advice not to undertake heavy lifting following a previous back injury and had not arranged the patient's bed for the most efficient lifting.

0%   **LINDSAY v TNT EXPRESS (UK) LTD**

1996 GWD 38–2231 (OH)

L was employed by TNT as a delivery driver. He injured his back delivering a 48kg television to a customer, who refused to assist. He had to manhandle the television off the lorry and carry it to the customer's house in a cramped and awkward position. He was regularly required to undertake heavy and awkward lifts, worked alone and was not provided with a barrow. It was found that L was required to make the best of a bad job and there was no contributory negligence.

5. UNSAFE MACHINERY

100%   **COPE v NICKEL ELECTRO**

[1980] CLY 1268 (QBD)

C, an experienced engineer, was called to NE's factory to repair a power press, the guards of which had been removed ready for C's inspection. C instructed the machine to be run and injured himself when he touched the flywheel. It was held that although there had been a breach of s 14 of the Factories Act 1961, C was in charge and solely responsible for the operation. He undertook the risk of not requiring that the guards be replaced when the machine was run. C was found to have been 100% contributorily negligent.

100%   **HUMPHRIES v SILENT CHANNEL PRODUCTS**

[1981] CLY 1209 (QBD)

H was employed by SCP as a tool setter. He was changing
some guides on a machine, when the machine made a
stroke and a blade cut his hand. Whilst the machine was
not guarded as it should have been, it was held that H
should have isolated the power to the machine before
working on it. In the circumstances, H was the sole author
of his misfortune.[2]

100%   **JAYES v IMI (KYNOCH) LTD**

[1985] ICR 155 (CA)

J was an experienced supervisor at IMI's factory. Other
employees were attending to a fault on a power press
machine. The guard was removed and the machine was
started to test it. As a belt inside the machine was moving,
J reached in and used a rag to stop grease spreading to the
belt. The rag became caught and J's finger was pulled into
the machine and injured. At the trial of the claim based
upon J's allegation that the dangerous part of the machine
should have been guarded, he admitted that he had done a
very foolish thing and was found to have been 100%
contributorily negligent. There comes a stage where the
claimant's degree of fault is so great that the court ceases to
make fine distinctions and holds that, in practical terms,
the fault is entirely that of the claimant.

---

2.   Cf *Stocker* v *Norprint Ltd* (1971) 115 SJ 58 (CA), where it was said that it was
     impossible to say that an accident was the sole fault of an employee where there
     had been a failure by the employer to fence dangerous machinery.

100%   **HEWSON v GRIMSBY FISHMEAL CO**

[1986] CLY 2255 (QBD)

H was an experienced mechanical shovel driver employed
by G. He was operating a mechanical system that became
jammed. Whilst attempting to clear the blockage with the
assistance of G's foreman, H's arm became trapped and he
was injured. H was found to have broken all of the relevant
rules for the safe clearance of blockages and was 100%
contributorily negligent.

90%   **HODKINSON v HENRY WALLWORK & CO LTD**

[1955] 1 WLR 1195, [1955] 3 All ER 236 (CA)

H was employed working at a machine, which stopped
working when the wire ropes used in the transmission
slipped off their pulleys. H knew that the established
practice in such circumstances was to summon the
maintenance crew to put the matter right. However, rather
than waiting for the maintenance crew, he obtained a
ladder and climbed up to the pulleys, which were some
nine feet above the ground. H had not switched the power
to the machine off and as he was replacing the ropes, the
machine started operating and his hand was crushed. It
was held that even though the pulleys were high above the
ground, they should have been fenced and that the
absence of fencing was a cause of the accident. However,
given that HWC could not have foreseen H's acts, his
contributory negligence in acting in defiance of the
established practice was assessed at 90%.

80%   **UDDIN v ASSOCIATED PORTLAND CEMENT MANUFACTURERS LTD**

[1965] 2 QB 582, [1965] 2 WLR 1183, [1965] 2 All ER 213 (CA)

U was a machinery attendant at APCM's factory. Adjacent to the machinery upon which he worked was a dust extractor plant. U was not forbidden to go into the area of the dust extractor plant, but he had no authority or reason to go there. U saw a pigeon by the dust extractor plant and left his work area and climbed a ladder to try to catch it. In the course of trying to catch the pigeon, U leant across a revolving shaft, got caught in the same and was severely injured. U's behaviour was described as "an action of extreme folly" and he was found to have been doing "an unauthorised act, in an unauthorised place, for his own purposes". There was found to have been a breach of the applicable Factories Act in failing to fence the machinery. However, U's contributory negligence was assessed at 80% and the Court of Appeal did not interfere with this finding, although the view was expressed that a higher percentage of blame might have been attributed to U.

80%   **WILLIAMS v SYKES & HARRISON LTD**

[1955] 1 WLR 1180, [1955] 3 All ER 225 (CA)

W was employed as a labourer at SH's foundry. He attempted to clean a moving roller in a sand preparation plant with a steel brush. There was no guard on the plant and W injured his hand when it was caught between a belt and the roller. W's contributory negligence was assessed at 80%.

75%   McCREESH v COURTAULDS PLC

[1997] PIQR P421 (CA)

M had been employed by C as a joiner for nine weeks when he injured himself on a circular saw. It was found that M had been given no instructions on the use of the saw, he was inadequately supervised and although a guard was available, it was never used. However, M, adopted a procedure for cutting wood, which he knew to be unsafe and was found to have been 100% to blame. This was varied on appeal to 75% on the basis that C had acquiesced in a dangerous practice.

75%   GRAY v CAMELOT HOODS

[1983] CLY 128 (CA)

G had just installed a fan at C's factory and had instructed that it be unfenced so that he could assess the force of the air intake. As he was doing so he placed his hand into contact with the revolving fan and was injured. G was found to have been contributorily negligent to the extent of 75%.

75%   LEACH v STANDARD TELEPHONES & CABLES LTD

[1966] 1 WLR 1392, [1966] 2 All ER 523 (QBD)

L used a rotating saw when he had no business to and had been instructed not to. He set the guard far too high and injured his thumb. The guard would not have been effective even had it been set lower. L's contributory negligence was assessed at 75%.

66.66%   **NAPIERALSKI v CURTIS (CONTRACTORS) LTD**

[1959] 1 WLR 835, [1959] 2 All ER 426 (QBD)

N was employed by C as a joiner. He stayed behind at the end of a working day to help a colleague make a cabinet for himself. In the course of making the cabinet, N used one of C's circular saws. N knew the saw to be defective and unsafe as it wobbled and the guard was too short and could not be fully lowered. N had complained about these defects to C previously. In the course of using the saw it wobbled and N's hand was injured when it caught the guard. Liability was not established, but the view was expressed that N would have been found to have been contributorily negligent to the extent of two thirds.

66.66%   **KERRY v CARTER**

[1969] 1 WLR 1372, [1969] 3 All ER 723 (CA)

K, aged 18, had been an apprentice to C, a farmer, for two and a half years. He had previously been given some instruction on the use of circular saws at technical college and had used one at another farm. K asked C if he could use a circular saw and said that he had used one before and been shown how to do it. C watched K use the saw for a few minutes and then left K alone. Shortly thereafter, K caught his hand in the saw and injured it. It was found that C was negligent in not making further inquiry into K's experience and supervising him more closely. However, K was negligent in misleading C about his previous experience and putting his hand across the blade of the saw. K's contributory negligence was assessed at two thirds.

66.66%   **GUNTER v JOHN NICHOLAS & SONS (PORT TALBOT) LTD**

[1993] PIQR P67 (CA)

G, an experienced wood machinist employed by JN, was working on a cutting machine. He turned the machine off to adjust the cutters and, as he knew that the cutters on the machine took some time to stop revolving, attended to other tasks. He returned to the cutting machine after a few minutes and saw that the top cutter had stopped rotating. G assumed that the bottom cutter had also stopped rotating and touched it. However, the bottom cutter was still rotating and G's hand was injured. G's claim against JN succeeded on the ground that the cutting machine should have been fitted with a brake. However, G knew that the bottom cutter often continued to revolve after the top one had stopped and did not check that it had stopped revolving. G's contributory negligence was found to have been two thirds.

50%   **DENYER v CHARLES SKIPPER AND EAST LTD**

[1970] 1 WLR 1087, [1970] 2 All ER 382 (CA)

D, aged 17, was injured whilst cleaning the cylinders of a lithographic printing machine. He had been given clear instructions not to touch the cylinders with a rag whilst they were still moving, yet he did so and his hand became caught and was injured. CSE were found liable for exposing D to a risk of injury from the moving parts of the machinery. However, D's carelessness and disobedience of the instructions he had received were found to have been a substantial cause of the accident and his contributory negligence was assessed at 50%.

50%   **CAKEBREAD v HOPPING BROS (WHETSTONE) LTD**

[1947] KB 641, [1947] 1 All ER 389 (CA)

C was working on a circular saw, which did not have a guard in accordance with the applicable regulations, as it did not extend close enough to the cutting edge of the saw. C did not place the guard as low as it could go and was injured when his hand made contact with the saw. C's contributory negligence was assessed at 50%.

50%   **CLAY v SOUTH COAST SHIPPING CO LTD**

[1970] 2 Lloyd's Rep 146 (QBD)

C was employed on a dredger. In the course of winding a rope around a revolving drum he placed his hand on top of the drum and his hand became trapped and injured. It was found that there was an unsafe system of work, but that C was 50% to blame.

50%   **COWELL v BAIRDWEAR LTD**

[1997] CLY 2606 (CC)

C, who was employed by B as a sewing machinist, was injured when the machine's needle penetrated her finger. C had suffered four similar injuries in a short period of time and on each occasion she had been reassessed and retrained in her working practices. It was found that whilst it was not unusual for a sewing machinist to occasionally suffer a needle in finger injury, it was highly unusual for one individual to suffer four such injuries in a short space of time. This indicated that C did not pay full attention and her contributory negligence was assessed at 50%.

0%   **CHARLES v S SMITH & SONS (ENGLAND) LTD**

[1954] 1 WLR 451, [1954] 1 All ER 499 (QBD)

C was employed as an attendant at an hydraulic mould press. He immobilised the machine by placing the starting handle in a neutral position, raised the guard and inserted his hand into the machine to test a locking nut. In the course of so doing, C inadvertently pressed his leg against the starting handle, causing the machine to operate and his hand was injured. It was found that there had been a breach of the Factories Act in failing to guard the machine. C was found not to have been contributorily negligent.

0%   **MOFFAT v ATLAS HYDRAULIC LOADERS**

1992 SLT 1123 (OH)

M was injured whilst cleaning a paddle mixing machine, which was still operating. The machine was unfenced and had been run without its guard for four months. M had cleaned the machine whilst it was operating for some months and this had either been acquiesced in by his employers or at least showed inadequate supervision by them. There were practical reasons for not turning the machine off during cleaning. There was found to have been no contributory negligence.

0%   **SCOTT v KELVIN CONCRETE (AYRSHIRE)**

1993 SLT 935 (OH)

S was attempting to rectify a fault in an hydraulic press. He stepped inside it and accidentally caused it to operate, causing him injuries. The machine had been designed with various safety features, all of which had been disabled over a period of time. S had failed to use the isolator button to switch the machine off, but his employers had allowed the machine to remain in a dangerous state and had grossly failed to take proper care. There was no contributory negligence.

0%   **MCNEILL v ROCHE PRODUCTS LTD (NO. 2)**

1989 SLT 498 (OH)

M was an experienced fireman carrying out a routine test on a pump at a factory. The practice had developed whereby the pump was turned off by using a fuel cock lever, which was less safe than using the stop button. In reaching for the fuel cock lever M put his hand through a mesh enclosing a cooling fan and was injured. It was held that M was performing a routine operation on a piece of familiar equipment, the dangerous part of which lay behind a guard. He had no duty to look where he was putting his hand and there was no finding of contributory negligence.

0%   **KANSARA v OSRAM (GEC) LTD**

[1967] 3 All ER 230 (CA)

K was employed adjusting a machine, although he was not concerned with its electrical parts. The power had to be turned on for the machine to be tested. In the course of working on the machine a screwdriver he was holding touched an un-insulated wire and K was injured. It was held that casual inadvertence by an employee is not necessarily contributory negligence and on the facts, there was no contributory negligence.

0%   **THUROGOOD v VAN DEN BERGHS & JURGENS LTD**

[1951] 2 KB 537, [1951] 1 All ER 682 (CA)

T was engaged in testing an electric fan, which had been removed from its normal position of being set into a wall behind a grill for maintenance. As T was touching the motor housing to see whether it was overheating with his left hand, his right hand came into contact with the fan's rotating blades and was injured. It was found that T's conduct was mere inadvertence, which did not amount to contributory negligence.

0%   **JOHNS v MARTIN SIMMS (CHELTENHAM) LTD**

[1983] 1 All ER 127 (QBD)

J's hand became trapped and injured whilst he was
checking an unfenced radiator fan in an engine. There was
found to have been no contributory negligence. It was said
that this was:

> "... the sort of accident that can happen by
> inadvertence and that is one of the reasons why
> regulations made under this statute are made, because
> workmen who are concentrating on doing a job may
> inadvertently get their hands in a position of danger by
> reason of a dangerous part of the machine, and that is
> why the law requires the dangerous part to be fenced."[3]

---

3.   [1983] 1 All ER 127 per Lawson J at 130.

0%   **JOHN SUMMERS & SONS LTD v FROST**

[1955] AC 740, [1955] 2 WLR 825, [1955] 1 All ER 870
(HL)

F was employed at JS's steelworks. He was grinding the end
of a metal bar on a rotating grinding machine by resting
the bar on the rest provided and holding the metal bar
against the grindstone. The revolving grindstone was
fenced, save for an arc about seven inches long so that the
object to be ground could be placed into contact with it. As
F was holding the metal bar against the grindstone it
slipped and his thumb came into contact with the
grindstone and was injured. If F had held the bar with his
fingers further away from the grindstone, he would not
have had sufficient control over it. It was held that JS were
in breach of their statutory obligations to fence dangerous
parts of machinery, notwithstanding that to have done so
would have rendered the grinding machine unusable. It
was argued that as there was no safe way for F to do the task
on this machine, he should used a hand file instead.
However, F was found to have acted reasonably in using
the machine. There was found to have been no
contributory negligence on F's part as he was not acting in
a foolhardy way and any criticisms that could be made of
him fell short of negligence.

> "There [was] no question of disobedience to orders, or
> of reckless disregard by a workman of his own safety. At
> most, there was a mere error of judgment by [F] as to
> how the work on which he was engaged could best be
> carried out, and possibly only a mere momentary
> inadvertence ... [which] fell short of negligent
> conduct."[4]

---

4.   [1955] AC 740 per Lord Keith at 777.

6. UNSAFE PLACE OF WORK & FALLS

SLIPPING

66.66%   **WILLOWS v CRAGGS**

[1999] CLY 2855 (CC)

W was employed as petrol pump attendant at C's garage when he slipped and fell, having stepped on an oil soaked piece of paper. The previous day another employee had spilled oil and placed paper over the spillage in an attempt to soak it up. It was found that oil soaking granules should have been put down immediately, but that W was at fault in knowingly walking briskly on a visible piece of paper. W was found to have been contributorily negligent to the extent of two thirds.

50%   **WILSON v ROLLS ROYCE PLC**

1998 SLT 247 (OH)

W, a maintenance engineer employed by RR, was called out to deal with a burst pipe. The water that had leaked from the pipe had frozen and in order to examine the pipe, W walked on the ice and slipped. The claim failed as RR were found not to have been negligent, but it was said that W's contributory negligence would have been at least 50% in choosing to walk on an icy area.

50%   PORTER v STRATHCLYDE RC

1991 SLT 446 (IH)

P, a nursery assistant, slipped on some food dropped by a child whilst carrying a baby. SRC was at fault in not having in place an adequate system for mopping up such spillages or warning of their presence. However, P knew that food on the floor was a common occurrence and the baby she was carrying did not obstruct her view. P's contributory negligence was assessed at 50%.

50%   LEASK v GLASGOW DC

1993 SLT 674 (OH)

L was injured when he slipped on oil or grease on a duckboard on which he was standing. As the system at L's place of work was for employees to keep their own work areas clean, contributory negligence would have been assessed at 50%.

50%   KING v R C O SUPPORT SERVICES LTD

[2001] ICR 608, [2001] PIQR P206 (CA)

K was employed by RCO at Y's premises spreading grit, when he slipped on the un-gritted part of Y's ice-covered yard. K's claim under the Manual Handling Operations Regulations 1992 succeeded against RCO, but his damages were reduced by 50% to take account of his contributory negligence. K's task was not a particularly difficult one and had he kept his concentration on what he was doing, he would not have slipped.

0%   RYAN v MANBRE SUGARS LTD

(1970) 114 SJ 492 (CA)

R slipped on a slippery step at MS' factory. The step was necessarily slippery and R knew that it required special care, but failed, due to pure inadvertence, to step over it. It was said that mere knowledge of a danger does not prove contributory negligence and something more than that is required.[5] In the circumstances, R was found not to have been contributorily negligent.

0%   JOHNSON v REA LTD

[1962] 1 QB 373, [1961] 1 WLR 1400, [1961] 3 All ER 816 (CA)

R were stevedores who were engaged in loading sacks of soda ash from a shed onto a ship. They had been doing this for a few days and some of the soda ash had seeped through the sacks and onto the floor of the shed, making it slippery. J was a driver's mate, who was not employed by R. He arrived at the docks with a delivery of chemicals, which were to be loaded onto the ship. R directed him to store the kegs of chemicals on the quay, for which purpose J was required to walk through the shed. Both J and R knew that the floor of the shed was slippery from the soda ash and as J was walking through the shed with the first keg he slipped and injured himself. There was found to have been no contributory negligence by J. He had no alternative but to walk through the shed and there was no evidence that he had walked carelessly or hurried.

---

5. However, it was said in the later case of *Boothman v British Northrop Ltd* (1972) 13 KIR 112 (CA) per Stephenson LJ at 121 that "there are cases in which mere knowledge might be enough."

TRIPPING

100%   **BACON v JACK TIGHE (OFFSHORE) & CAPE SCAFFOLDING**

[1987] CLY 2568 (CC)

B tripped on a scaffolding clip, which had been left on a catwalk on an oil rig and injured himself. It was held that the duty on B was higher than the duty on either his employers or the scaffolding contractors. An oil rig was fraught with potential hazards and B should have seen the clip. B was found to have been 100% contributorily negligent.

33.33%   **SULLIVAN v HWF LTD**

Current Law Oct/2001 (CC)

S was a director and employee of HWF. He tripped on a bolt left on the floor by another employee and injured himself. S was responsible for the implementation and enforcement of health and safety procedures at HWF and had carried out a risk assessment, which warned particularly of the dangers of bolts being left on the floor. Contributory negligence was assessed at one third in respect of S's failure to see the bolt.

33.33%   **FOLEY v ENSO-GUTZEIT OSAKEYHTIO**

[1962] 1 Lloyd's Rep 247 (QBD)

F was a stevedore loading cargo onto EGO's vessel. He tripped over a cable, which was securing cargo to a hook on the deck. F had no reason to suspect that a wire would be there as the cargo was normally lashed down after the stevedores had left the ship. Nonetheless, F's contributory negligence was assessed at one third. It was said that where someone is working on a ship, he must keep his eyes open.

25%   ## BOOTHMAN v BRITISH NORTHROP LTD

(1972) 13 KIR 112 (CA)

B was employed as a fitter and welder at BN's factory. He was required to use an electric welding torch and in the course of his work he needed to turn the cylinders that he was welding. This inevitably had the effect of twisting the power lead to the welding torch and causing it to kink on the floor. There was a device which would have prevented the kinking, but this had been out of action for some time. Shortly after putting the welding torch down, B tripped over the twisted lead and injured himself. It was found that BN had been negligent in failing to provide B with a safe place of work. However, B had been engaged in this work for two or more months and although he was on piece-work, it must have been obvious to him that there was some risk and that additional care was required. B's contributory negligence was assessed at 25%.

ROSSI v PORT OF LONDON AUTHORITY

[1956] 1 Lloyd's Rep 478 (QBD)

R was injured at work when a fellow employee tripped and the load that he had been carrying struck R. It was said:

> "There is no obligation upon a person walking along, say, a railway platform, or in a ballroom, to watch where he is placing his feet. He is entitled to rely on the general condition of the area. But if you are engaged in working in a place where you know that dangers exist and, if you do not keep a proper look out, are likely to fall over, if you hurt yourself or somebody else as a result of that not looking out, then it amounts to negligence. It is a question of reasonable care. A reasonably careful man, working on top of a pile of timber at the dockside, before getting hold of a piece of timber at all for the purpose of lifting it, would obviously look to see the sort of place he had to traverse when carrying this piece of timber."[6]

---

6.   [1956] 1 Lloyd's Rep 478 per Lynskey J at 480.

FALLING

100%   ## MANWARING v BILLINGTON

[1952] 2 All ER 747 (CA)

M was employed by B as a builder. He was instructed not to climb any ladder without first putting sacking under it and tying it securely at the top to prevent it slipping. M set up a ladder with the assistance of another employee, who had received similar instructions. M ascended the ladder without placing sacking under it or tying it at the top. The ladder slipped and M fell, sustaining injuries. It was found that B was in breach of the applicable regulations, which placed on employers the duty of ensuring that ladders were footed and securely fixed. It was held that B's statutory duty had not been delegated to M, but that B was only in breach of the regulations because of the failure of M to perform duties, which were properly and reasonably assigned to him. M had failed to carry out his instructions, and, with appreciation of his own omissions, had proceeded to climb the ladder, which then slipped. M's injuries were caused solely by his own negligence.

60%   ## BETTS v TOLKEY

Unreported, 2002 (CA) *Digested in Health & Safety Law 2.1*

B fell while walking down some unlit steps at her employer's premises. She had been feeling her way down along the wall when she lost her footing, fell and sustained injuries. The stairs were in pitch darkness and B's contributory negligence in carrying on regardless was assessed at 60%.

50%   **BOYLE v KODAK LTD**

[1969] 1 WLR 661, [1969] 2 All ER 439 (HL)

B, an experienced painter, was employed by K painting a 30 feet high oil storage tank. He used a ladder to reach the top of the tank and the applicable regulations placed a duty on both B and K to secure the ladder at the top by lashing it before using it. An external iron staircase on the side of the oil tank gave access to the top of the ladder, but instead of using this, B climbed the ladder to lash it at the top. The ladder fell before he managed to do this and B was injured. It was found that in failing to instruct B to use the staircase in circumstances where no danger was apparent, K was in breach of its duty. On the basis that neither party was gravely to blame (given the remoteness of the danger), B's contributory negligence was assessed at 50%.

50%   **MCMATH v RIMMER BROTHERS (LIVERPOOL) LTD**

[1962] 1 WLR 1, [1961] 3 All ER 1154 (CA)

M, a builder, went up a ladder on a building site. He knew that the employee whose job it was to foot the ladder was improperly absent from the site, but went ahead and took the risk of the ladder slipping. It did slip and M was injured. It was held that both M and his employers were in breach of statutory duty and M's contributory negligence was assessed at 50%.

50%   **LANE v SHIRE ROOFING COMPANY (OXFORD) LTD**

[1995] PIQR P417 (CA)

L was employed by SRC re-roofing a porch. He fell from the
top of a ladder and injured himself when he over-reached
to cut a slate and lost his balance. It was found that the
ladder was not appropriate and was unsuitable for the
purpose. However, as L had refused SRC's offer of a trestle
or scaffold tower and insisted on using a ladder and had
over-reached, his contributory negligence was assessed at
50%.

50%   **BLANCHFLOWER v CHAMBERLAIN**

[1996] CLY 2997 (CA)

B was injured in the course of his employment with C. B
was standing on a trailer, attempting to cover a load with a
tarpaulin. The tarpaulin rucked up in the middle and as B
stood on the load and pulled the tarpaulin free he lost his
balance and fell. It was found that despite B's experience,
he should have been given some instruction and was not
provided with a safe system of work. However, the risk was
obvious and avoidable. Contributory negligence was
assessed at 50%.

50%   **PARKER v P F C FLOORING SUPPLIES LTD**

[2001] PIQR P115 (QBD)[7]

P, a director and employee of PFC, slipped and fell through
a sky light on a roof whilst attempting to remove a cable
left on the roof by vandals. It was held that it was
reasonably foreseeable that an employee might venture
onto the roof in such circumstances. However, P had taken
it upon himself to go into a situation of obvious danger as
he knew the roof was slippery. Accordingly, he was equally
at fault for the breach of the Workplace (Health, Safety and
Welfare) Regulations 1992 and was as responsible as PFC
for the accident. P's contributory negligence was assessed at
50%.

50%   **HARRISON v METROPOLITAN-VICKERS ELECTRICAL CO LTD**

[1954] 1 WLR 324, [1954] 1 All ER 404 (CA)

H was employed in MVE's foundry. He and another
employee were walking backwards carrying a ladle of
molten metal when he fell into an unfenced pit in the floor
adjoining a gangway and was injured. The pit had been
there for days and seen by H many times. The trial judge
found that H's contributory negligence amounted to 50%.
The Court of Appeal did not overturn the judge's decision,
but would not have found him guilty of contributory
negligence.

---

7.   Affirmed by the Court of Appeal at Current Law Dec/2001.

33.33%   **SOLE v W J HALLT LTD**

[1973] QB 574, [1973] 2 WLR 171, [1973] 1 All ER 1032
(QBD)

S was contracted to fix plasterboards to a ceiling in a house
that was in the course of being built. The stairwell had no
guard rails or boards available to cover it. In the course of
looking up at the ceiling S stepped back and fell into the
stair well. Contributory negligence was assessed at one
third.

33.33%   **ROSS v ASSOCIATED PORTLAND CEMENT MANUFACTURERS
LTD**

[1964] 1 WLR 768, [1964] 2 All ER 452 (HL)

D was instructed to repair a safety net suspended below an
aerial ropeway some 20 feet above the ground. This was an
unusual task and D was neither provided with instructions
nor proper equipment such as a platform, although he
could have used any equipment that was available. Rather
than using a moveable platform, D used a ladder, which
was unsuitable for the task. He rested the ladder against the
netting, which partially collapsed and D fell and was fatally
injured. D's contributory negligence was held to have been
one third.

33.33%   **MULLARD v BEN LINE STEAMERS LTD**

[1970] 1 WLR 1414, [1971] 2 All ER 424 (CA)

M was working on two hatch covers on a ship's deck.
Between the two hatches was an open third hatch, which,
in breach of regulations was unfenced and the
compartment below was in total darkness. Whilst moving
between the hatches, M fell through the open hatch and
was injured. It was found that M had ample experience of
walking on ships in darkness, but the Court of Appeal held
that it would defeat the purpose of the regulations to
demand too strict a duty of care from an employee where
an accident is caused partly by an employee's negligence,
but mostly by an employer's breach of the regulations. M
was held to have been one third to blame.

30%   **KING v SMITH**

[1995] ICR 339, [1995] PIQR P48 (CA)

K was employed as a window cleaner by S. S's rules required window cleaners to clean high windows from the inside or by sitting on the sill. If this could not be done, window cleaners were only to stand on external window sills where they were securely attached to the building by a safety harness. K was cleaning a high window, which he felt could not be cleaned from the inside due to the top sash window sticking. The presence of furniture near the window meant that he could not sit on the sill. Accordingly, K went onto the external sill to clean the window notwithstanding that there was no means of attaching a safety harness to the building. As he was attempting to come back into the building his hand slipped on a piece of paper pinned inside the window frame and he fell, sustaining injuries. It was held that S should have absolutely forbidden employees from going onto external sills where there was no means of attaching a safety harness. However, K's contributory negligence in not trying very hard to free the sticking top sash window (which could have been done) and simply going out onto the external sill to get the job done as quickly as possible was assessed at 30%. The Court of Appeal did not interfere with the trial judge's apportionment, but would have found a slightly greater measure of contributory negligence if hearing the case themselves.

25%   **SKELTON v A V P DEVELOPMENTS LTD**

(1970) 8 KIR 927 (CA)

S was an electrician, working on a ceiling. He was standing and walking along a trestle and when he reached the end of it he stood on the bar of some partly dismantled scaffolding, which collapsed and he was injured. It was found that his employers were in breach of the applicable regulations, but that S was contributorily negligent to the extent of 25% in failing to look where he was putting his foot.

25%   **DONAGHEY v BOULTON & PAUL LTD**

[1968] AC 1, [1967] 3 WLR 829, [1967] 2 All ER 1014
(HL)

D was working on the sloping roof of a hanger replacing
asbestos sheeting. Crawling boards were available, but not
used. D and another employee were pulling on a sheet of
asbestos to remove it. As the sheet came free, D lost his
balance and fell through a hole in the roof caused by their
earlier removal of another asbestos sheet. It was found that
BP were in breach of the applicable regulations in not
ensuring that crawling boards were used, but that D's
contributory negligence amounted to 25%.

20%   **BYRNE v E H SMITH (ROOFING) LTD**

[1973] 1 All ER 490 (CA)

B was working on a fragile roof, which was accessed by
walking along a narrow slippery gutter. It was possible to
walk along safely by placing one foot on the gutter and the
other on the part of the roof supported by a purlin, which
could be identified by a line of bolts. B turned and placed
his weight bearing foot on an unsupported part of the roof
and fell through. It was held that B had not been provided
with a safe means of access to his place of work, but as he
must have turned carelessly his contributory negligence
was assessed at 20%.

20%   **DAVISON v APEX SCAFFOLDS**

[1956] 1 QB 551, [1956] 2 WLR 636, [1956] 1 All ER
473 (CA)

D was employed erecting scaffolding to clean the roof of a
station. The necessary materials for erecting the scaffolding
were sent from AS' store to the site, but in the course of the
project some materials from other scaffolding contractors
on the site got mixed up with AS' materials. D knew that
AS only used a particular kind of coupler, but in the course
of erecting the scaffolding he used a different coupler,
which was a slightly different size. The effect of this was
that, although the coupler appeared to be securely screwed,
it failed to tighten a clip around a vertical pole. The
scaffolding collapsed and D was killed. It was held that D
was himself in breach of the applicable regulations in
knowingly using someone else's materials when his
employers had provided him with all the necessary
materials. He was failing to co-operate in complying with
the regulations by using materials which turned out not to
be suitable. His contributory negligence was assessed at
20%.

0%   **WESTWOOD v POST OFFICE**

[1974] AC 1, [1973] 3 WLR 287, [1973] 3 All ER 184
(HL)

W and other employees often went onto the roof of PO's
building for a break. One day the normal access to the roof
was blocked, but it was possible to get onto the roof
through the lift motor room. PO tolerated the practice of
employees going onto the roof, but did not know that
access was ever gained through the lift motor room. The
door to the lift motor room had a notice saying "only the
authorised attendant is permitted to enter". W accessed the
roof through the lift motor room, but on his way back fell
through a trap door and was killed. PO were found to be in
breach of the Offices, Shops and Railway Premises Act
1963. W had been disobedient in entering the lift motor
room, but not negligent and so was not guilty of
contributory negligence in relation to PO's breach of
statutory duty. However, if the case had been decided in
negligence and not breach of statutory duty, a finding of
contributory negligence might have been made.

0%   **SMITH v AUSTIN LIFTS LTD**

[1959] 1 WLR 100, [1959] 1 All ER 81 (HL)

S, who was employed by AL as a fitter, was sent to overhaul
the lift at a customer's premises. Access to the machinery
was via a ladder and through some double doors, which
were about 12 feet above the level of the roof. S had been
to these premises many times before and knew that the
hinge on the left hand door was defective and he had
complained about this. On his last visit he had left the
doors tied together with wire, as they could not be bolted
closed. However, when he returned to the premises he
noticed that someone had jammed the left hand door
closed and left the right hand door open, so that he could
not get in through both doors. As S reached the top of the
ladder he tested the left hand door for a handhold and it
seemed safe. He grasped it higher up to help himself in, but
the door gave way on him and he fell, injuring himself. It
was found that S had been exposed to a trap and did not
have full appreciation of the danger. There was no finding
of contributory negligence.

0%   **GENERAL CLEANING CONTRACTORS LTD v CHRISTMAS**

[1953] AC 180, [1953] 2 WLR 6, [1952] 2 All ER 1110
(HL)

C was an experienced window cleaner. In accordance with
the normal practice, he was standing on a narrow external
window sill holding onto the bottom of the top sash
window. The lower sash window was slightly open, but it
fell closed unexpectedly causing the woodwork at the top
of the frame to trap C's fingers. This had the effect of
causing C to lose his balance and fall, injuring himself.
Whilst safety belts were available, this particular building
did not have any hooks for them to be attached to. It was
argued that C should have ensured that it was safe to rely
on the window for a hand hold and further that he should
have wedged the lower window open with a block. There
was found to have been an unsafe system of work and there
was no finding of contributory negligence against C. It was
said:

> "Where a practice of ignoring an obvious danger has
> grown up I do not think that it is reasonable to expect
> an individual workman to take the initiative in
> devising and using precautions."[8]

---

8.   [1953] AC 180 per Lord Reid at 194. See also *Holmes* v *T & J Harrison Ltd* [1962] 1
Lloyd's Rep 455 (CA).

0%   **GRANT v SUN SHIPPING CO LTD**

[1948] AC 549, [1948] 2 All ER 238 (HLS)[9]

G, a stevedore, was moving oil drums along the deck of a ship. He knew that repairers had removed some of the hatch covers from the deck. As he was rolling an oil drum along the deck he found himself in an area of darkness and went to attend to the lights, which had been taken down. As he was walking towards the lights he fell through an open hatch cover and was injured. The accident was found to have been caused by the negligence and breach of statutory duty of the ship owners and the repairers. G was found not to have been contributorily negligent. He was entitled to assume that the repairers would not have left the hatch cover off and failed to replace the lighting when they left the area.

> "Almost every workman constantly, and justifiably, takes risks in the sense that he relies on others to do their duty, and trusts that they have done it. I am far from saying that everyone is entitled to assume, in all circumstances, that other persons will be careful. On the contrary, a prudent man will guard against the possible negligence of others, when experience shows such negligence to be common. Where, however, the negligence is a breach of regulations, made to secure the safety of workmen, which may be presumed to be strictly enforced in the ordinary course of a ship's discipline, I am not prepared to say that a workman is careless if he assumes that there has been compliance with the law."[10]

---

9. This case arose out of an accident which occurred before the coming into force of the LR(CN)A 1945 and so had contributory negligence been found, it would have afforded a complete defence.
10. [1948] AC 549 per Lord Du Parcq at 567.

0%   **O'KEEFE v JOHN STEWART & CO SHIPPING LTD**

[1979] 1 Lloyd's Rep 182 (QBD)

O was the boatswain on a cargo ship. He was footing a
ladder for a seaman who, whilst working up the ladder,
appeared to get himself into difficulty and seemed to be in
imminent danger of falling. O went up the ladder to assist
the seaman without getting someone else to foot the ladder
for him. The ladder slipped and O was injured. There was
found to have been no contributory negligence. The risk to
the seaman far outweighed the slight risk of the ladder
slipping.

OTHERS

80%   **STAPLEY v GYPSUM MINES LTD**

[1953] AC 663, [1953] 3 WLR 279, [1953] 2 All ER 478
(HL)

S was working with another employee, D, in GM's mine.
They approached a roof, which they recognised to be
dangerous. They informed their foreman, who instructed
them not to work under it until they had brought it down.
S and D were unable to get the roof down easily and
decided to press on with their work. D left the area and S
went to work under the roof. D returned after half an hour
to find S dead under the collapsed roof. S's contributory
negligence was assessed at 80%.

50%   **WRIGHT v IMPERIAL CHEMICAL INDUSTRIES LTD**

(1965) 109 SJ 232 (QBD)

W was employed in ICI's mine, in which an unforeseeably
high build up of methane gas occurred after blasting. W lit
a cigarette and was injured in the ensuing fire. It was found
that ICI should have tested for gas before allowing W into
the area, but that W's contributory negligence amounted to
50%.

25%   **MCNAUGHTON v MICHELIN TYRE PLC**

2001 SLT (Sh Ct) 67 (SH)

M walked into a protruding wall bracket for a shelf that was
no longer in use at his place of work. The claim failed, but
the opinion was expressed that although M had been
distracted by his duties, contributory negligence would
have been assessed at around 25% as the bracket had been
near eye level.

7. UNSAFE SYSTEM OF WORK

50%   **CARGILL v P R EXCAVATIONS**

[2000] CLY 4228 (QBD)

PRE emloyed C as a general labourer. He was working with another employee benching the base of a manhole cover in an excavation approximately 1.8 metres deep, 2 metres wide and 2.4 metres long. No steps were taken to shore up the excavation by using wooden batons or compacting the excavated soil. The soil had been extracted from the pit with a mechanical excavator operated by the other employee. C was injured when struck by a large lump of soil, which fell into the excavation. It was found that:

(1) C and the other employee were of similar status and working together in a position of parity;

(2) the other employee (for whom PRE was vicariously liable) was negligent as the spoil was placed close to the excavation and there was no attempt to shore the excavation up or prevent material from falling into it;

(3) C had attended a two day safety awareness course;

(4) C had disregarded oral and written instructions as to a safe system of work; and

(5) C was aware of the proximity of the spoil and the danger that it posed and nonetheless entered the excavation and worked with that knowledge.

C was held to have been contributorily negligent to the extent of 50%.

50%   **BOYLE v KODAK LTD**

[1969] 1 WLR 661, [1969] 2 All ER 439 (HL)

B, an experienced painter, was employed by K painting a
30 feet high oil storage tank. He used a ladder to reach the
top of the tank and the applicable regulations placed a duty
on both B and K to secure the ladder at the top by lashing
it before using it. An external iron staircase on the side of
the oil tank gave access to the top of the ladder but instead
of using this, B climbed the ladder to lash it at the top. The
ladder fell before he managed to do this and B was injured.
It was found that in failing to instruct B to use the staircase
in circumstances where no danger was apparent, K was in
breach of its duty. On the basis that neither party was
gravely to blame (given the remoteness of the danger), B's
contributory negligence was assessed at 50%.

50%   **WALSH v ROLLS ROYCE**

Unreported, 1982 (CA)

W, an employee with 25 years' experience, devised a system
with a fellow employee whereby W walked backwards
carrying a 21 foot ladder, relying on the fellow employee
(also carrying a ladder) to be a look out for obstructions. W
was injured and held to have been contributorily negligent
to the extent of 50% as being the "author of a bad and
rather silly system of work".

50%   **WILLIAMS v PORT OF LIVERPOOL STEVEDORING CO LTD**

[1956] 1 WLR 551, [1956] 2 All ER 69 (QBD)

W and five other employees were unloading bags from a barge. They were instructed to unload according to the usual safe method, which they did. However, when the supervisor left they started to unload and stack the bags using a different and dangerous method. The stack of bags collapsed and injured W. It was held that W had been contributorily negligent to the extent of 50% as his consent to the dangerous and disobedient system had been essential to the whole gang adopting that method.

50%   **HEFFER v ROVER CAR CO**

[1964] CLY 2555 (QBD)

RCC kept petrol in open tins without markings, which were similar to those used to store non-flammable liquids. They also did not prohibit smoking. H and a fellow employee were fooling around and H threatened to strike some matches and the fellow employee threatened to throw the contents of a tin (which no-one realised was petrol) over H. They both did as they had threatened and H was badly burned. H's contributory negligence in lighting matches when he knew that the contents of the tin, which the fellow employee had threatened to throw over him, might be petrol was assessed at 50%.

50%   **WRIGHT v IMPERIAL CHEMICAL INDUSTRIES LTD**

(1965) 109 SJ 232 (QBD)

W was employed in ICI's mine in which an unforeseeably high build up of methane gas occurred after blasting. W lit a cigarette and was injured in the ensuing fire. It was found that ICI should have tested for gas before allowing W into the area, but that W's contributory negligence amounted to 50%.

50%   **MCINTYRE v STRATHCLYDE RC**

1994 SLT 933 (OH)

M was instructed by his foreman to remove some
shuttering. Both knew that trestles or scaffold would be
required to provide a working platform for the work to be
done safely. The foreman left the site and M looked for
suitable materials, but none were readily available and so
he carried out the task in an unsafe manner and was
injured. It was held that the foreman should have ensured
that suitable equipment was supplied, but that M was
equally to blame for having carried on with the task when
he had been unable to find the equipment required.

50%   **BLANCHFLOWER v CHAMBERLAIN**

[1996] CLY 2997 (CA)

B was injured in the course of his employment with C. B
was standing on a trailer, attempting to cover a load with a
tarpaulin. The tarpaulin rucked up in the middle and as B
stood on the load and pulled the tarpaulin free he lost his
balance and fell. It was found that despite B's experience,
he should have been given some instruction and was not
provided with a safe system of work. However, the risk was
obvious and avoidable. Contributory negligence was
assessed at 50%.

33.33%   **REILLY v BRITISH TRANSPORT COMMISSION**

[1957] 1 WLR 76, [1956] 3 All ER 857 (QBD)

R and W were employed tightening bolts on a railway line. They were working without a look-out and whilst they were both engaged in tightening a bolt, they were struck and killed by a train. R and W had failed to notice a signal showing that a train was approaching and took no notice of the train's whistle as it approached. It was found that ignoring the whistle was not, of itself, negligent as they were obviously engrossed in their work and oblivious to all else. However, contributory negligence was found in their failure to check the signal and it was said that this temporary and probably unaccustomed lapse carried a lesser share of the responsibility than BTC's failure to assess the situation and send a look-out man. Contributory negligence was assessed at one third.

33.33%   **FRASER v WINCHESTER HEALTH AUTHORITY**

(2000) 55 BMLR 122, (1999) *The Times*, July 12 (CA)

F was a 21-year-old residential support worker employed by WHA who was required to go on a camping trip with a patient. She injured herself when she attempted to change a gas cylinder near a lit candle. She had not been instructed in the use of camping equipment, which was found to amount to a breach of duty in circumstances where she was inexperienced and had heavy responsibilities. F had appreciated the risk and known what she was doing was dangerous. She was found to have been contributorily negligent to the extent of one third.

30%   **KING v SMITH**

[1995] ICR 339, [1995] PIQR P48 (CA)

K was employed as a window cleaner by S. S's rules required window cleaners to clean high windows from the inside or by sitting on the sill. If this could not be done, window cleaners were only to stand on external window sills where they were securely attached to the building by a safety harness. K was cleaning a high window, which he felt could not be cleaned from the inside due to the top sash window sticking. The presence of furniture near the window meant that he could not sit on the sill. Accordingly, K went onto the external sill to clean the window notwithstanding that there was no means of attaching a safety harness to the building. As he was attempting to come back into the building his hand slipped on a piece of paper pinned inside the window frame and he fell, sustaining injuries. It was held that S should have absolutely forbidden employees from going onto external sills where there was no means of attaching a safety harness. However, K's contributory negligence in not trying very hard to free the sticking top sash window (which could have been done) and simply going out onto the external sill to get the job done as quickly as possible was assessed at 30%. The Court of Appeal did not interfere with the trial judge's apportionment, but would have found a slightly greater measure of contributory negligence if hearing the case themselves.

25%   BALL v RICHARD THOMAS & BALDWINS LTD

[1968] 1 WLR 192, [1968] 1 All ER 389 (CA)

B, an experienced worker, was required to lift some pieces of metal with a crane. He placed the hook of the crane under the metal and signalled the crane driver to lift. However, as the crane took the strain the hook flew out and struck B, injuring him. RTB were found to have been in breach of statutory duty as the hook was not of adequate strength. However, B was found to have been negligent in standing less than nine feet from the hook. He knew that it was dangerous to stand too close and the accident was easily avoidable, as it would have been easy for B to have stood a safe distance away. B's contributory negligence was assessed at 25%.

20%   BEGGS v MOTHERWELL BRIDGE FABRICATORS LTD

1998 SLT 1215 (OH)

B, a factory worker, was driving a fork lift truck over an uneven road when the forks got caught in old railway lines, which were protruding from the road. This caused the fork lift truck to stop suddenly and B suffered fatal injuries when he was propelled from the fork lift truck. B had not had specific training in driving a fork lift truck over uneven ground and used the road infrequently. B's contributory negligence in failing to set the forks at a proper height was assessed at 20%.

0%   **MACHRAY v STEWARTS & LLOYDS LTD**

[1965] 1 WLR 602, [1964] 3 All ER 716 (QBD)

M, an experienced rigger employed by SL at a steelworks, was subject to the direction of his foreman, or in his absence, a charge-hand, who essentially relied on M so far as rigging techniques were concerned. A large section of pipe needed to be moved urgently and as there was no crane available, M looked for sets of chain pulley blocks. However, none were available and so M borrowed a set of wooden blocks from other contractors on the site. In the course of lifting the pipe it swung out, injuring M. It was said that in using the wooden blocks, M used a method which was obviously less safe than his preferred method. However, there was no contributory negligence on M's part as it was found that he used the wooden blocks:

> "not for the sake of saving himself trouble but in order to get on with his employer's business, and [he was] prevented from doing the work in the way in which he would have preferred to do it by the employer's breach in not providing him with the proper [equipment]."[11]

0%   **BYERS v HEAD WRIGHTSON & CO LTD**

[1961] 1 WLR 961, [1961] 2 All ER 538 (QBD)

B was a steel erector who was tasked with moving a welding set. He attempted to take it across an improvised plank bridge over a trench. The plank sagged and he was injured when the welding set fell on top of him. It was held that there was no contributory negligence and said that where an employee is required to make a decision which is too difficult for him and so makes the wrong decision and is injured, he should not be found guilty of contributory negligence.

---

11   [1965] 1 WLR 602 per McNair J at 610.

0%   **TURNER v LANCASHIRE CC**

[1980] CLY 1886 (QBD)

T was a trainee fireman on a training course. He was
injured when a ladder was over extended. The exercise was
conducted unsafely and there was no contributory
negligence on the part of T in a strictly disciplined and
closely structured situation as he was only a recruit acting
upon orders.

0%   **JONES v R W POWIS & SONS**

[1981] CLY 296 (CA)

J was loading a container weighing half a ton onto a lorry.
The system for loading the container onto the lorry was
unsafe and it began to slide off the tailboard of the lorry. By
way of immediate reaction, J attempted to prevent the
container from falling and was injured. J was held not to
have been contributorily negligent in the circumstances.

0%   **SMITH v STAGES**

[1988] ICR 201 (CA)[12]

M and S had been working together and in order to get the job finished they worked all day on a Sunday and then carried on through Sunday night. They finished work at 8.30 am on the Monday morning and got straight into S's car for the long drive home. On the way home M was injured in an accident caused by S's negligent driving. In proceedings against the employers on the basis that they were vicariously liable for the negligent driving of S, it was alleged that M had been contributorily negligent in allowing himself to be driven by S, when he knew that S had not had enough sleep. However, M was held not to have been contributorily negligent. The Court of Appeal approved[13] the trial judge's observation that:

> "I cannot accept that [M] was in a condition, himself, to apply rational judgement to the risks involved in travelling in S's car at the time due to his own deprivation of sleep and fatigue. This itself was caused by the wholly excessive hours he was required [by his employers] to work ... I decline to condemn a man as negligent of his own safety when the charge is made against him by employers who themselves produced the conditions which deprived him of the capacity to care properly for his own safety."

---

12. The finding in relation to contributory negligence was not challenged on the appeal to the House of Lords reported at [1989] AC 928, [1989] 2 WLR 529, [1989] 1 All ER 833.
13. [1988] ICR 201 per Glidewell LJ at 213.

0%   GENERAL CLEANING CONTRACTORS LTD v CHRISTMAS

[1953] AC 180, [1953] 2 WLR 6, [1952] 2 All ER 1110 (HL)

C was an experienced window cleaner. In accordance with the normal practice, he was standing on a narrow external window sill holding onto the bottom of the top sash window. The lower sash window was slightly open, but it fell closed unexpectedly causing the woodwork at the top of the frame to trap C's fingers. This had the effect of causing C to lose his balance and fall, injuring himself. Whilst safety belts were available, this particular building did not have any hooks for them to be attached to. It was argued that C should have ensured that it was safe to rely on the window for a hand hold and further that he should have wedged the lower window open with a block. There was found to have been an unsafe system of work and there was no finding of contributory negligence against C. It was said:

> "Where a practice of ignoring an obvious danger has grown up I do not think that it is reasonable to expect an individual workman to take the initiative in devising and using precautions."[14]

0%   HERTON v BLAW KNOX LTD

(1968) 112 SJ 963 (QBD)

H was a trained lathe operator employed by BK. He was injured whilst operating a machine in the manner which he had been taught by BK. BK accepted that the method of operation was unsafe, but alleged that H had been contributorily negligent in not realising the risk and eliminating it. It was held that there was no contributory negligence. It did not lie in BK's mouth to criticise the procedure taught by them.

---

14. [1953] AC 180 per Lord Reid at 194. See also *Holmes v T & J Harrison Ltd* [1962] 1 Lloyd's Rep 455 (CA).

0%   **WRIGHT v RICHARD THOMAS & BALDWINS LTD**

(1966) 1 KIR 327

W was repairing a carriage at RTB's steelworks when
another employee moved the carriage without warning
and crushed W. It was alleged that W was guilty of
contributory negligence in failing to keep a proper lookout.
However, it was held that an employee is not contributorily
negligent in failing to keep a look out if he is entitled to
assume that fellow employees will not move the
machinery, which causes his injuries.

0%   **MULLANEY v CHIEF CONSTABLE OF WEST MIDLANDS POLICE**

Unreported, 2001 (CA)

M was a probationary police officer who was seriously injured when he was assaulted by someone he was attempting to arrest for importuning in a public lavatory. It was held that CCWMP was liable for the failure of fellow officers to respond to radio calls and come to M's assistance. Subject to public policy considerations, CCWMP was under a duty not to expose officers to an unnecessary risk of injury. This included a duty to exercise reasonable care to ensure that a safe system of work was provided. It was alleged that M was guilty of contributory negligence in: (1) entering the lavatories by himself when M and the other officers involved in the operation had been told to operate in pairs and (2) persisting in his efforts to arrest the suspect after he had become violent. It was found that M was guilty of a misjudgement in going into the lavatories alone, but was not guilty of contributory negligence. He had allowed his enthusiasm for his duty to overcome any caution that he might otherwise have had. The Court of Appeal approved the trial judge's remark that:

> "police officers should not be discouraged from doing their duty by fear of a finding of contributory negligence against them if, in consequence of a misjudgement, they sustain injury."

M was a very inexperienced officer doing his best in circumstances in which he had no reason to expect an attack of such a nature and in which he could reasonably expect back up if he called for assistance. The allegation that M should not have persevered in the arrest was also rejected. M was doing no more than he, in the heat of the moment and with some bravery, thought was his duty. Accordingly, there was no contributory negligence.

8. UNSUITABLE EQUIPMENT OTHER THAN MACHINERY

50%   **HEFFER v ROVER CAR CO**

[1964] CLY 2555 (QBD)

RCC kept petrol in open tins without markings, which
were similar to those used to store non-flammable liquids.
They also did not prohibit smoking. H and a fellow
employee were fooling around and H threatened to strike
some matches and the fellow employee threatened to
throw the contents of a tin (which no-one realised was
petrol) over H. They both did as they had threatened and
H was badly burned. H's contributory negligence in
lighting matches when he knew that the contents of the
tin, which the fellow employee had threatened to throw
over him, might be petrol was assessed at 50%.

50%   **MCINTYRE v STRATHCLYDE RC**

1994 SLT 933 (OH)

M was instructed by his foreman to remove some
shuttering. Both knew that trestles or scaffold would be
required to provide a working platform for the work to be
done safely. The foreman left the site and M looked for
suitable materials, but none were readily available and so
he carried out the task in an unsafe manner and was
injured. It was held that the foreman should have ensured
that suitable equipment was supplied, but M was equally to
blame for having carried on with the task when he had
been unable to find the equipment required.

50%   **WHEELER v COPAS**

[1981] 3 All ER 405 (QBD)

W entered into a labour only contract to undertake
building works at C's property, under which C was to
provide the necessary materials and equipment. W
required a long ladder and was given a choice of two by C.
One of the ladders was too long and W selected the shorter
one, which was a fruit-picking ladder. The ladder was too
flimsy for heavy building work and collapsed with W on it,
causing him to fall and injure himself. C was found to have
been negligent in providing a ladder, which was wholly
unsuitable for its intended purpose. However, W was an
experienced builder and the ladder was obviously
inadequate. His contributory negligence was assessed at
50%.

33.33%   **ROSS v ASSOCIATED PORTLAND CEMENT MANUFACTURERS
LTD**

[1964] 1 WLR 768, [1964] 2 All ER 452 (HL)

D was instructed to repair a safety net suspended below an
aerial ropeway some 20 feet above the ground. This was an
unusual task and D was neither provided with instructions
nor proper equipment such as a platform, although he
could have used any equipment that was available. Rather
than using a moveable platform, D used a ladder, which
was unsuitable for the task. He rested the ladder against the
netting, which partially collapsed and D fell and was fatally
injured. D's contributory negligence was held to have been
one third.

25%   BALL v RICHARD THOMAS & BALDWINS LTD

[1968] 1 WLR 192, [1968] 1 All ER 389 (CA)

B, an experienced worker, was required to lift some pieces
of metal with a crane. B placed the hook of the crane under
the metal and signalled the crane driver to lift. However, as
the crane took the strain the hook flew out and struck B,
injuring him. RTB were found to have been in breach of
statutory duty as the hook was not of adequate strength.
However, B was found to have been negligent in standing
less than nine feet from the hook. He knew that it was
dangerous to stand too close and the accident was easily
avoidable as it would have been easy for B to have stood a
safe distance away. B's contributory negligence was assessed
at 25%.

20% **DAVISON v APEX SCAFFOLDS**

[1956] 1 QB 551, [1956] 2 WLR 636, [1956] 1 All ER 473 (CA)

D was employed erecting scaffolding to clean the roof of a station. The necessary materials for erecting the scaffolding were sent from AS' store to the site, but in the course of the project some materials from other scaffolding contractors on the site got mixed up with AS' materials. D knew that AS only used a particular kind of coupler, but in the course of erecting the scaffolding he used a different coupler, which was a slightly different size. The effect of this was that, although the coupler appeared to be securely screwed, it failed to tighten a clip around a vertical pole. The scaffolding collapsed and D was killed. It was held that D was himself in breach of the applicable regulations in knowingly using someone else's materials when his employers had provided him with all the necessary materials. He was failing to co-operate in complying with the regulations by using materials which turned out not to be suitable. His contributory negligence was assessed at 20%.

0%   **MACHRAY v STEWARTS & LLOYDS LTD**

[1965] 1 WLR 602, [1964] 3 All ER 716 (QBD)

M, an experienced rigger employed by SL at a steelworks, was subject to the direction of his foreman, or in his absence, a charge-hand, who essentially relied on M so far as rigging techniques were concerned. A large section of pipe needed to be moved urgently and as there was no crane available, M looked for sets of chain pulley blocks. However, none were available and so M borrowed a set of wooden blocks from other contractors on the site. In the course of lifting the pipe it swung out, injuring M. It was said that in using the wooden blocks, M used a method which was obviously less safe than his preferred method. However, there was no contributory negligence on M's part as it was found that he used the wooden blocks:

> "not for the sake of saving himself trouble but in order to get on with his employer's business, and [he was] prevented from doing the work in the way in which he would have preferred to do it by the employer's breach in not providing him with the proper [equipment]."[15]

0%   **BYERS v HEAD WRIGHTSON & CO LTD**

[1961] 1 WLR 961, [1961] 2 All ER 538 (QBD)

B was a steel erector who was tasked with moving a welding set. He attempted to take it across an improvised plank bridge over a trench. The plank sagged and he was injured when the welding set fell on top of him. It was held that there was no contributory negligence and said that where an employee is required to make a decision which is too difficult for him and so makes the wrong decision and is injured, he should not be found guilty of contributory negligence.

---

15. [1965] 1 WLR 602 per McNair J at 610.

CHAPTER TEN
CHILDREN

For the principles involved in assessing the applicable standard of care when considering the contributory negligence of children, reference should be made to Chapter 3 above. When considering the examples set out below it should be borne in mind that the Scottish Courts have generally been readier to make higher findings of contributory negligence against children than the Courts in England and Wales have been.

1. CROSSING THE ROAD

75%   **MORALES v ECCLESTON**

[1991] RTR 151 (CA)

M, an eleven-year-old boy, followed a football out onto a road without looking in either direction. D was driving his car at 20 mph in a stream of traffic and collided with M, who was already over half way across the road. Taking account of M's age, he was found to have been contributorily negligent to the extent of 75%.

75%   **FOSKETT v MISTRY**

[1984] RTR 1 (CA)

M was driving his car at a reasonable speed in open parkland when F, aged 16, ran down a slope and out into the road, colliding with M's car. M should have appreciated the potential danger and warned F of his presence, but F was contributorily negligent to the extent of 75% in running out.

66.66%   **HARVEY v CAIRNS**

1989 SLT 107 (OH)

A six-year-old girl was killed when she stepped from the pavement into the path of a car. The car was being driven by an unqualified and unsupervised driver at 30 mph, which was normal for that road, but still excessive. The driver should have anticipated that the child might run out into the road. It was held that the girl was two thirds to blame.

60%   **FUTTER v BRYCELAND**

2000 GWD 9–339 (OH)

F, aged 15, was hit by a car driven by B whilst running across a road at the back of a group of boys. In the hour before the accident it had snowed to a depth of between one and three inches. A 20 mph speed limit was set for the road between the date of the accident and trial. It was found that:

(1) B was travelling at not less than 20 mph, which was too fast given the nature of the road, snowy conditions and presence of the group of boys running across the road;

(2) B was not keeping a proper look out;

(3) F was at an age where he could be held to be capable of taking proper care for his own safety and had materially contributed to the accident by failing to check that it was safe to cross the road;

(4) if B's only fault had been to drive too fast, F's share of the responsibility would have been very high; but

(5) as B had failed to keep a proper look out, F was 60% to blame.

50%   **McKINNELL v WHITE**

1971 SLT 61 (OH)

S, a five-year-old boy, let go of his elder brother's hand and
ran from the pavement across a main road whereupon he
was struck by W's car. W was found to have been negligent
and S's contributory negligence in running out was
assessed at 50%. It was said that the danger of running
across a main road was very obvious and must have been
within the understanding of S. It was also said that the fact
of S letting go of his brother's hand and running off made
his actions rather more deliberate and more obviously
negligent than if he had been alone.

33.33%   **ARMSTRONG v COTTRELL**

[1993] PIQR P109 (CA)

A group of girls were hovering at the side of a road,
obviously intending to cross. A, aged twelve, moved into
the road, but hesitated and was struck by C's car. C should
have reduced her speed and sounded her horn to warn of
her presence. Bearing in mind A's age, contributory
negligence was assessed at one third.

33.33%   **ROBERTS v PEARSON**

Unreported, 1991 (CA)

R, aged twelve, was struck by P's motorcycle whilst crossing
the road from a central reservation. P was travelling too fast
and not keeping a proper look out. However, R's
contributory negligence was assessed at one third. It was
said that a twelve-year-old boy is less able to gauge the
speed of an approaching vehicle and is likely to be less
inhibited than an adult.

20%   **MCCLUSKEY v WALLACE**

1998 SLT 1357 (IH)

M, a ten-year-old girl, was injured by a car driven by W whilst she was crossing the road. M had not noticed W's oncoming vehicle when she crossed the road and W had similarly not been paying attention. It was said that a person driving a car is always much more dangerous to others than a pedestrian and might, therefore, be much more to blame than a pedestrian. M was found to have been 20% to blame. No special account appears to have been taken of her age.

0%   **GOUGH v THORNE**

[1966] 1 WLR 1387, [1966] 3 All ER 398 (CA)

G, aged 13, was waiting to cross a busy main road with her brothers aged 17 and 10. A lorry stopped and the driver put out a hand to stop other traffic and waved G and her brothers across. G stepped out beyond the lorry without looking and was struck by T's car, which was passing the lorry. T was found to have been negligent in driving too fast and not observing the lorry driver's signal. It was held that it was not negligent of G to rely on the lorry driver in the circumstances and so there was no reduction for contributory negligence. It was said:

> "A child has not the road sense or the experience of his or her elders. He or she is not to be found guilty unless he or she is blameworthy."[1]

An adult probably would have been found guilty of contributory negligence in proceeding beyond the lorry without checking that it was safe to do so.

---

1.   [1966] 1 WLR 1387 per Lord Denning MR at 1390.

0%   ANDREWS v FREEBOROUGH

[1967] 1 QB 1, [1966] 3 WLR 342, [1966] 2 All ER 721
(CA)

A, aged nearly eight, was a bright child and well aware of
the hazards of traffic. She was standing on the kerb waiting
to cross a road when she was caught by F's passing car,
which was being driven too close to the kerb, and fatally
injured. There was no finding of contributory negligence
against A and it was said that even if A had stepped out into
the path of F's car:

> "I should have needed a good deal of persuasion before
> imputing contributory negligence to the child having
> regard to her tender age."[2]

Further:

> "The little girl was only eight years of age, and in my
> judgment it is not possible to say that she was guilty of
> contributory negligence in the circumstances of this
> case. It is true that she was thought by her parents to
> be sufficiently trained and traffic-conscious to be fit to
> be trusted not only to cross highways safely herself but
> also to be put in charge of her four-year-old brother on
> such a journey. But even if she did step off [the kerb]
> into the car, it would not be right to count as
> negligence on her part such a momentary, though
> fatal, act of inattention or carelessness."[3]

---

2.   [1967] 1 QB 1 per Wilmer LJ at 8.
3.   [1967] 1 QB 1 per Davies LJ at 16.

0%   **JONES v LAWRENCE**

[1969] 3 All ER 267 (QBD)

J, aged seven, ran out from behind a parked vehicle, apparently without looking, across a road to get to a fun-fair. He was struck by a motorcycle driven by L, which was going too fast. There was found to have been no contributory negligence on J's part. There was evidence that children of his age are prone to forget what they have been taught about matters such as road safety when something else is uppermost in their mind and his conduct was only that to be expected of a seven-year-old.

2. CLIMBING & TRESPASSING

66.66%   **ADAMS v SOUTHERN ELECTRICITY BOARD**

(1993) *The Times*, October 21 (CA)

A, a 15-year-old boy, was electrocuted whilst climbing a high voltage electrical transformer. The anti-climbing device was in a defective condition, but A was held to have been contributorily negligent to the extent of two thirds.

60%   **DAVIES v KNOWSLEY METROPOLITAN BOROUGH COUNCIL**

Unreported, 1999 (QBD)

D, aged eleven, went onto the roof of a boiler building at his school, which he knew to be out of bounds. He jumped on a sky light and sustained injuries when he fell through it. It was found that D was quite capable of understanding the risks of jumping on a sky light and his contributory negligence was assessed at 60%.

33.33%   **DAWSON v SCOTTISH POWER PLC**

1999 SLT 672 (OH)

D, an eleven-year-old boy, was injured when he climbed into an electricity substation to retrieve a football. The fence around the substation was covered with spikes and notices stating "Danger of Death. Keep Out", although the fence was only four feet high. SP were held liable on the basis that the fence was not high enough to prevent the foreseeable risk of children climbing over. However, D realised that he was taking a risk in crossing the fence and had previously been warned not to do so by his father. D was held one third to blame.

20%   **TYPE v MERTHYR TYDFIL BC**

[1990] CLY 1684 (CC)

An eleven-year-old boy was swinging from a tree in a park, when the branch broke and he fell into a hole beneath the tree. Contributory negligence was assessed at 20%.

0%   **DEVINE v NORTHERN IRELAND HOUSING EXECUTIVE**

[1992] NI 74 (NICA)

A ten-year-old boy sustained injuries when he fell from a garage roof. It was held that it was possible for a child aged ten to be found contributorily negligent depending on the circumstances of the case, although no such finding was made on the facts.

0%   **FRENCH v SUNSHINE HOLIDAY CAMP**

(1963) 107 SJ 595 (QBD)

F, aged six, climbed on a low wall surrounding a flowerbed covered by thin glass at a restaurant. On three occasions she was instructed to get down, but she climbed up for a fourth time and was injured when she fell through the glass. F was found not to have been contributorily negligent, as she did not know of the danger from the glass.

0%   **OULETTE v DAON DEVELOPMENT CORPORATION**

[1988] 4 WWR 366 (Canada)

O, a five-year-old girl, was injured when she fell from the top of a free standing escalator to the floor below in a shopping mall. The escalator had been designed in such a way that it had been possible for O to grab the moving hand rail at the bottom of the escalator and be pulled up a ledge located outside the enclosed stairway to the top of the escalator. At the top, O fell when attempting to climb from the ledge into the enclosed stairway of the escalator. Given her age, O was found not to have been contributorily negligent.

0%   **BUCKLAND v GUILDFORD GAS LIGHT AND COKE CO**

[1949] 1 KB 410, [1948] 2 All ER 1086 (KBD)

B, a 13-year-old girl, strayed from a path across a field and climbed an easily climbable oak tree, which was found to be an allurement to children. The dense foliage made high voltage electrical wires just above the tree difficult to see and B was electrocuted upon reaching the top of the tree. It was held that contributory negligence on the part of B had not been made out.

3. DANGEROUS GAMES

50%   **C v IMPERIAL DESIGN LTD**

[2001] Env LR 593 (CA)

C, aged 13, was playing with some friends on an open area of land close to ID's factory. He came across a container that had a residue of waste solvent in it, which had been negligently discarded by ID. C set fire to the solvent, which exploded causing him to suffer severe burns. C knew that setting fire to the container was dangerous, but did not expect there to be an explosion. A finding had to be made "as to whether [C] expected that there would be an explosion and, if he did not do so, whether it was reasonable for him not to have foreseen that risk."[4] It was further said:

> "The question ... is, [did C take] such care of his own safety as it is reasonable to expect of a 13-year-old child? In this case the answer is obviously that he [did] not ... The issue is one of apportionment ... there are two matters to be taken into account: the relative causative potency of what each of the parties did and their respective blameworthiness."[5]

On the former issue, C was indeed more responsible than ID. On the latter issue, however, C was simply too young and inexperienced to recognise the real risk of explosion. Overall, C's contributory negligence was assessed at 50%.

---

4.   [2001] Env LR 593 per Arden LJ at 605.
5.   [2001] Env LR 593 per Hale LJ at 603.

33.33%   **EVANS v SOULS GARAGES LTD**

[2001] TLR 51 (QBD)

E and his friend, both aged 13, purchased some petrol from
SG's garage. They inhaled the petrol and some of it spilled
onto E's trousers. E's friend then threw a match and the
petrol ignited causing E to suffer extensive burns. SG was
held to have been negligent in supplying the petrol to E,
but E's contributory negligence was assessed at one third. E
was at fault in acquiring the petrol, which he knew to be
inflammable, and although he might not have known of
its volatility or that someone sniffing it would do
something dangerous, by sniffing the petrol in a joint
venture with B, the boys became less responsible and that
played some part in the accident.

33.33%   **HARRISON v MINISTRY OF DEFENCE**

[1998] CLY 3929 (CC)

H, a 14-year-old cadet, was instructed to run up and down
a steep embankment in a race. The cadets were given no
instructions or warnings. Most of the cadets slid down the
embankment on their behinds, but the more adventurous
ran straight up and down. H ran and tripped over a stump
or root and fractured his arm. The defence of *volenti non fit
injuria* was not made out having regard to H's age and the
fact that he was acting under orders. However, as H knew
that running straight up and down increased the risk of
falling, his damages were reduced by one third on account
of his contributory negligence.

25%   ## JOLLEY v SUTTON LBC

[2000] 1 WLR 1082, [2000] 3 All ER 409 (HL)[6]

A small wooden boat had been abandoned on SLBC's land. It became rotten and derelict and J, aged 14, attempted to renovate it with a friend. He jacked the boat up to repair holes in the hull using his father's car jack and some wood. However, whilst he was underneath the boat, it fell on top of him causing him severe injuries. It was found that the boat was an allurement to children and SLBC were held liable as occupiers of the land. J's contributory negligence was assessed at 25%.

0%   ## YACHUK v OLIVER BLAIS CO LTD

[1949] AC 386, [1949] 2 All ER 150 (PC)

Y, a boy aged nine, bought a small quantity of petrol from OB's petrol station, which he said was needed for his mother's stranded car, but in fact he wanted for a game. In due course Y set fire to the petrol and burnt himself. In an action for negligence against OB, it was held that Y had not been contributorily negligent, as he had no knowledge of the danger inherent in petrol. It was said:

> "If one gives to a child an explosive substance, and the child, with a limited knowledge in respect to the likely effect of the explosion, is tempted to meddle with it to his injury, it cannot be said in answer to a claim on behalf of the child that he did meddle to his own injury, or that he was tempted to do that which a child of his years might reasonably be expected to do."[7]

---

6. The question of contributory negligence was not raised on the appeals to the Court of Appeal or the House of Lords.
7. [1949] AC 386 per Lord Du Parcq at 397.

0%   **GALBRAITH'S CURATOR AD LITEM v STEWART**

1998 SLT 1305 (OH)

G, an eight-year-old boy, and other children played on a number of concrete pipes left unsecured overnight on S's construction site. G was injured when he fell off a pipe. It was held that there was no general rule to determine the question of a child's contributory negligence, the particular danger and the capacity of the child to appreciate the risk had to be considered and in the instant case, there was no contributory negligence proved.

0%   **GLASGOW CORPORATION v TAYLOR**

[1922] 1 AC 44 (HLS)

T, aged seven, was poisoned when he ate attractive looking, but poisonous berries growing on a shrub in a public park. The berries were an allurement to children and GC, who were aware of their dangerous nature, had given no warnings. It was held that T had not been contributorily negligent.

4. SEAT BELTS AND CYCLING HELMETS

0%   **A v SHORROCK**

Current Law Oct/2001 (QBD)

A, aged 14, was injured when he rode his bicycle onto a
road from the pavement and was struck by S's car. Liability
was not established, but it was indicated that A would not
have been found to have been contributorily negligent in
failing to wear a safety helmet. There was no legal
requirement for him to do so and he was not engaged in
any particularly hazardous kind of riding, during which it
might be thought prudent to wear a helmet.

0%   **DUCHARME v DAVIES**

[1984] 1 WWR 699 (Canada)

D was responsible for causing a car accident injuring two
parents and their three-year-old child, none of whom were
wearing seatbelts. The awards to the parents were reduced
by 15% to take account of their contributory negligence,
but the award to the child was not reduced. It was held that
an infant was incapable of contributory negligence and
that the negligence of a parent in failing to ensure that a
child is restrained by a seat belt cannot be imputed to the
child. No claim was made against the parents for a
contribution on the basis that they were joint tortfeasors.[8]

---

8.   Such a claim was made in *Jones* v *Wilkins* [2001] PIQR P179, [2001] RTR 283 (CA),
     where the child's mother's responsibility (together with the child's aunt who was
     driving) was assessed at 25% under the Civil Liability (Contribution) Act 1978. See
     page 247 below.

5. OTHERS

20%   **MINTER v D A H CONTRACTORS (CAMBRIDGE) LTD**

[1983] CLY 2544 (QBD)

M, a nine-year-old boy, was injured when he rode his bicycle into a pile of hardcore, which had been negligently left in the road by DHC. M was "a good rider" and his contributory negligence was assessed at 20%.

10%   **CRAIG v STRATHCLYDE REGIONAL COUNCIL**

1998 Housing LR 104 (SH)

A nine-year-old boy was injured whilst carrying a bicycle down some stairs in complete darkness. SRC were under a duty to light the stairway and C was held to have been contributorily negligent to the extent of 10%.

CHAPTER ELEVEN
PRODUCT LIABILITY

See also page 66 above for consideration of the Consumer Protection Act 1987.

33.33%   **DEVILEZ v BOOTS PURE DRUG CO**

(1962) 106 SJ 552 (QBD)

D purchased a bottle of corn solvent from BPD. After using the product he dropped the bottle and the cork came out, which allowed the contents to spill onto D, causing him injury. It was held that BPD should have placed a warning as to the dangers of the product on the bottle and secured the bottle in a better way than with a cork. However, D's contributory negligence in not calling a doctor soon enough or appreciating the possible need for care when handling the bottle was assessed at one third.

33.33%   **WEBBER v McCAUSLAND**

Current Law 47–51/6765, (1948) 98 LJ 360 (CC)

W purchased a bottle of hair dye from M. The bottle had conditions printed on it, which stated that the dye should not be used without having first read the booklet, which accompanied the bottle. However, W's bottle had been supplied without a booklet. W used the dye and contracted dermatitis. His contributory negligence in not having read the conditions on the bottle was assessed at one third.

33.33%   **KAYE v ALFA ROMEO (GB)**

(1984) 134 NLJ 126[1]

K was injured in a road traffic accident, for which he was found to have been one third to blame. In his claims against the manufacturer and supplying agents of his car arising out of their negligence in fitting seat belts which partially failed, his damages were correspondingly reduced by one third.

HODGSON v IMPERIAL TOBACCO LTD

[1999] CLY 459 (QBD)

H and others commenced a class action against IT alleging that they had developed lung cancer after smoking IT's tobacco products over a number of years. The applications to disapply the primary limitation period were dismissed as none of the applicants had acted promptly or reasonably. It was observed that the claims were speculative due to the difficulties in establishing causation and counteracting the defence of *volenti non fit injuria* and allegations of contributory negligence.

0%   **RE SPARKLING MINERAL WATER BOTTLE**

[1999] ECC 534 (Austria)

The claimant was injured when the cap from a bottle of sparkling mineral water flew into his eye. The bottle had been left in a car on a hot day for several hours, causing a build up of pressure. In proceedings under Austrian product liability legislation it was found that there was no warning on the bottle and that the claimant was not liable for contributory negligence.

---

1.   See also *Kaye* v *Motorway Sports Cars* (1984) 134 NLJ 451.

CHAPTER TWELVE
PROFESSIONAL NEGLIGENCE

1. ACCOUNTANTS & AUDITORS

50%   **NELSON GUARANTEE CORPORATION LTD v HODGSON**

[1958] NZLR 609 (New Zealand)

NGC's claim against its auditor for failing to spot an employee's embezzlement failed, but it was said that NGC would have been found to have been contributorily negligent to the extent of 50%.

40%   **DAIRY CONTAINERS LTD v NZI BANK LTD**

[1995] 2 NZLR 30 (New Zealand)

DCL was the victim of a fraud perpetrated by senior employees and claimed against its auditors and bankers. DCL was found to have been 40% contributorily negligent as against its auditors in failing to protect its own interests by the directors' failing to monitor DCL's affairs. Its contributory negligence was not confined to hampering the audit.

33.33%   **AWA LTD v DANIELS T/A DELOITTE HASKINS & SELLS**

(1995) 16 ACSR 607 (Australia)[1]

AWA claimed that its auditors, D, were negligent in failing to report serious deficiencies in AWA's internal control system, which allowed an employee to incur large losses for AWA. AWA had been contributorily negligent in failing to employ specialist managers, ignoring advice about the weakness in its system, failing to have proper internal controls, failing to have those deficiencies reported to the board and failing to supervise the employee responsible for the transactions causing the loss. AWA's damages were reduced by one third to take account of its contributory negligence. It was found that AWA's negligence was not only that of its directors, but also that of the senior management.

30%   **DE MEZA & STUART v APPLE VAN STRATEN SHENA & STONE**

[1974] 1 Lloyd's Rep 508 (QBD)[2]

A firm of solicitors instructed auditors to complete consequential loss insurance certificates. Errors were made on the forms and the solicitors were under insured when their offices were damaged by fire. It was found that the solicitors' contributory negligence in failing to spot the obvious errors amounted to 30%.

---

1.   See also the first instance decisions at (1992) 7 ACS R 759 and (1992) 9 ACS R 383.
2.   The question of contributory negligence was not considered by the Court of Appeal at [1975] 1 Lloyd's Rep 498.

20%   PECH v TILGALS

(1994) 28 ATR 197 (Australia)

P claimed on the basis that his accountants had been negligent in failing to prepare accurate tax returns. P failed to read the tax returns and check their accuracy before signing them and his contributory negligence was assessed at 20%.

0%   WALKER v HUNGERFORDS

(1987) 19 ATR 745 (Australia)

A clerk at the client company made an arithmetical error in completing a tax return. However, there was no reduction for contributory negligence in a claim against the accountants, as it was reasonable for him to believe that the accountants would check the figures.

0%   HENDERSON v MERRETT SYNDICATES LTD (NO. 2)

[1996] 1 PNLR 32 (QBD)

Auditors were unable to argue that Lloyds' names should be held contributorily negligent on the basis of the negligence of the managing agents employed by them. It was said:

> "It makes a nonsense of the purpose for which the auditors were employed if the names' claims against the auditors are defeated by reason of the very negligence to which the auditors were supposed to be alerting the names."[3]

---

3.   [1996] 1 PNLR 32 per Cresswell J at 40. Although cf *Pride Valley Foods Ltd* v *Hall & Partners (Contract Management) Ltd* (2001) 76 Con LR 1 (CA), the facts of which are set out below and *Astley* v *Austrust Ltd* [1999] Lloyd's Rep PN 758 (Australia) at page 201 below.

2. ARCHITECTS & RELATED PROFESSIONALS

50%   **PRIDE VALLEY FOODS LTD v HALL & PARTNERS (CONTRACT MANAGEMENT) LTD**

(2001) 76 Con LR 1 (CA)

PVF engaged project managers to design a factory. The project managers were negligent in failing to advise PVF that certain panels, which it wished to use in the factory, would allow a fire to spread rapidly. A fire started, partly as the result of PVF's negligence. The Court of Appeal upheld the trial judge's assessment of contributory negligence at 50%, although the view was expressed that as the consequences of the fire were only as serious as they were as a result of the project managers' failure to guard against that very risk, the reduction might have been assessed at one third.

0%   **CARDY & SON v TAYLOR**

[1994] CLY 324 (CC)

T brought proceedings against his builder, C, alleging defective workmanship and design. C joined the architects who had designed the alterations to T's property as third parties. In C's claim against the architects, it was found that C had not been contributorily negligent in failing to check the architect's survey and/or not conducting his own survey.

3. DOCTORS

In the UK there are no reported decisions where contributory negligence has been found in a claim against a medical practitioner.

66.66%   ## CROSSMAN v STEWART

(1978) 5 CCLT 45 (Canada)

S, a doctor, prescribed drugs for C's skin condition but negligently failed to warn her of the risks associated with use of the drug for a prolonged period. C, who worked as a medical receptionist, was able to purchase the drug privately from a drug salesman and continued to use it for a long time after S had stopped prescribing it. S was found to have been negligent in failing to appreciate from test results that C was probably still using the drug. C's contributory negligence was assessed at two thirds; her conduct in using a drug without a prescription was described as foolhardy.

50%   ## FREDETTE v WIEBE

(1986) 29 DLR (4th) 534 (Canada)

The claimant underwent an unsuccessful termination of a pregnancy by reason of her doctor's negligence. However, she failed to attend her follow up examination, which would have revealed that she was still pregnant. Her contributory negligence was assessed at 50%.

30%   ## FERGUSON v HENSHAW

[1989] BCJ No. 1 199 (Canada)

The claimant carelessly misused oral contraceptives, which had been negligently prescribed. As a result she became pregnant. Her contributory negligence was assessed at 30%.

25%   **HÔPITAL NOTRE-DAME DE L'ESPÉRENCE v LAURENT**

[1978] 1 SCR 605 (Canada)

L went to see a doctor, who negligently failed to diagnose
a fracture at the head of her femur. However, L did not seek
further medical treatment for over three months and her
contributory negligence was assessed at 25%.

20%   **BRUSHETT v COWAN**

(1990) 3 CCLT (2d) 195, [1991] 2 Med LR 271 (Canada)

B, a former nursing assistant, was discharged from hospital
following surgery to her leg without having been warned
by C, her orthopaedic surgeon, not to put weight on her
injured leg. While not using her crutches she fell and re-
injured her leg. It was found that C was liable for not
warning B not to put weight on her leg, but B's
contributory negligence in failing to ask amounted to 20%.

0%–50%   **FOOTE v ROYAL COLUMBIAN HOSPITAL**

(1982) 38 BCLR 222*

A doctor negligently failed to warn hospital staff that a 15-
year-old epileptic patient, whose medication had been
changed, might have a seizure at any time. The patient had
a bath unsupervised and suffered injuries when she had a
seizure. There was found to have been no contributory
negligence on the part of the patient. However, it was said
that if it had been shown that the patient had understood
instructions not to bathe unsupervised, there would have
been a reduction of 50%.

---

*   See also the decision on appeal at 19 ACW 5 (2d) 304.

4. INSURANCE BROKERS

75%   **MORASH v LOCKHART & RITCHIE LTD**

(1979) 95 DLR (3d) 647 (Canada)

Brokers negligently failed to send M a renewal form for his fire insurance or to inform him that the policy was expiring. However, M's contributory negligence in failing to take any action for 18 months after the policy expired was assessed at 75%.

75%   **FORSIKRINGSAKTIESELSKAPET VESTA v BUTCHER**

[1986] 2 All ER 488 (QBD)

Brokers negligently failed to deal with a request from insurers to contact the re-insurers about an exclusion clause. The insurers failed to chase the brokers and their contributory negligence was assessed at 75%. The Court of Appeal[4] did not interfere with the finding, but plainly considered the reduction to be at the very highest end of the reasonable range and one member of the Court said he was somewhat surprised by the level of the reduction.

50%   **FIRESTONE CANADA INC v AMERICAN HOME ASSURANCE CO**

(1989) 67 OR (2d) 471 (Canada)

FC's manager had read a clause in an insurance contract, which did not accord with his requirements, but he did nothing take the matter any further. FC's contributory negligence was assessed at 50%.

---

4.   [1988] 3 WLR 565, [1988] 2 All ER 43. The question was not considered by the House of Lords at [1989] AC 852, [1989] 2 WLR 290, [1989] 1 All ER 402.

33.33%   **TUDOR JONES v CROWLEY COLOSSO LTD**

[1996] 2 Lloyd's Rep 619 (QBD)

C, insurance brokers, were instructed by M (also insurance brokers) to place insurance cover in respect of T's building development. The policy did not cover building works for which a completion certificate had been issued before any damage occurred. A hurricane damaged a completed part of the development. It was found that C were negligent in allowing the exclusion to appear in the policy, but M were contributorily negligent to the extent of one third in failing to inspect the terms properly before approving the policy.

20%   **YOUELL v BLAND WELCH & CO LTD**

[1990] 2 Lloyd's Rep 431 (QBD)

Insurers received a copy of a contract of reinsurance on three occasions, but did not notice that the reinsurance cover did not match the terms of the insurance they had granted. The reinsurance contracted had been drafted in such a way as to make the relevant provisions difficult to understand. The insurers' contributory negligence was assessed at 20%.

0%   **J W BOLLOM & CO LTD v BYAS MOSLEY & CO LTD**

[1999] Lloyd's Rep PN 598 (QBD)

BM had been JWB's property insurance brokers for 30 years. A fire broke out at JWB's premises and their insurers refused to pay the claim in full as JWB's alarm had been switched off in breach of a clause in the policy. In an action brought by JWB, BM admitted a duty to take reasonable steps to bring the relevant clause in the policy to JWB's notice, but alleged contributory negligence. JWB were found not to have been contributorily negligent, not being under a duty to guard against BM's negligence, which was not foreseeable. JWB were entitled to assume that BM would act with reasonable care and skill and were not negligent in not guarding against the possibility that they had not done so.

0%   **SHARP AND ROARER INVESTMENTS LTD v SPHERE DRAKE INSURANCE PLC**

[1992] 2 Lloyd's Rep 501 (QBD)

When arranging yacht insurance, brokers asked S whether he or his family would live on the yacht over winter, but were negligent in failing to ask whether anyone else would. The yacht's crew did live on the boat over winter and the insurers relied on a houseboat exclusion clause. There was no contributory negligence on S's part for failing to appreciate the effect of the exclusion clause.

5. LENDERS

HOUSING LOAN CORPORATION PLC v WILLIAM H BROWN LTD

[1999] Lloyd's Rep PN 185 (CA)

The correct approach in cases of lender's contributory negligence is to consider whether or not there are instances of fault on the lender's part which were partly causative of the damage suffered. Thereafter, one must determine the causative potency of each factor and its blameworthiness. It was said that whilst it will not necessarily amount to negligence where a lender has not followed its own lending guidelines, they might be illustrative of sensible precautions.

90%

NATIONWIDE BUILDING SOCIETY v ARCHDEACONS

[1999] Lloyd's Rep PN 549 (Ch D)

A were solicitors acting for both NBS and a borrower on a house purchase. A were found to have been negligent in providing an unconditional report on title, which failed to show that the property had been purchased three months earlier for a lesser sum. However, NBS had been contributorily negligent to the extent of 90% as: (1) the borrower's employer's reference showed a lower income than had been declared, (2) NBS's interviews with the borrower showed confusion, uncertainty and inconsistent answers on his part, (3) further references showed that the borrower's income fell below that required by NBS's lending criteria and (4) an employee of NBS had advised that the borrower's application for a loan should be turned down.

66.66%   **NATIONWIDE BUILDING SOCIETY v LITTLESTONE & COWAN**

[1999] Lloyd's Rep PN 625 (Ch D)

LC, a firm of solicitors, were found to have been negligent in failing to disclose information to NBS, which would have cast doubt on the accuracy of a valuation of a property undertaken by NBS, upon the security of which NBS made a loan. NBS were found to have been contributorily negligent to the extent of two thirds in circumstances where they had themselves overvalued the property, failed adequately to investigate the borrower's ability to repay the loan and advanced over 75% of the property's perceived value.

50%   **NATIONWIDE BUILDING SOCIETY v VANDERPUMP & SYKES**

[1999] Lloyd's Rep PN 422 (Ch D)

VS were a firm of solicitors acting for the borrower on the purchase of a house and also NBS, the mortgagees. VS were found to have been negligent in not reporting various suspicious matters to NBS. However, NBS were found to have been 50% contributorily negligent in making a loan of 95% of the valuation of the property when they had not investigated the many credit searches undertaken against the borrower by several financial institutions and had ignored a warning from their own valuer that there was reason to doubt the borrower's honesty.

40%   **NATIONWIDE BUILDING SOCIETY v JR JONES (A FIRM)**

[1999] Lloyd's Rep PN 414 (Ch D)

A firm of solicitors acting for the borrower and lender on a house purchase were found to have been negligent in not reporting to NBS that this was a back to back transaction with an uplift. However, NBS's award was reduced by 40% on account of their contributory negligence in failing to obtain bank references, credit references or accounts or to investigate the unusual circumstances of a non-property owning 28-year-old with no dependants proposing to occupy a property with four reception rooms, three kitchens, five bedrooms and two en-suite bathrooms.

20%   PLATFORM HOME LOANS LTD v OYSTON SHIPWAYS LTD

[2000] 2 AC 190, [1999] 2 WLR 518, [1999] 1 All ER
833 (HL)

Valuers negligently overvalued a borrower's property at
£1.5m, when it was worth only £1m. The lender lent
£1.05m to the borrower on the security of the property.
However, the borrower defaulted and after the lender had
sold the property, it suffered a loss on the transaction of
£611K. On SAAMCO/BBL[5] principles, the loss recoverable
from the valuer was effectively capped at £500K, being the
extent of the over valuation. It was argued that the lender
had been contributorily negligent in lending at a loan to
value ratio of 70% and in failing to check the price at
which the borrower had purchased the property. The
lender's contributory negligence was assessed at 20%. The
House of Lords held that the 20% reduction was to be
applied to the overall loss (i.e. £611K reducing it to £489K)
and not to the otherwise recoverable damages of £500K (so
as to reduce them to £400K). To apply the reduction
otherwise would be to make the same reduction twice over.
Where the lender's imprudence was partly responsible for
the overall loss, but did not cause or contribute to the
overvaluation, it is the overall loss alone that should be
reduced. Therefore, where only part of the overall loss is
recoverable in damages on SAAMCO/BBL principles, the
damages should not be reduced twice (once to take account
of the SAAMCO/BBL "cap" and then again for contributory
negligence). Rather, the total amount of the loss should be
reduced to take account of any contributory negligence
and the claimant awarded that reduced figure or the
damages recoverable on SAAMCO/BBL principles,
whichever is the lower.

---

5.   See *South Australia Asset Management Corporation* v *York Montague Ltd* (*Banque
     Bruxelles Lambert SA* v *Eagle Star Insurance Co Ltd*) [1997] AC 191, [1996] 3 WLR 87,
     [1996] 3 All ER 365 (HL). See page 14 above.

0%   **H I T FINANCE v LEWIS & TUCKER LTD**

[1993] 2 EGLR 231 (QBD)

HITF advanced around £1.5m against the security of a property, which had been negligently valued at £2.2m. It was said:

> "The cushion apparently provided by the property, on the basis of [the valuation] was accordingly £660,000. In such circumstances, even if the borrowers turned out to be complete men of straw, the lenders were entitled to regard themselves as being more than adequately covered not merely in respect of the capital sum lent, but also any likely loss of interest, and indeed all the costs and expenses likely to be incurred in foreclosing upon and realising the security ... it is very difficult to see how such a lender could properly be characterised as being imprudent ... [However,] I am not suggesting that the prudent lender, merely because he has the comfort of more than adequate security, is entitled to shut his eyes to any obviously unsatisfactory characteristics of the proposed borrower."[6]

0%   **COVENTRY BUILDING SOCIETY v WILLIAM MARTIN & PARTNERS**

[1997] 2 EGLR 146 (QBD)

WMP negligently overvalued a property over which CBS took a charge as security for a non-status loan whereby CBS did not enquire into the borrower's ability to service the loan. It was held that whilst CBS had been negligent in failing to enquire into the borrower's means, there was no reduction for contributory negligence, as their conduct did not cause any loss.

---

6.   [1993] 2 EGLR 231 per Wright J at 235.

0%   **LEEDS PERMANENT BUILDING SOCIETY v WALKER, FRASER & STEELE**

1995 SLT (S Ct) 72 (SH)

LPBS sued valuers alleging that they had negligently overvalued a property. They confined their claim to losses flowing from the valuation and made no claim in respect of other losses arising from a forced sale of the property. It was said that LPBS had been contributorily negligent in that they had inadequately considered the borrowers' ability to repay the loan. However, the defence of contributory negligence failed as the allegations of fault against LPBS were not causative of the loss for which they sought to recover.

6. SOLICITORS

See also the section on lenders at page 194 below.

80%   **FASKEN CAMPBELL GODFREY v SEVEN-UP CANADA INC**

(2000) 182 DLR (4th) 315 (Canada)

Solicitors failed to advise a trustee that he required the beneficiaries' consent to enter into a transaction that benefited himself. There was no loss, but as the trustee was a former partner in the firm of solicitors, his contributory negligence would have been assessed at 80%.

75%   **MCLELLAN v FLETCHER**

(1987) 3 PN 202, (1987) 13 NLJ 593 (QBD)

Solicitors failed to ensure that life insurance cover
(arranged by the client) had commenced or warn the client
as to the risks of completing a transaction without such
cover being in effect. However, the client failed to pay the
first premium on the policy so as to bring it into effect and
his contributory negligence was assessed at 75%.

50%   **CLARK BOYCE v MOUAT**

[1992] 2 NZLR 559 (New Zealand)[7]

Solicitors acted in breach of duty by accepting instructions
from a mother and her son, which generated a conflict of
interests. However, the client told the solicitors that she
relied upon and trusted her son and was found to have
been contributorily negligent to the extent of 50% in not
following the solicitors' recommendation to seek
independent advice.

50%   **DOIRON v CAISSE POPULAIRE D'INKERMAN LTEE**

(1985) 17 DLR (4th) 660 (Canada)

Solicitors failed to obtain personal guarantees for a loan.
The lenders did not inspect the documents to ascertain that
the guarantees were missing or give particularly clear
instructions. Their contributory negligence was assessed at
50%.

---

7. However, the finding of liability was reversed by the Privy Council on appeal and
    so the assessment of contributory negligence was not considered. The Privy
    Council decision is reported at [1994] 1 AC 428, [1993] 3 WLR 1021, [1993] 4 All
    ER 268.

50%   **MACDONELL v M & M DEVELOPMENTS LTD**

(1998) 157 DLR (4th) 240 (Canada)

Solicitors failed to inform a client that he was required to give contractual notification of a share transfer. However, as the client had ignored his accountant's advice to give such notification, his contributory negligence was assessed at 50%.

50%   **ASTLEY v AUSTRUST LTD**

[1999] Lloyd's Rep PN 758 (Australia)

Solicitors failed to advise a trustee about excluding his personal liability in the event a trading trust failed. The trustee was contributorily negligent to the extent of 50% in failing to properly assess the viability of the proposed investment, even though the solicitor's duty was to protect against that very loss. The High Court of Australia held there to be no absolute rule that a client is entitled to rely on his professional advisers to do their duty. Whilst the role and duty of the defendant will be relevant factors, the question remains whether or not the claimant took reasonable care. However, it was held that the Australian contributory negligence legislation did not allow apportionment in contractual cases and so there was no reduction.[8]

---

8.   However, there has since been legislation expressly enabling the defence to be raised in contractual claims.

25% **LAWRIE v GENTRY DEVELOPMENTS INC**

(1990) 72 OR (2d) 512 (Canada)

Solicitors were held to be liable in respect of their failure to prepare certain documents on time. However, the client's contributory negligence in being dilatory returning the documents to the solicitors was assessed at 25%.

25% **SKIRZYK v CRAWFORD**

(1990) 64 Man R (2d) 220 (Canada)

A solicitor failed to pursue personal injury litigation diligently. The client was found to have been contributorily negligent to the extent of 25% in also failing to deal with the matter expeditiously.

0% **EARL v WILHELM**

(2000) 183 DLR (4th) 45, [2001] WTLR 1275 (Canada)

Solicitors were negligent in failing to ensure that beneficiaries received the land intended by a testator. In a claim by the beneficiaries, the Saskatchewan Court of Appeal reversed a reduction based upon the testator's contributory negligence in failing to give clear instructions, holding it to be irrelevant.[9] There was no contributory negligence on the part of the testator as he did not owe his beneficiaries a duty of care and the beneficiaries had not contributed to any loss they had sustained.

---

9. Although see the dissenting judgment of Sir Murray Stuart-Smith in *Gorham* v *British Telecommunications Plc* [2000] 1 WLR 2129, [2000] 4 All ER 867 (CA).

0%   **BRITISH RACING DRIVERS' CLUB LTD v HEXTALL ERSKINE & CO**

[1996] 3 All ER 667 (Ch D)

There was no contributory negligence on the part of a company where solicitors failed to advise its board of directors that a particular transaction required the members' approval.

0%   **CENTRAL TRUST CO v RAFUSE**

(1986) 31 DLR (4th) 481 (Canada)

R, a firm of solicitors, failed to advise CT that there were limitations on a company's ability to borrow and give security to purchase its own shares. It was held that even though the company was acting through legally qualified officers, there was no contributory negligence as those officers were concerned with the business side of the transaction and had left the legal side to the solicitors.

0%   **MANOTARN LTD v ROSE & BIRD**

[1995] EGCS 142 (QBD)

M, a property investment company, alleged its solicitors were negligent in not drawing a break clause in a lease to its attention. M had failed to read the lease and so notice the break clause itself. There was no contributory negligence.

0%   **UCB CORPORATE SERVICES LTD v CLYDE & CO**

[2000] 2 All ER (Comm) 257, [2000] PNLR 841 (CA)

Solicitors negligently failed to obtain an enforceable guarantee. There was no contributory negligence by the bank in withdrawing a charge over an additional property belonging to the guarantor as: (1) this was not causative of any loss and (2) the bank was not to blame in thinking that it was adequately protected by the guarantee.

7. FAILURE TO CARRY OUT A SURVEY

There are conflicting decisions as to whether or not a purchaser's failure to
have a house structurally surveyed can amount to contributory negligence.
It was held that a failure to do so could amount to contributory negligence
in *Yianni* v *Edwin Evans & Sons*,[10] but held that such a failure did not
constitute contributory negligence in *Sutherland* v *C R Maton & Son Ltd*.[11]

0%   **LOW v R J HADDOCK LTD**

[1985] 2 EGLR 247, (1985) 6 Con LR 122 (OR)

L was the owner of a house, which sustained damage due
to the extraction of moisture from the subsoil by a nearby
tree on the highway. The local authority was found liable
in nuisance and negligence. L had been contributorily
negligent in failing to have the house structurally surveyed
prior to purchasing the same. It was said:

> "A purchaser who commits most of his life's savings
> and undertakes to repay a large loan in order to buy a
> house which he has not had surveyed is taking a
> terrible chance."[12]

However, as no cracks would have been visible at the time,
the failure to commission a survey did not cause any loss
and so there was no reduction.

---

10. [1982] QB 438, [1981] 3 WLR 843, [1981] 3 All ER 592 (QBD), see page 206 below.
    See also *Perry* v *Tendring DC* [1985] 1 EGLR 260 (QBD).
11. [1979] 2 EGLR 81 (QBD).
12. [1985] 2 EGLR 247 per HHJ Newey QC at 243.

0%   **YIANNI v EDWIN EVANS & SONS**

[1982] QB 438, [1981] 3 WLR 843, [1981] 3 All ER 592 (QBD)

Y applied to a building society for a loan to purchase a property. He paid a valuation fee to the building society, which instructed EE, surveyors, to carry out the valuation. The building society's literature stated that borrowers who desired a survey for their own protection or information should instruct their own surveyor. However, Y did not instruct a surveyor and relied on the fact of the building society making an offer of a loan as being indicative that the property was worth at least that amount. EE's survey was negligent and after completion it became apparent that the property was subject to significant structural defects, which would cost more than the purchase price to correct. The argument that Y had been contributorily negligent was rejected. The property was at the lower end of the market and so, as Y was likely to be of modest means, he was not negligent in relying on the valuation and in failing to obtain an independent valuation. However, it was observed that had the warning from the building society been in stronger terms and contained a warning that it would be dangerous to rely on the building society's valuer's report, a finding of contributory negligence might well have been made.[13]

0%   **KIJOWSKI v NEW CAPITAL PROPERTIES**

(1987) 15 Con LR 1 (QBD)

Purchasers were not contributorily negligent in failing to have a house structurally surveyed before purchasing the same in circumstances where the house was relatively new and contained no obvious defects, which would have led a reasonable purchaser to require an expert's inspection.

---

13. See also *Davies* v *Parry* [1988] 1 EGLR 147 (QBD).

CHAPTER THIRTEEN
ROAD TRAFFIC ACCIDENTS

1. COLLISIONS AT JUNCTIONS

80%   **DOWLING v DARGUE**

[1997] CLY 3769 (CC)

C was riding a motorcycle overtaking stationary traffic at
about 10 mph on the wrong side of the road. The traffic
had stopped to allow D to turn right from a side road onto
the major road upon which C was travelling. A collision
occurred as D was completing her manoeuvre. C was held
to have been contributorily negligent to the extent of 80%.

80%   **POWELL v MOODY**

(1966) 110 SJ 215 (CA)

P was driving his motorcycle along the offside of a queue of
stationary traffic in a major road. M slowly entered the
major road from a side road, having been invited to do so
by a driver in the stationary queue, who left a gap for M to
pull out. A collision ensued and the trial judge held P 80%
to blame. Whilst the Court of Appeal did not interfere with
the apportionment, Salmon LJ indicated that he would
have apportioned liability equally.

75%   **DOLBY v MILNER**

[1996] CLY 4430 (CA)

An accident occurred when D turned right out of a side
road and collided with M's motorcycle. M was travelling at
excessive speed and failed to take evasive action, but as D
was under a continuing obligation to give way and M had
been visible from 95 yards away, D was found to have been
contributorily negligent to the extent of 75%.

75%   **RICHARDS v QUINTON**

Unreported, 2000 (CA)

A collision occurred between R on his bicycle and Q's car when Q drove from a driveway and onto a cycle path, which he had to cross to get to the road. It was held that R had the better opportunity to avoid the collision and should have acted when he saw Q's car emerge. R's contributory negligence was assessed at 75%.

75%   **KOTECHA v LONDON BOROUGH OF HARROW**

[1995] CLY 1812 (CC)

K drove his car out of a minor road and into collision with another vehicle on a major road. LBH, the highway authority, had recently resurfaced the minor road and there were no "give way" markings on the road or other signs. In his claim against LBH, K's contributory negligence was assessed at 75%.

66.66%   **PATEL v EDWARDS**

[1970] RTR 425 (CA)

P was riding his bicycle, which was followed by a car, which was followed by E on his motorcycle. The car indicated to turn left and P pulled out to turn right in front of the car and collided with E, who was overtaking the car. It was said that in cases of such collisions, regard should be paid to the ease with which each vehicle can be brought to a stop. P's contributory negligence was assessed at two thirds.

66.66%   ## COX v DIXON

(1984) 134 NLJ 236, 451 (QBD)

C, a policeman, was chasing a motorcycle in an unmarked car. He was driving at 60 mph in an area subject to a 30 mph limit and collided with D, who came out of a side turning. C was found to have been two thirds to blame for the accident.

60%   ## GRIFFIN v MERSEY REGIONAL AMBULANCE SERVICE

[1998] PIQR P34 (CA)

G drove through a busy junction controlled by traffic lights that were green in his favour and collided with an ambulance that was turning right against a red light. The ambulance was on an emergency call and had its lights and siren on. G had not seen the ambulance as his view was obstructed by a van, which had stopped to let the ambulance through. The ambulance was found liable for not waiting a little longer to check that no vehicles were crossing its path and travelling faster than it should have done. However, G was held to have been contributorily negligent to the extent of 60% in not appreciating the presence of the ambulance or realising that the van had stopped to allow it through.

50%   ## THOMPSON v SPEDDING

[1973] RTR 312 (CA)

S was driving his car, followed by X, who was followed by T. S decided to turn right and braked sharply. X stopped safely, but T could not stop in time and hit X's car. T's contributory negligence in travelling too close to X to stop safely was assessed at 50%.

40%   **HORTON v MORGAN & HEAVY TRANSPORT (EEC)**

[1978] CLY 331 (CA)

H, a provisional licence holder, was riding his motorcycle
along an icy road when he collided with a tanker. The
tanker was turning right across the road into a side road. H
must have seen the manoeuvre being executed by the slow
moving taker, but the tanker driver was more to blame for
failing to keep a proper look out. The tanker driver had the
higher duty when executing what was described as "a
notoriously dangerous manoeuvre". H was found to have
been contributorily negligent to the extent of 40%.

33.33%   **KENFIELD MOTORS LTD v HAYLES & REES**

[1998] CLY 3919 (CC)

K's employee was driving along a main road, intending to
turn right into a side road. He crossed to the wrong side of
the road 40 yards before the junction and intended to
travel past the side road, stop and then reverse into the side
road so that he could exit the side road more easily the next
day. H was stationary at the junction in the side road
intending to turn left into the main road. H looked to the
right and began pulling out of the junction, whereupon the
two vehicles collided. H had not looked sufficiently to the
left before pulling out, but K's driver was carrying out a
dangerous manoeuvre on the wrong side of the road and
was held to have been contributorily negligent to the
extent of one third.

33.33%   **WADSWORTH v GILLESPIE**

[1978] CLY 2534 (QBD)

G was stationary at a "give way" sign at the exit from a minor road into a major road. W was driving his motorcycle along the major road with his left turn indicator signalling. G entered the major road in reliance on the signal and collided with W, who was unaware that his indicator was flashing and carried straight on. W's contributory negligence was assessed at one third.

33.33%   **RUBERY v HARBROE & COHEN**

[1997] CLY 3771 (CC)

R was driving a minibus and trailer out of a garage onto a single carriageway road. He had emerged to a point half way across the near side carriageway and was intending to turn left. H was waiting in a side road to R's left intending to turn right onto the road. H was unable to see traffic approaching due to the position of R's vehicle and H indicated to R that it was safe to pull out. R pulled out around H's vehicle and collided with C who had been overtaking H. It was held that all three drivers were one third to blame.[1]

---

1.   However, this approach has been disapproved of. The claimant's contributory negligence should be assessed and then the question of contribution between defendants should be considered separately. The two stages should not be combined as appears to have happened in this case. To combine the two stages can lead to an erroneous award e.g. treating the claimant's negligence as being equal to that of the defendants would lead to a reduction of 50%, which is plainly not the same as holding the claimant one third to blame. See *Fitzgerald* v *Lane* [1989] AC 328, [1988] 3 WLR 356, [1988] 2 All ER 961 (HL), considered at pages 83 above and 234 below.

20%   **HAMIED v EASTWICK**

Unreported, 1994 (CA)

H was driving his vehicle along a major road when E pulled out of a minor road ahead of him intending to turn right into the major road. It was found that H had been exceeding the speed limit by 5–10 mph and whilst that was not necessarily negligent, H was driving along a busy road in a built up area with lots of side roads and a prudent driver must bear in mind the possibility of someone emerging from a side road. In driving faster than he should have done, H gave himself less time and opportunity to take avoiding action. H's contributory negligence was assessed at 20%.

0%   **SINGH v NIXON & COSTELLO**

(1974) 21 WIR 203 (Guyana)

A driver crossing a green light owes a duty only to persons lawfully in the intersection. If a driver unlawfully in the intersection wishes to allege contributory negligence, he must show that the claimant ought to have seen him.[2]

---

2. See also *Miller* v *Evans* [1975] RTR 70 (CA), *Hopwood Homes* v *Kennerdine* [1975] RTR 82 (CA) and *Davis* v *Hassan* (1967) 117 NLJ 72 (CA).

2. COLLISIONS OTHER THAN AT JUNCTIONS

50%   **BAKER v MARKET HARBOROUGH INDUSTRIAL CO-OPERATIVE SOCIETY LTD**

[1953] 1 WLR 1472 (CA)

Where a collision occurs in the centre of a straight road between two motor vehicles travelling in opposite directions, the inference, in the absence of any other evidence,[3] is that each driver was equally to blame. It was further said[4] that even if one of the vehicles was over the centre line and thus to blame, the absence of any avoiding action by the other driver made that vehicle also to blame. Once both were to blame, and there was no means of distinguishing between them, the blame should be cast equally on each.

50%   **JENKINS v HOLT**

[1999] RTR 411 (CA)

J drove his car into collision with H, who had commenced a U turn into the path of J's car. It was found that both parties would have seen each other if they had been exercising reasonable care. Blame was apportioned equally on the basis that J neglected to avoid the danger created by H. It was said:

> "Put in terms of negligence, the defendant created the danger of a collision and the [claimant] failed to avoid it. In these circumstances it seems to me that blame falls equally on both parties."[5]

---

3. Both drivers died.
4. [1953] 1 WLR 1472 per Denning LJ at 1477.
5. [1999] RTR 411 per Sedley LJ at 416.

50%   **SMITH v MITCHELL**

[1978] CLY 328 (CA)

S, a police motorcyclist, was injured when he collided with
M's car on a wet road. M had pulled out to her right
suddenly to avoid a stationary car at a time when S was too
close behind her. However, S should have anticipated such
a manoeuvre by M and was found to have been
contributorily negligent to the extent of 50%.

50%   **DAWRANT v NUTT**

[1961] 1 WLR 253, [1960] 3 All ER 681 (QBD)

D was a passenger in the side-car of a motorcycle being
driven by her husband after dark. Both D and her husband
knew that the motorcycle's lights were not working. There
was a collision with a car driven by N, in which D was
injured and her husband was killed. D brought proceedings
against N, both on her own behalf and as her husband's
adminstratrix. It was held that both a driver and a
passenger are subject to a duty to take care for their own
safety, although this does not mean that they will both be
guilty of the same degree of contributory negligence as
against a third party. D's damages were reduced by 25% and
the damages on behalf of her husband's estate were
reduced by 50%.

25%   **BOC LTD v GROVES**

1993 SLT 360 (OH)

A car driver lost control of his car, causing it to overturn. A
lorry approaching at speed failed to take reasonable steps to
avoid a collision. The lorry driver was found to have been
contributorily negligent to the extent of 25%.

0%   **CORNWELL v AUTOMOBILE ASSOCIATION**

[1989] CLY 2535 (CC)

C was travelling at 60 mph and collided with the rear of an
AA vehicle on a motorway. The AA vehicle was escorting a
slow moving defective car and pulled out from the hard
shoulder at 15 mph, as the hard shoulder did not continue
under a bridge. There was found to have been no
contributory negligence on C's part.

3. OBSTRUCTIONS

75%   **HANNAM v MANN**

[1984] RTR 252 (CA)

H was riding his motorcycle at about 20 mph behind a car
along a well lit stretch of road at night. As the car
approached a junction it indicated right and H assumed
that it was intending to turn off into a side street. H
overtook the car on the near side. However, the car had
only been indicating an intention to pull out around M's
stationary car, which was unlit. H collided with M's car. It
was found that M's car should have been lit and that this
would have drawn attention to it, but that H would have
seen it if he had been keeping a proper look out. H's
contributory negligence was assessed at 75%.

70%   **FOSTER v MAGUIRE**

Unreported, 2001 (CA)

M parked his van and trailer in the cycle lane of a busy dual carriageway in poor weather conditions with his hazard warning lights showing. F rode her bicycle into collision with M's trailer, as she had not seen the vehicle until it was too late. It was held that M had created a source of danger with a foreseeable risk of injury. However, the vehicle would have been visible to F for at least one minute and she was found to have been contributorily negligent to the extent of 70%.

60%   **SUTHERLAND v GARDINER**

1981 SLT 237 (OH)

S was riding his motorcycle around a bend in a road when he collided with G's stationary car, which had been parked about four feet out from the kerb. It was found that G had created a hazard and had not been entitled to assume that other road users would exercise reasonable care. However, S had not kept a proper look out and his contributory negligence was assessed at 60%.

50%   **DRURY v CAMDEN LBC**

[1972] RTR 391 (QBD)

C left an unlit skip on a road at night. D drove his scooter into it and was injured. Both parties were held equally to blame.

50%   **AMEEN v HUNTER**

2000 SLT 954

A's vehicle came to a halt in the outside lane of a dual carriageway, probably due to a flat tyre. A's car had been jerking for some time, but she had continued to drive. She said that she had switched on her hazard warning lights, but there was no evidence that they were on. H collided with the rear of A's vehicle and was convicted of careless driving. It was held that both parties were equally to blame.

50%   **JAMES v DURKIN (CIVIL ENGINEERING CONTRACTORS)**

[1983] CLY 2541 (QBD)

J's estate claimed following his death when he drove a 12 feet high lorry into a bridge 11 feet 6 inches high. The lorry should have had a notice in the cab warning of its height, but J approached the bridge too fast at 25–30 mph and his contributory negligence was assessed at 50%.

40%   **SAPER v HUNGATE BUILDERS LTD**

[1972] RTR 380 (QBD)

HB left a skip on a road at night. It was positioned 60 yards from the blind crest of a hill, opposite a street lamp. The skip was also lit with two lamps, but was not obvious. K drove his car into the skip and was held 40% to blame as an alert motorist would have seen it in time to avoid a collision.

20%   **DAVIES v CARMARTHENSHIRE CC**

[1971] RTR 112 (CA)

CCC widened a busy road, but left a lamp-post so that it was near the centre of the road. The only warning of its presence was a sign warning of road works ahead. D was driving along the road when she was dazzled by the sun and collided with the lamp-post. The lamp-post could ordinarily be seen from 100 yards away, but it was foreseeable that a motorist driving towards the setting sun could face difficulties. It was said that where a highway authority leaves an obstacle in a busy road without sufficient warning to motorists, the negligence of the highway authority is likely to be far greater than that of a motorist who collides with it. D's contributory negligence was assessed at 20%.

20%   **BLACKHALL v MACINNES**

1997 SLT 649 (OH)

B stopped her car due to a puncture in an offside tyre. The car was parked close to the kerb of a dual carriageway with a 70 mph speed limit. Visibility was poor and the traffic on the road was heavy. B did not consider attempting to drive the car off the road and onto the verge. She was attempting to change the tyre, when she was struck by a car driven by M. B was held to have been contributorily negligent to the extent of 20%.

0%   **CULLIP v HORSHAM DC**

Unreported, 1981 (CA)

C, a motorcyclist, was found to have been negligent in coming round a blind bend so as to collide with a stationary dust lorry. However, C's fault was so small in comparison to that of the driver of the dust lorry in parking where he did, that C's share of the responsibility for the accident was assessed at nil.

4. PASSENGERS

100%   **PITTS v HUNT**

[1991] 1 QB 24, [1990] 3 WLR 542, [1990] 3 All ER 344 (CA)

A motorcycle pillion passenger was injured in a collision. He had encouraged the intoxicated, uninsured and unlicensed rider to ride in a reckless manner. The action arose directly *ex turpi causa* and P was precluded from recovering.

75%   **DONELAN v DONELAN & GENERAL ACCIDENT FIRE AND LIFE ASSURANCE**

[1993] PIQR 205 (QBD)

C persuaded his girlfriend, D, to drive his unfamiliar car after they had both been drinking heavily. C was dominant and put D in a position of great difficulty. There was a collision and C's contributory negligence was assessed at 75%.

50%   **TAYLOR v LESLIE**

1998 SLT 1248 (OH)

T was a passenger in a car being driven by L. T was aware that L was 16, unlicensed, uninsured and driving the car without the owner's consent. L was urged to drive faster by T, who was leaning out of the passenger door. The car collided with another vehicle, injuring T. T was held to have been contributorily negligent to the extent of 50%.

50%   **NETTLESHIP v WESTON**

[1971] 2 QB 691, [1971] 3 WLR 370, [1971] 3 All ER 581 (CA)

N, an experienced driver, gave W a driving lesson whereby W controlled the steering wheel and pedals and N controlled the gear lever and handbrake. Whilst driving along, W panicked and collided with a lamp post, injuring N. It was held that the standard of care expected of a learner driver was the same as that expected of anybody else and this was not affected by N's knowledge of W's inexperience. Further, where an instructor and leaner driver were jointly controlling the driving, they were, *prima facie*, jointly responsible for the accident and absent evidence that one or the other was to blame, both should be held equally to blame.

40%   **GREGORY v KELLY**

[1978] RTR 426 (QBD)

G was a passenger in a car being driven by K, which was involved in an accident. G was not wearing a seat belt and knew that the car had defective brakes. It was held that the matter had to be looked at generally and justice had to be done by broadly sharing out the blame. G's contributory negligence was assessed at 40%.

33.33%   **CURRIE v CLAMP**

2002 SLT 196 (OH)

C was a passenger in a car being driven by X without the
owner's consent and when C knew that X had been
drinking. The car was involved in a collision caused by X's
negligence. C's contributory negligence was assessed at one
third as he knew or ought to have known that X was unfit
to drive in view of the quantity of alcohol he had
consumed.

33.33%   **HILL v CHIVERS**

1987 SLT 323 (OH)

H was a front seat passenger in a car that was driven by C
out of a minor road and into the path of a bus. H was not
wearing his seat belt and had accepted a lift from C when
he had been obviously affected by alcohol. H's
contributory negligence totalled one third.

33.33%   **STINTON v STINTON**

[1995] RTR 167 (CA)[6]

The claimant was a passenger in a car driven by his brother,
with whom he had spent the day drinking heavily. The car
was driven into a collision with a lamp post and it was
found that the claimant's conduct involved
blameworthiness to the greatest extent possible short of
direct participation in the actual performance. His
contributory negligence was assessed at one third.

---

6.   See also the first instance decision at [1993] PIQR P135.

25%   **DAWRANT v NUTT**

[1961] 1 WLR 253, [1960] 3 All ER 681 (QBD)

D was a passenger in the side-car of a motorcycle being driven by her husband after dark. Both D and her husband knew that the motorcycle's lights were not working. There was a collision with a car driven by N, in which D was injured and her husband was killed. D brought proceedings against N, both on her own behalf and as her husband's adminstratrix. It was held that both a driver and a passenger are subject to a duty to take care for their own safety, although this does not mean that they will both be guilty of the same degree of contributory negligence as against a third party. D's damages were reduced by 25% and the damages on behalf of her husband's estate were reduced by 50%.

25%   **PRIOR v KYLE**

(1965) 52 DLR (2d) 272 (Canada)

P, aged 17, was a passenger in K's car. She did not object when K and another driver decided to race, although P thought it likely that the race would take place on a deserted road. The cars raced and P was injured in a collision with a third car. Her contributory negligence was assessed at 25%.

25%   **MEAH v McCREAMER**

[1985] 1 All ER 367 (QBD)

The claimant was a passenger in a car being driven by the defendant, who was drunk. The car was involved in an accident as a result of the defendant's negligence and the claimant was injured. It was found that had the claimant not himself been affected by drink, it would have been obvious to him that the defendant was not in a fit state to drive. Contributory negligence was assessed at 25%.

20%   **OWENS v BRIMMELL**

[1977] QB 859, [1977] 2 WLR 943, [1976] 3 All ER 765
(QBD)

O and B went out on a pub crawl in B's car. They both
drank a considerable amount and on the way home there
was an accident caused by B's negligence. O's contributory
negligence was assessed at 20%. As B alone was controlling
the car, he bore a far greater degree of responsibility for the
accident. Contributory negligence will be found either
where the claimant travels as a passenger in a car driven by
someone whom he knows to have consumed alcohol in
such a quantity as to impair his ability to drive safely, or
where the claimant knows that he will later be a passenger
and yet goes drinking with the driver in such a way as to
not only diminish the driver's ability to drive safely, but
also to reduce the claimant's own capacity to appreciate the
danger.

20%   **GREEN v GAYMER**

Unreported, 1999 (QBD)

The claimant was a pillion passenger on a motorcycle being
driven by the defendant. The motorcycle was involved in a
collision as a result of the defendant's negligence. The
claimant's contributory negligence in riding with the
defendant, when he knew him to have been drinking, was
assessed at 20%.

20%   **DAVIES v SWAN MOTOR CO (SWANSEA) LTD**

[1949] 2 KB 291, [1949] 1 All ER 620 (CA)

D, contrary to his employer's regulations, was riding on the side steps of a dustcart when an accident occurred between the dustcart and an overtaking bus, crushing D. The accident was caused by the fault of both the driver of the dustcart and the driver of the bus. It was found that D had taken up a very dangerous and unnecessary position on the dustcart and his contributory negligence was assessed at 20%.

15%   **W v HARDMAN**

Current Law Jul/2001 (CC)

W was a passenger in a vehicle driven by a person whom he knew to have been drinking alcohol. Additionally, W was not wearing a seat belt. The car was involved in a collision and W suffered minor physical injuries, but significant psychiatric injuries. W's contributory negligence was assessed at 15%.

10%   **PRIESTLEY v McKEOWN**

Unreported, 1998 (QBD)

P died in an accident caused by M's negligent driving. M had given P a lift to a petrol station and on the way there had driven dangerously in an attempt to impress P. At the petrol station P complained to M about his driving, but nevertheless got back into his car for the return journey, which is when the accident occurred. In a claim by P's dependant child the court approved a reduction of 10% on account of P's contributory negligence on the basis that M had driven badly to the petrol station and yet P got back into the car for the return journey.

0%   **LIMBRICK v FRENCH AND FARLEY**

[1993] PIQR P121 (QBD)[7]

L was a passenger in a car being driven by her boyfriend. He had been drinking and was uninsured. There was an accident and it was alleged that L had allowed her boyfriend to drive her when she knew that he was unfit to drive. It was held that the burden of proving such knowledge was on the boyfriend and he had failed to discharge that burden.

0%   **BRIGNALL v KELLY**

Unreported, 1994 (CA)

B was injured whilst a passenger in a vehicle being driven by K. The accident was the sole fault of K, who had been drinking heavily. B, who was sober, had only seen K drink one pint of lager, had had a sensible conversation with him and had seen no signs to suggest to him that K was drunk. There was found to have been no contributory negligence, as it was not shown that B was in any way guilty of a want of proper care for his own safety. It was said:

> "For my part I refuse to accept the proposition that if a man in a public house observes another man drink one pint of lager and give no sign of intoxication, he cannot accept a lift from him without interrogating him as to exactly how much he has had to drink."[8]

---

7.   See also *Malone v Rowan* [1984] 3 All ER 402 (QBD).
8.   Per McCowan LJ.

0%   **TRAYNOR v DONOVAN**

[1978] CLY 2612 (QBD)

T was a front seat passenger in a car driven by D, who had
been drinking. She was not wearing a seat belt and suffered
injuries in an accident caused by D's negligent driving. It
was found that T would have suffered different, but equally
severe injuries had she been wearing a seat belt and also
that the fact that D had been drinking had not been
apparent to T. There was no reduction for contributory
negligence.

0%   **SMITH v STAGES**

[1988] ICR 201 (CA)[9]

M and S had been working together and in order to get the job finished they worked all day on a Sunday and then carried on through Sunday night. They finished work at 8.30 am on the Monday morning and got straight into S's car for the long drive home. On the way home M was injured in an accident caused by S's negligent driving. In proceedings against the employers on the basis that they were vicariously liable for the negligent driving of S, it was alleged that M had been contributorily negligent in allowing himself to be driven by S, when he knew that S had not had enough sleep. However, M was held not to have been contributorily negligent. The Court of Appeal approved[10] the trial judge's observations that:

> "I cannot accept that [M] was in a condition, himself, to apply rational judgement to the risks involved in travelling in S's car at the time due to his own deprivation of sleep and fatigue. This itself was caused by the wholly excessive hours he was required [by his employers] to work ... I decline to condemn a man as negligent of his own safety when the charge is made against him by employers who themselves produced the conditions which deprived him of the capacity to care properly for his own safety."

---

9. The finding in relation to contributory negligence was not challenged on the appeal to the House of Lords reported at [1989] AC 928, [1989] 2 WLR 529, [1989] 1 All ER 833.
10. [1988] ICR 201 per Glidewell LJ at 213.

STOREBRAND SKADEFORSIKRING AS v FINANGER

[2000] Lloyd's Rep IR 462, [1999] 3 CMLR 863 (EFTA Court of Justice)

F was a passenger in car driven by a person she knew to be intoxicated. Provisions of Norwegian law prevented claims for compensation where the injured party knew that the driver was under the influence of alcohol. It was held that as third party motor insurance enabling an injured third party to obtain compensation was compulsory throughout the EEA, a national law denying compensation to a passenger in a motor vehicle in F's circumstances was incompatible with EEA law. Further, whilst a reduction for contributory negligence is permissible in exceptional circumstances, a disproportionate reduction would be incompatible with the Motor Vehicle Insurance Directives.[11]

5. PEDESTRIANS

80%   **WATSON v SKUSE**

Unreported, 2001 (CA)

W was crossing a road at a pedestrian crossing when he was run over by a lorry driven by S. S had been stationary at traffic lights by the crossing and W walked out onto the crossing when the lights were red against him. When the lights turned to green for S, W was directly in front of the lorry where S could not see him. It was held that there was a high degree of care expected of the driver of a lorry, but that W had acted foolishly in the manner in which he had chosen to cross the road and his contributory negligence was assessed at 80%.

---

11. First Council Directive 72/166, Second Council Directive 84/5 & Third Council Directive 90/232.

75%   **BRYCE v McKIRDY**

1999 SLT 988 (OH)

B was working as a foreman on a building site on the side
of a road. He had been standing in the road facing the
building site when he stepped backwards into the path of
M's car. M had seen B standing with his back to the road
and realised that he might be careless and step back into
the road, but had not warned of her presence. However, B
had failed to take reasonable care to keep a proper look out
for traffic and was found to have been 75% responsible for
the accident.

75%   **MORALES v ECCLESTON**

[1991] RTR 151 (CA)

M, an eleven-year-old boy, followed a football out onto a
road without looking in either direction. D was driving his
car at 20 mph in a stream of traffic and collided with M,
who was already over half way across the road. Taking
account of M's age, he was found to have been
contributorily negligent to the extent of 75%.

75%   **BERTOLI v FARRELL**

Unreported, 1995 (CA)

B, a foreign student, was standing at the side of a road
outside a public house talking to a friend in a taxi. B moved
away from the taxi to cross the road, but being more used
to the traffic in Spain, looked in the wrong direction and
was hit by F's car. It was found that F should have noticed
B at the side of the road and been aware of the potential
hazard associated with the several taxis outside the public
house. B's contributory negligence was assessed at 75%.

75%   **FOSKETT v MISTRY**

[1984] RTR 1 (CA)

M was driving his car at a reasonable speed in open parkland when F, aged 16, ran down a slope and out into the road, colliding with M's car. M should have appreciated the potential danger and warned F of his presence, but F was contributorily negligent to the extent of 75% in running out.

66.66%   **HARVEY v CAIRNS**

1989 SLT 107 (OH)

A six-year-old girl was killed when she stepped from the pavement into the path of a car. The car was being driven by an unqualified and unsupervised driver at 30 mph, which was normal for that road, but still excessive. The driver should have anticipated that the child might run out into the road. It was held that the girl was two thirds to blame.

66.66%   **DONOGHOE v BLUNDELL**

[1986] CLY 2254 (CC)

D was injured when he was run over by a car as he lay in the road, drunk. His contributory negligence was assessed at two thirds.

60%   **FUTTER v BRYCELAND**

2000 GWD 9–339 (OH)

F, aged 15, was hit by a car driven by B whilst running across a road at the back of a group of boys. In the hour before the accident it had snowed to a depth of between one and three inches. A 20 mph speed limit was set for the road between the date of the accident and trial. It was found that:

(1) B was travelling at not less than 20 mph, which was too fast given the nature of the road, snowy conditions and presence of the group of boys running across the road;

(2) B was not keeping a proper look out;

(3) F was at an age where he could be held to be capable of taking proper care for his own safety and had materially contributed to the accident by failing to check that it was safe to cross the road;

(4) if B's only fault had been to drive too fast, F's share of the responsibility would have been very high; but

(5) as B had failed to keep a proper look out, F was 60% to blame.

50%   **FITZGERALD v LANE**

[1989] AC 328, [1988] 3 WLR 356, [1988] 2 All ER 961
(HL)

The claimant crossed a road at a pelican crossing. Traffic
was stopped in the lane closest to the pavement, but
moving freely in the next lane and the two lanes on the
opposite side of the road. Despite the lights being green for
the traffic and red against the claimant, he did not wait and
walked at a brisk pace across the crossing. He passed in
front of a stationary car in the closest lane and into the
path of the first defendant's moving car in the next lane.
He was struck by the first defendant's car and thrown onto
the other side of the road, where he was struck by the
second defendant's moving car. The two drivers were found
to have been negligent in travelling at 30 mph and failing
to keep a look out for pedestrians trying to cross the road.
The House of Lords expressed the view that the trial judge's
finding that the defendants were twice as much to blame as
the claimant was clearly wrong. The claimant was
substantially the author of his own misfortune and the
Court of Appeal's order that the claimant's damages be
reduced by 50% was generous to the claimant.

50%   **DAVIDSON v SCOTT**

1987 SLT 480 (OH)

D was working at road works, which severely restricted the
width of the road. D stepped backwards into the path of a
car. The car driver was found to have had a special duty to
guard against the risk of injury to a workman, but D was
found to have been contributorily negligent to the extent
of 50%.

50%   **MALCOLM v FAIR**

1993 SLT 342 (OH)

A drunk pedestrian started to cross a road without having seen a car approaching at a reasonable speed. The driver failed to notice the pedestrian until it was too late and both parties were found equally to blame.

50%   **WIDDOWSON v NEWGATE MEAT CORPORATION**

[1998] PIQR P138 (CA)

W, who suffered from a serious mental disorder, was injured whilst wearing dark clothing and walking along a dual carriageway at night when a van driven by S collided with him. S and W did not give evidence at the trial and the circumstances leading up to the accident were not known and nor was it known where W had been going or why he was walking along the dual carriageway at night. Despite his illness, the medical evidence indicated that W was appreciative of danger and aware of road safety. It was found that W was not wearing any light-coloured or reflective clothing and a person who showed proper care for his own safety would have stepped onto the verge when he saw S's headlights. W's contributory negligence was assessed at 50%.

50%   **McKINNELL v WHITE**

1971 SLT 61 (OH)

S, a five-year-old boy, let go of his elder brother's hand and ran from the pavement across a main road whereupon he was struck by W's car. W was found to have been negligent and S's contributory negligence in running out was assessed at 50%. It was said that the danger of running across a main road was very obvious and must have been within the understanding of S. It was also said that the fact of S letting go of his brother's hand and running off made his actions rather more deliberate and more obviously negligent than if he had been alone.

33.33%   **ARMSTRONG v COTTRELL**

[1993] PIQR P109 (CA)

A group of girls were hovering at the side of a road, obviously intending to cross. A, aged twelve, moved into the road but hesitated and was struck by C's car. C should have reduced her speed and sounded her horn to warn of her presence. Bearing in mind A's age, contributory negligence was assessed at one third.

33.33%   **LUNT v KHELIFA**

Unreported, 2001 (QBD)

L, who had consumed a large quantity of alcohol, stepped out into a road directly into the path of K's car. It was found that K had not been keeping a proper look out and had failed to notice L crossing in front of him. L's contributory negligence was assessed at one third.

33.33%   **ROBERTS v PEARSON**

Unreported, 1991 (CA)

R, aged twelve, was struck by P's motorcycle whilst crossing
the road from a central reservation. P was travelling too fast
and not keeping a proper look out. However, R's
contributory negligence was assessed at one third. It was
said that a twelve-year-old boy is less able to gauge the
speed of an approaching vehicle and is likely to be less
inhibited than an adult.

33.33%   **MARKOWSKI v ELSON**

Current Law Oct/2001 (CC)

An ambulance was parked illegally outside some shops. M,
an elderly lady, crossed the road in front of the ambulance,
which she was unable to see around. She did not stop to
check that the road was clear before stepping out beyond
the ambulance and was struck by E's car. It was held that
the operators of the ambulance were negligent in parking it
in such a position, but M's contributory negligence in
failing to check that it was clear to cross the road was
assessed at one third.

33.33%   **SKOLIMOWSKI v HAYNES**

[1983] CLY 2525 (QBD)

S started to cross the road at a pelican crossing when the
green man was showing. He was slightly disabled and
continued to cross unaware that the red man had started
showing. He was knocked down by H, who should have
been alive to the risk of pedestrians, but S was found to
have been contributorily negligent to the extent of one
third in not being alert to the red man and failing to stand
still between lanes when trapped.

33.33%   **McDONALD v CHAMBERS**

2000 SLT 454 (OH)

M was knocked down by C's car on a pedestrian crossing. M stepped onto the crossing before establishing that the traffic had stopped. C had driven through an amber traffic light despite seeing M pressing the control button at the crossing. M's contributory negligence was assessed at one third.

30%   **COOK v THORNE**

Unreported, 2001 (CA)

C, who had been drinking heavily, was a passenger in a car, which stopped in the road so that he could get out and vomit. As C was vomiting in the middle of the road he was struck by T's car, which was approaching from the other direction. T had been blinded by the headlights on the car in which C had been travelling and had slowed from around 40 mph to about 30 mph. It was held that T should have slowed to a far greater extent when blinded, but that C had been contributorily negligent to the extent of 30%.

25%   **BAKER v WILLOUGHBY**

[1970] AC 467, [1970] 2 WLR 50, [1969] 3 All ER 1528 (HL)

B was intending to cross a road. He saw a car approaching about 100 yards away and assumed that he had time to cross, but was struck by W's car, which he had not seen and which was overtaking the car he had seen. A clear view of each other was available to both parties. B's contributory negligence was assessed at 25%. The court had to consider causation and blameworthiness:

> "A pedestrian has to look to both sides as well as forwards. He is going at perhaps 3 mph and at that speed he is rarely a danger to anyone else. The motorist has not got to look sideways though he may have to observe over a wide angle ahead: and if he is going at a considerable speed he must not relax his observation, for the consequences may be disastrous."[12]

Accordingly, W was more blameworthy than B.

---

12. [1970] AC 467 per Lord Reid at 490.

20%   **HURT v MURPHY**

[1971] RTR 186 (QBD)

H started to cross a road after having checked that there were no cars approaching for over 100 yards. She continued to cross the road without checking again for approaching traffic. M, who was later convicted of causing death by dangerous driving, approached in his car at over 60 mph and struck H. H's contributory negligence in not continuing to check for traffic as she crossed the road was assessed at 20%.

20%   **WHITE v CHAPMAN**

Unreported, 2001 (QBD)

W was struck by C's car as she was crossing a road. W had crossed the road at a place where there was no central island or specified neutral zone and without ensuring that she could walk straight across the road without having to stop in the middle. Her contributory negligence was assessed at 20%.

20%   **CLIFFORD v DRYMOND**

[1976] RTR 134 (CA)

C stepped onto a crossing when D's car was 75–90 feet away and travelling at 26–30 mph. She was knocked over by D when she was about 10 feet onto the crossing. It was held that if C had not looked at the car before stepping onto the crossing to check that it was reasonable to do so, she was guilty of contributory negligence. If she had looked, she should have seen that D's car was near enough and travelling at such a speed as to create a doubt as to whether or not D would stop and allow her precedence. C's contributory negligence was assessed at 20%.

20%   **McCLUSKEY v WALLACE**

1998 SLT 1357 (IH)

M, a ten-year-old girl was injured by a car driven by W while she was crossing the road. M had not noticed W's oncoming vehicle when she crossed the road and W had similarly not been paying attention. It was said that a person driving a car is always much more dangerous to others than a pedestrian and might, therefore, be much more to blame than a pedestrian. M was found to have been 20% to blame. No special account appears to have been taken of her age.

0%   **GOUGH v THORNE**

[1966] 1 WLR 1387, [1966] 3 All ER 398 (CA)

G, aged 13, was waiting to cross a busy main road with her brothers aged 17 and 10. A lorry stopped and the driver put out a hand to stop other traffic and waved G and her brothers across. G stepped out beyond the lorry without looking and was struck by T's car, which was passing the lorry. T was found to have been negligent in driving too fast and not observing the lorry driver's signal. It was held that it was not negligent of G to rely on the lorry driver in the circumstances and so there was no reduction for contributory negligence. It was said:

> "A child has not the road sense or the experience of his or her elders. He or she is not to be found guilty unless he or she is blameworthy."[13]

An adult probably would have been found guilty of contributory negligence in proceeding beyond the lorry without checking that it was safe to do so.

---

13. [1966] 1 WLR 1387 per Lord Denning MR at 1390.

0%   **CHAPMAN v POST OFFICE**

[1982] RTR 165 (CA)

A pedestrian struck by a car's wing mirror was not guilty of contributory negligence where he was standing on the kerb with his back to the traffic or even where he went an inch or two onto the road.

0%   **TREMAYNE v HILL**

[1987] RTR 131 (CA)

T crossed diagonally over two roads at a complex junction at night and was struck by a car driven by H, who had gone through a red traffic light. It was held that any failure of T to keep a proper look out did not amount to contributory negligence as T was entitled to assume that H would stop at the red traffic light. A pedestrian is entitled to cross a road anywhere provided that he takes reasonable care for his own safety.

0%   **JONES v LAWRENCE**

[1969] 3 All ER 267 (QBD)

J, aged seven, ran out from behind a parked vehicle, apparently without looking, across a road to get to a fun-fair. He was struck by a motorcycle, driven by L, which was going too fast. There was found to have been no contributory negligence on J's part. There was evidence that children of his age are prone to forget what they have been taught about matters such as road safety when something else is uppermost in their mind and his conduct was only that to be expected of a seven-year-old.

0%   **ANDREWS v FREEBOROUGH**

[1967] 1 QB 1, [1966] 3 WLR 342, [1966] 2 All ER 721
(CA)

A, aged nearly eight, was a bright child, well aware of the
hazards of traffic. She was standing on the kerb waiting to
cross a road when she was caught by F's passing car, which
was being driven too close to the kerb, and fatally injured.
There was no finding of contributory negligence against A
and it was said that even if A had stepped out into the path
of F's car:

> "I should have needed a good deal of persuasion before
> imputing contributory negligence to the child having
> regard to her tender age."[14]

Further:

> "The little girl was only eight years of age, and in my
> judgment it is not possible to say that she was guilty of
> contributory negligence in the circumstances of this
> case. It is true that she was thought by her parents to
> be sufficiently trained and traffic-conscious to be fit to
> be trusted not only to cross highways safely herself but
> also to be put in charge of her four-year-old brother on
> such a journey. But even if she did step off [the kerb]
> into the car, it would not be right to count as
> negligence on her part such a momentary, though
> fatal, act of inattention or carelessness."[15]

---

14. [1967] 1 QB 1 per Wilmer LJ at 8.
15. [1967] 1 QB 1 per Davies LJ at 16.

6. SEAT BELTS AND CRASH HELMETS

SEAT BELTS

50%　　　**HITCHENS v BERKSHIRE COUNTY COUNCIL**

Unreported, 2000 (CA)

A taxi driver, who was not wearing a seat belt, was involved in an accident, in the course of which he was ejected from his vehicle and suffered fatal injuries. Had he been wearing a seat belt he would, at worst, have suffered minor injuries. In claims brought by his spouse and young children it was argued that the damages should be reduced beyond the levels set out in *Froom* v *Butcher*[16] as the wearing of seat belts had become compulsory since the time of that decision. The trial judge stated that he considered himself bound by authority to order a reduction of 15%. However, were he not so bound, he would have ordered a reduction of between 50% and 70%. The decision was appealed to the Court of Appeal, but before the matter came on for hearing, it was settled on the basis of a 50% reduction for contributory negligence. The Court of Appeal approved the settlement on those terms.

40%　　　**GREGORY v KELLY**

[1978] RTR 426 (QBD)

G was a passenger in a car being driven by K, which was involved in an accident. G was not wearing a seat belt and knew that the car had defective brakes. It was held that the matter had to be looked at generally and justice had to be done by broadly sharing out the blame. G's contributory negligence was assessed at 40%.

---

16. [1976] QB 286, [1975] 3 WLR 379, [1975] 3 All ER 520 (CA), see page 246 below.

33.33%   **HILL v CHIVERS**

1987 SLT 323 (OH)

H was a front seat passenger in a car that was driven by C
out of a minor road and into the path of a bus. H was not
wearing his seat belt and had accepted a lift from C when
he had been obviously affected by alcohol. H's
contributory negligence totalled one third.

25%   **PATIENCE v ANDREWS**

[1983] RTR 447 (QBD)

The court must consider the injuries suffered and then
consider the appropriate reduction depending on the
extent to which those injuries had been caused or
contributed to by the claimant's failure to wear a seat belt.
However, a detailed consideration of the injuries that
would have been sustained had a seat belt been worn is not
required. On the facts a 25% reduction was considered
appropriate.

20%   **FROOM v BUTCHER**

[1976] QB 286, [1975] 3 WLR 379, [1975] 3 All ER 520 (CA)

The Court of Appeal laid down what have become guidelines for assessing contributory negligence in the ordinary case of not wearing a seat belt.[17] It was said that where the injuries would have been altogether prevented by the wearing of a seat belt, the damages should be reduced by 25%. Where the injuries would have been a good deal less severe, the reduction should be 15%. Where the wearing of a seat belt would have made no difference at all, the damages should not be reduced. In that case the accident was wholly caused by B's negligence. F sustained head and chest injuries and a broken finger in the accident. All except the last of these injuries would probably have been avoided had F been wearing a seat belt. The trial judge's assessment of a 20% reduction overall (if there was contributory negligence, which the Court of Appeal confirmed that there was) was not interfered with.

15%   **W v HARDMAN**

Current Law Jul/2001 (CC)

W was a passenger in a vehicle driven by a person whom he knew to have been drinking alcohol. Additionally, W was not wearing a seat belt. The car was involved in a collision and W suffered minor physical injuries, but significant psychiatric injuries. W's contributory negligence was assessed at 15%.

---

17. It has been held that the same principles apply to passengers seated in the front and those in the rear of a vehicle, *Biesheuval* v *Birrell*, unreported, 1988 (QBD).

15%–0%   **DUCHARME v DAVIES**

[1984] 1 WWR 699 (Canada)

D was responsible for causing a car accident injuring two
parents and their three-year-old child, none of whom were
wearing seatbelts. The awards to the parents were reduced
by 15% to take account of their contributory negligence,
but the award to the child was not reduced. It was held that
an infant was incapable of contributory negligence and
that the negligence of a parent in failing to ensure that a
child is restrained by a seat belt cannot be imputed to the
child. No claim was made against the parents for a
contribution on the basis that they were joint tortfeasors.

0%   **JONES v WILKINS**

[2001] PIQR P179, [2001] RTR 283 (CA)

J, aged two, was sitting on her mother's knee in the front
passenger's seat of a car being driven by J's aunt. She was
restrained only by the lap belt part of her mother's seat
belt. The car was involved in a collision caused by W's
negligence, in which J was seriously injured. It was found
that if J had been wearing an approved child restraint, the
risk of injury would have been practically eliminated.
Liability was apportioned under the Civil Liability
(Contribution) Act 1978 so that W bore 75% of the
responsibility and J's mother and aunt were 25% to blame
for J's injuries.

0%   **NEILL v DOHERTY & AKRAM**

[1997] CLY 3772 (QBD)

N was a passenger in the rear of a taxi that was involved in a collision with another vehicle. The force of the accident was very severe and N was ejected from the vehicle. N, who was found to have failed to take reasonable care by not wearing a seat belt, was paralysed. However, as it was found that N's paralysing spinal injury occurred on the initial impact and before N was ejected from the vehicle, no reduction was made for contributory negligence, as N's negligence had had no causative effect.

0%   **ALLEN v DANDO**

[1977] CLY 738 (QBD)

A suffered minor physical injuries in a road traffic accident. No reduction was made in respect of his contributory negligence in failing to wear a seat belt as no causal connection had been established between the failure to wear a seat belt and the physical injuries sustained.[18]

0%   **TRAYNOR v DONOVAN**

[1978] CLY 2612 (QBD)

T was a front seat passenger in a car driven by D, who had been drinking. She was not wearing a seat belt and suffered injuries in an accident caused by D's negligent driving. It was found that T would have suffered different but equally severe injuries had she been wearing a seat belt and also that the fact that D had been drinking had not been apparent to T. There was no reduction for contributory negligence.

---

18. See also *Barker* v *Murdoch* 1977 SLT (Notes) 75 (OH). The question of contributory negligence was not considered on the appeal at 1979 SLT 145 (IH).

0%   **JONES v MORGAN**

[1994] CLY 3344 (QBD)

J, a taxi driver, was involved in a collision for which M was responsible. J had not been wearing a seat belt, which he was exempt from doing whilst carrying fare paying passengers. He had been advised by his employer not to wear a seat belt when carrying passengers late at night as it made it harder to evade an attack. It was held that it would be unreasonable to have an invariable policy of not wearing a seat belt as some customers could be assessed as not posing a threat. However, J did not know this female passenger, whom he had picked up late at night. It was held to have been reasonable for J not to have worn a seat belt in the circumstances and there was no reduction for contributory negligence, even though his injuries would have been much less severe had he been wearing a seat belt.[19]

0%   **HOADLEY v DARTFORD DC**

[1979] RTR 359 (CA)

Where there was no statutory obligation to fit seat belts to a vehicle, it was a question of fact and not of law whether a person had failed to take proper care for his own safety. On the facts of the case there was no reduction for contributory negligence.

---

19. See also *Pace* v *Cully* 1992 SLT 1073 (OH), where the taxi driver was not wearing a seat belt on police advice.

0%   **HOGAN & RYAN v SMITH**

Unreported, 1991 (QBD)

H and R were passengers in the rear seat of S's vehicle, which was involved in an accident as a result of S's negligence. Seat belts were fitted to the rear seats, although H and R did not realise this and had not worn seat belts in the rear of a vehicle before. It was held that there was no contributory negligence. However, the accident occurred in 1989 and it was said that had it occurred after the wearing of rear seat belts became compulsory, a reduction along the lines suggested in *Froom* v *Butcher*[20] would have been made.[21]

0%   **CONDON v CONDON**

[1978] RTR 483 (QBD)

A phobia, supported by medical evidence, might be a valid reason for the sufferer not to wear a seat belt and in those circumstances, there would be no reduction for contributory negligence in respect of injures suffered in a road traffic accident.

---

20. [1976] QB 286, [1975] 3 WLR 379, [1975] 3 All ER. 520 (CA), see page 246 above.
21. Similarly, it was held that the same principles apply to passengers seated in the front and those seated in the rear of a vehicle in *Biesheuval* v *Birrell*, unreported, 1988 (QBD).

0%   **MACKAY v BORTHWICK**

1982 SLT 265 (OH)

M was a passenger in a car involved in an accident. She was not wearing a seat belt as she suffered from a hiatus hernia and found it uncomfortable. She tolerated the discomfort on long journeys, but it was not her practice to wear a seat belt on short journeys, such as the one she was on at the time of the accident. It was held that she was not guilty of contributory negligence in the circumstances.

CRASH HELMETS

15%   **O'CONNELL v JACKSON**

[1972] 1 QB 270, [1971] 3 WLR 463, [1971] 3 All ER 129 (CA)

O was riding his moped when he was involved in a collision with J's car, which was found to have been wholly J's fault. O was not wearing a crash helmet and suffered head injuries. The injuries would have been less severe if O had been wearing a crash helmet. At that time there was no legal requirement that a crash helmet be worn. However, O was found to have been contributorily negligent to the extent of 15%.

10%   **CAPPS v MILLER**

[1989] 1 WLR 839, [1989] 2 All ER 333 (CA)

C was riding a moped with a crash helmet on, but the chin strap was unfastened. An accident was caused by M at a time when C was stationary, during which C's helmet came off and his head struck the road. C's contributory negligence was assessed at 10%.

0%   **A v SHORROCK**

Current Law Oct/2001 (QBD)

A, aged 14, was injured when he rode his bicycle onto a
road from the pavement and was struck by S's car. Liability
was not established, but it was indicated that A would not
have been found to have been contributorily negligent in
failing to wear a safety helmet. There was no legal
requirement for him to do so and he was not engaged in
any particularly hazardous kind of riding, during which it
might be thought prudent to wear a helmet.

CHAPTER FOURTEEN
SELF HARM & DRUNKENNESS

For further cases where drunkenness was a factor in road traffic accidents, reference should be made to Chapter 13 above.

100%　　**ROWE v HERMAN**

[2000] CLY 4243 (CC)

R tripped over a metal plate on the pavement near his home whilst drunk. His action against the highway authority failed as it was found that they had carried out a reasonable system of inspection. However, it was said that R's contributory negligence would have been assessed at 100%, as he knew about the plate, which he regarded as a hazard and would have been able to avoid if sober.

80%   **STRACHAN v HIGHLAND COUNCIL**

1999 GWD 38–1863 (SP)

S, while under the influence of drink, had stepped over a section of dilapidated fence from a car park maintained by HC and onto a path, where he was walking near the edge of a cliff in the early hours of the morning. He lost his footing and fell to the shore below. It was found that:

(1) HC knew people would be in the vicinity of the cliff;

(2) the cliff was a natural and obvious hazard;

(3) even a dilapidated fence was a visible barrier;

(4) where a normal adult deliberately chose to cross an obvious barrier and proceed to a place of obvious danger, he was the sole author of his own misfortune; and

(5) if that were wrong, S would have been found to have been contributorily negligent to the extent of 80%.

75%   **JEBSON v MINISTRY OF DEFENCE**

[2000] 1 WLR 2055, [2001] RTR 22, [2000] PIQR P201 (CA)

J was one of a group of soldiers who went on an organised off duty trip. It was foreseeable that the soldiers would get drunk and behave in a foolhardy manner. On the way back, J attempted to climb onto the roof of the lorry, but lost his footing and fell. It was held that the MOD should have provided some supervision and that where there was a duty of care in relation to a person who was likely to be intoxicated, liability could not be avoided on the grounds of that person's drunkenness. However, J's contributory negligence was assessed at 75%.

75%   **LOGUE v FLYING COLOURS LTD**

Unreported, 2001 (CC)

L was on holiday in Ibiza. He went out one night and had a considerable amount to drink, returning to his hotel room at 6 am. He awoke at 9 am and lost his balance and fell as he was getting out of bed. He put a hand out to stop his fall and it went through the glass patio window of his bedroom, causing him injuries. The glass was not toughened and whilst it was in accordance with the local Spanish standards, it was not compliant with British standards or UK Building Regulations. The claim under the Package Travel, Package Holidays and Package Tours Regulations 1992 failed as it was found that there had been no improper performance of the contract, local standards having been complied with. Contributory negligence would have been assessed at 75%, as L had been considerably affected by drink and this was a major cause of the accident.

66.66%   **BARRETT v MINISTRY OF DEFENCE**

[1995] 1 WLR 1217, [1995] 3 All ER 87 (CA)

A naval airman died after becoming so drunk at a naval base that he passed into a coma and asphyxiated on his own vomit. In a claim brought by his widow it was found that the deceased was the only person responsible at law for his collapse. No one was better placed to judge the amount which he could consume than the individual himself. It was unreasonable to blame anyone else for his lack of self control. However, once he had collapsed and was incapable of looking after himself, the MOD failed to provide adequate medical care. The deceased's contributory negligence was assessed at two thirds.

66.66% **DONOGHOE v BLUNDELL**

[1986] CLY 2254 (CC)

D was injured when he was run over by a car as he lay in the road, drunk. His contributory negligence was assessed at two thirds.

50% **REEVES v COMMISSIONER OF POLICE OF THE METROPOLIS**

[2000] 1 AC 360, [1999] 3 WLR 363, [1999] 3 All ER 897 (HL)

R brought a claim arising out of L's suicide whilst in police custody. It was found that the police owed a duty to take reasonable care to prevent L, a known suicide risk, committing suicide in police custody. The police had been negligent in leaving open the hatch of L's cell door, as it was reasonably foreseeable that he would tie his shirt to it and strangle himself. The defence of *volenti non fit injuria* failed, as it would have been inconsistent with the duty owed by the police to find that it was negated by L's decision to commit suicide. On the question of causation it was found that both the police's failure to protect L from himself and L's deliberate decision to end his life were the causes of L's death. L was of sound mind and had a responsibility for his own life. He was found to have been contributorily negligent to the extent of 50%.

50%   **BRANNAN v AIRTOURS PLC**

[1999] CLY 3945 (CA)

B went on a package holiday organised by A, during which
A organised a dinner with unlimited free wine. There were
revolving ceiling fans seven feet above the floor and guests
were asked not to climb on the tables and warned about
the fans. B, who had had a considerable amount to drink,
although was not drunk, climbed onto his table and was
injured by a fan. It was found that the risk of people
drinking too much and consequently having less regard for
their own safety was foreseeable and that A should have
ensured that the tables were not positioned underneath the
fans. B's contributory negligence was reduced to 50% on
appeal.

50%   **MALCOLM v FAIR**

1993 SLT 342 (OH)

A drunk pedestrian started to cross a road without having
seen a car approaching at a reasonable speed. The driver
failed to notice the pedestrian until it was too late and both
parties were found equally to blame.

33.33%   **LUNT v KHELIFA**

Unreported, 2001 (QBD)

L, who had consumed a large quantity of alcohol, stepped
out into a road directly into the path of K's car. It was found
that K had not been keeping a proper look out and had
failed to notice L crossing in front of him. L's contributory
negligence was assessed at one third.

33.33%   **CURRIE v CLAMP**

2002 SLT 196 (OH)

C was a passenger in a car being driven by X without the owner's consent and when C knew that X had been drinking. The car was involved in a collision caused by X's negligence. C's contributory negligence was assessed at one third as he knew or ought to have known that X was unfit to drive in view of the quantity of alcohol he had consumed.

33.33%   **STINTON v STINTON**

[1995] RTR 167 (CA)

The claimant was a passenger in a car driven by his brother, with whom he had spent the day drinking heavily. The car was driven into a collision with a lamp post and it was found that the claimant's conduct involved blameworthiness to the greatest extent possible short of direct participation. His contributory negligence was assessed at one third.

30%   **COOK v THORNE**

Unreported, 2001 (CA)

C, who had been drinking heavily, was a passenger in a car, which stopped in the road so that he could get out and vomit. As C was vomiting in the middle of the road he was struck by T's car, which was approaching from the other direction. T had been blinded by the headlights on the car in which C had been travelling and had slowed from around 40 mph to about 30 mph. It was held that T should have slowed to a far greater extent when blinded, but that C had been contributorily negligent to the extent of 30%.

25%   **SCOLLEN v LEISURE HOLIDAYS LTD**

Unreported, 1992 (CA)

S, who had been drinking, suffered fatal injuries when he fell over a retaining wall at a holiday camp whilst wandering in the dark. His contributory negligence was assessed at 25%.

20%   **OWENS v BRIMMELL**

[1977] QB 859, [1977] 2 WLR 943, [1976] 3 All ER 765 (QBD)

O and B went out on a pub crawl in B's car. They both drank a considerable amount and on the way home there was an accident caused by B's negligence. O's contributory negligence was assessed at 20%. As B alone was controlling the car, he bore a far greater degree of responsibility for the accident. Contributory negligence will be found either where the claimant travels as a passenger in a car driven by someone whom he knows to have consumed alcohol in such a quantity as to impair his ability to drive safely, or where the claimant knows that he will later be a passenger and yet goes drinking with the driver in such a way as to not only diminish the driver's ability to drive safely, but also to reduce the claimant's own capacity to appreciate the danger.

0%   **FOULDER v CANADIAN PACIFIC STEAMSHIPS LTD**

[1969] 1 All ER 283, [1968] 2 Lloyd's Rep 366 (QBD)

F was employed on CPS' vessel. Negligently and in breach
of the applicable regulations, the shower provided for F
discharged scalding water and did not have an anti-
scalding mixing valve enabling F to select an appropriate
water temperature. F, who had been drinking, entered the
shower and was scalded by the very hot water. It was held
that F had not been contributorily negligent in failing to
test the water temperature before entering the shower.

CHAPTER FIFTEEN
SLIPPING, TRIPPING & FALLING

For examples of cases involving slips, trips or falls at work, reference should be made to Chapter 9.

1. SLIPPING

0%   **BITTNER v TAIT-GIBSON OPTOMETRISTS**

(1964) 44 DLR (2d) 113 (Canada)

B, a police officer, slipped on a patch of ice as he rushed to investigate a suspected crime. It was held that there was no contributory negligence as the risk was outweighed by the end to be achieved.

0%   **STOWELL v THE RAILWAY EXECUTIVE**

[1949] 2 KB 519, [1949] 2 All ER 193 (KBD)

S drove to a railway station to meet his family, who were arriving there by train. As he was walking along a platform he slipped on a patch of oil on the ground and injured himself. There was found to have been no contributory negligence. It was said:

> "What is acting reasonably must depend on the circumstances of each particular case. If one is walking along a dockside where one expects mooring ropes to be out and other obstructions about the dock or quayside, then one would have to walk gingerly and watch every step more or less, but if one is walking down a railway platform, provided for the purpose of those who use the trains, one is entitled to expect that the platform will be free from any obstruction. It would not be reasonable to require that those using the platforms should be looking down at their feet at every step they take."[1]

---

1.   [1949] 2 KB 519 per Lynskey J at 525.

2. TRIPPING

100%   **ROWE v HERMAN**

[2000] CLY 4243 (CC)

R tripped over a metal plate on the pavement near his
home whilst drunk. His action against the highway
authority failed as it was found that they had carried out a
reasonable system of inspection. However, it was said that
R's contributory negligence would have been assessed at
100%, as he knew about the plate, which he regarded as a
hazard and would have been able to avoid if sober.

25%   **DINGLEY v BROMLEY LBC**

[2000] CLY 4244 (CC)

D parked her car in a disabled parking space in a town
centre road. Her foot became wedged in a pothole in the
parking bay, causing her to fall. The pothole had been
present for three months and D knew of its existence. Her
contributory negligence was assessed at 25%.

25%–10%   **GALLAGHER v STRATHCLYDE RC**

1996 SLT 255 (OH)

Claims against a sewerage authority failed on the facts in
cases where two people had tripped over a broken slab.
However, the opinion was expressed that contributory
negligence would have been assessed at 10% in the case of
the person who had no knowledge of the defect and whose
accident occurred in the dark and 25% in the case of the
person injured in daylight who had not been keeping a
look out.

20%   ## BROWN v EDINBURGH CITY COUNCIL

1999 SLT (Sh Ct) 43 (SH)

B tripped in a pothole in a pavement, which was difficult to see. B was familiar with the pavement and aware that there were holes, although he was unaware of this particular hole. His contributory negligence was assessed at 20%.

20%   ## EVITT v CLANCY & CO

Unreported, 1980 (CA)

E, a local man who knew that there were roadworks in the road he was crossing, was injured when he fell into a trench dug in the road. There had been barriers around the trench, but vandals had removed these. E's contributory negligence was assessed at 20%.

ROSSI v PORT OF LONDON AUTHORITY

[1956] 1 Lloyd's Rep 478 (QBD)

R was injured at work when a fellow employee tripped and the load that he had been carrying struck R. It was said:

> "There is no obligation upon a person walking along, say, a railway platform, or in a ballroom, to watch where he is placing his feet. He is entitled to rely on the general condition of the area. But if you are engaged in working in a place where you know that dangers exist and, if you do not keep a proper look out, are likely to fall over, if you hurt yourself or somebody else as a result of that not looking out, then it amounts to negligence. It is a question of reasonable care. A reasonably careful man, working on top of a pile of timber at the dockside, before getting hold of a piece of timber at all for the purpose of lifting it, would obviously look to see the sort of place he had to traverse when carrying this piece of timber."[2]

0% ### HYMANSON v GREATER MANCHESTER COUNCIL

Unreported, 1981 (CA)

H was crossing a busy road with his secretary when he put his foot in a 2.5 inches deep hole in the road and injured himself. It was found that H had not been contributorily negligent. It was placing too high an obligation on a pedestrian to look carefully down at his feet while crossing a road.

---

2.   [1956] 1 Lloyd's Rep 478 per Lynskey J at 480.

0%   **PYNE v WILKENFELD**

(1981) 26 SASR 441 (Australia)[3]

P was injured in a road traffic accident caused by W's negligence. As a result of her injures, P was required to wear a cervical collar. P then tripped on a path because she was unable to see immediately in front of her as the collar restricted her vision. It was held that the tripping accident arose causally from the road traffic accident and that W was liable for both accidents. There was found to have been no contributory negligence.

0%   **NIMMO v SECRETARY OF STATE FOR SCOTLAND**

[2000] CLY 6173 (OH)

N tripped on a large piece of angle iron while crossing a prison yard in poor visibility when he stepped onto a surrounding path. The path had not been obstructed when N had walked along it four hours earlier. N was held not to have been at fault in assuming the path still to be clear of obstructions.

---

3.   See also *Wieland* v *Cyril Lord Carpets Ltd* [1969] 3 All ER 1006 (QBD), a case concerning similar facts where contributory negligence was not raised and the argument that the subsequent injuries were too remote was rejected. Cf *McKew* v *Holland & Hannen & Cubbitts (Scotland) Ltd* [1969] 3 All ER 1621 (HLS), where subsequent injuries were held to be too remote as the claimant's conduct in taking an unreasonable risk constituted a *novus actus interveniens*. See page 78 for the facts.

0%   **HOWARD v WALKER & CRISP**

[1947] KB 860, [1947] 2 All ER 197 (KBD)

H tripped and injured herself whilst walking over a
forecourt at dusk. The concrete on the forecourt was
uneven and broken. It was found that there had been no
contributory negligence. It was said:

> "I see no reason to attribute any negligence to [the
> claimant]. It is true she knew the place and it is true she
> knew, if she had thought about it at the time, that the
> concrete was broken, but a person who enters or leaves
> a shop in the evening can hardly be expected to keep
> her eyes on the ground."[4]

0%   **ALMEROTH v W E CHIVERS & SONS LTD**

[1948] 1 All ER 53 (CA)

A tripped on a heap of slates lying in the gutter by the kerb.
The pile of slates was lower than the height of the kerb.
There was no contributory negligence. It was held that a
pedestrian walking along a pavement or crossing a road on
which there is no traffic and stepping up onto a kerb, is not
obliged to keep his eyes on the ground to see whether or
not there is any obstacle in his path.[5]

---

4. [1947] 2 All ER 197 per Lord Goddard CJ at 198.
5. See also the speech of Lord Reid in *Haley* v *London Electricity Board* [1965] AC 778
    at 790, [1964] 3 WLR 479, [1964] 3 All ER 185 (HL), where it was said "I agree ...
    that a person walking along a pavement does not have to keep his eyes to the
    ground to see whether or not there is an obstacle in his path."

0%   ## GOODMAN v LUTON BOROUGH COUNCIL

Unreported, 1989 (QBD)

G was walking along a pavement when she tripped over a paving stone that was sticking up by about an inch. The allegation of contributory negligence failed. It was said:

> "Anybody using a footpath or pavement or a highway has to exercise reasonable care for his or her own safety and they have to look out for obvious dangers ... [The claimant] was walking along the pavement on her way to work, striding out, no doubt, as it was a cold morning; she may have been guilty of inadvertence in not spotting the tripping place ... but I do not think she was guilty of any negligence."[6]

---

6.   Per Lord Hooson QC.

3. FALLING

80%   **STRACHAN v HIGHLAND COUNCIL**

1999 GWD 38–1863 (SP)

S, while under the influence of drink, had stepped over a section of dilapidated fence from a car park maintained by HC and onto a path, where he was walking near the edge of a cliff in the early hours of the morning when he lost his footing and fell to the shore. It was found that:

(1) HC knew that people would be in the vicinity of the cliff;

(2) the cliff was a natural and obvious hazard;

(3) even a dilapidated fence was a visible barrier;

(4) where a normal adult deliberately chose to cross an obvious barrier and proceed to a place of obvious danger, he was the sole author of his own misfortune; and

(5) if that were wrong, S would have been found to have been contributorily negligent to the extent of 80%.

75%   **LOGUE v FLYING COLOURS LTD**

Unreported, 2001 (CC)

L was on holiday in Ibiza. He went out one night and had a considerable amount to drink, returning to his hotel room at 6 am. He awoke at 9 am and lost his balance and fell as he was getting out of bed. He put a hand out to stop his fall and it went through the glass patio window of his bedroom, causing him injuries. The glass was not toughened and whilst it was in accordance with the local Spanish standards, it was not compliant with British standards or UK Building Regulations. The claim under the Package Travel, Package Holidays and Package Tours Regulations 1992 failed as it was found that there had been no improper performance of the contract, local standards having been complied with. Contributory negligence would have been assessed at 75%, as L had been considerably affected by drink and this was a major cause of the accident.

50%   **GABBEDEY v BUTLER'S WHARF LTD**

[1962] 1 Lloyd's Rep 444 (QBD)

G was descending a steep flight of steps at BW's quay when he slipped and fell. The steps were defective, but G's contributory negligence in descending the steps with his back to them was assessed at 50%.

50%   ### A C BILLINGS & SONS v RIDEN

[1958] AC 240, [1957] 3 WLR 496, [1957] 3 All ER 1 (HL)

ACB were building contractors who dug up the sloping ramp leading to the front door of a house and removed the railings that had been either side of the ramp. As no plank was provided, the only practicable way to get to the house was to approach through the neighbouring property by passing through some shrubs, over a muddy patch and then to step up two or three feet to the remaining part of the ramp by the front door. R, aged 71, visited the house one evening and entered via the means described above. It was dark when she attempted to leave the property by the same route and she had no torch and refused an offer of assistance. She fell on attempting to step down from the ramp into the neighbouring property. R's contributory negligence was assessed at 50%. She should have accepted the offer of assistance and taken greater care when climbing down to the neighbouring property.

33.33%   ### RAE v MARS (UK) LTD

[1990] 3 EG 80 (QBD)

R, a surveyor, was inspecting premises. The occupiers failed to warn him that the floor level of an unlit storeroom was three feet below the level of the doorway. R fell as he entered the storeroom. As R had failed to switch on his torch or cast his eyes to the ground, he was found to have been contributorily negligent to the extent of one third.

25%   ## SAYERS v HARLOW UDC

[1958] 1 WLR 623, [1958] 2 All ER 342 (CA)

S found herself locked in a toilet cubicle as a result of a defective lock. She tried to escape by climbing over the door and placed a foot on a revolving toilet roll. She realised that she was not going to be able to escape this way and tried to climb down. In so doing, she put weight on the toilet roll, which revolved and she fell. It was held that it was reasonable in the circumstances for S to have explored the possibility of escaping in the way that she did. However, S was careless in allowing her balance to depend upon the toilet roll and her contributory negligence was assessed at 25%.

25%   ## SCOLLEN v LEISURE HOLIDAYS LTD

Unreported, 1992 (CA)

S, who had been drinking, suffered fatal injuries when he fell over a retaining wall at a holiday camp whilst wandering in the dark. His contributory negligence was assessed at 25%.

10%   ## CRAIG v STRATHCLYDE REGIONAL COUNCIL

1998 Housing LR 104 (SH)

A nine-year-old boy was injured while carrying a bicycle down some stairs in complete darkness. SRC were in breach of a duty to light the stairway, but C was held to have been contributorily negligent to the extent of 10%.

4. OTHERS

0%   **VOLLANS v SIMCO SUPERMARKETS**

[1982] CLY 2142 (CC)

V sustained injuries when he mistook a plate-glass window next to an exit at SS' shop for an open door. The window normally bore advertisements, but these had been taken down so that the window could be cleaned. It was held that the removal of the advertisements had created a foreseeable risk of injury and there was no contributory negligence.

CHAPTER SIXTEEN
SPORTS

1. DIVING INTO SHALLOW WATER

100%   **DODGESON v AIRTOURS PLC**

[1992] CLY 3217 (CC)

D was injured when he dived into the shallow end of a swimming pool on holiday, without first checking its depth. It was held that checking the depth was a matter of common sense and D was the sole author of his misfortune.

70%   **BANKS v BURY BC**

[1990] CLY 3284 (QBD)

C was injured when he dived into the shallow end of a public swimming pool. The depth was difficult to gauge visually, but C had not taken steps to check it. There was an inadequate sign showing the depth, which was written on the side of the pool and easily obscured by other swimmers. C conceded substantial contributory negligence, which was found to amount to 70%.

66.66%   **TOMLINSON v CONGLETON BOROUGH COUNCIL**

(2002) *The Times*, March 22 (CA)

T, aged 18, went to a park on a hot day with some friends. He ignored warning signs forbidding swimming and dived into a shallow lake, suffering serious injuries when his head struck the bottom. The warning signs were habitually flouted and it was held that CBC were in breach of the duty imposed on them by the Occupiers' Liability Act 1984. The trial judge's assessment of two thirds contributory negligence was not interfered with.

66.66%   **HARRISON v THANET DISTRICT COUNCIL**

[1998] CLY 3918 (QBD)

H injured himself diving into the shallow sea from a promenade, which TDC had been negligent in failing to inspect and assess the risk thereof. Diving into water of an unknown depth was said to be foolhardy and H was found to have been contributorily negligent to the extent of two thirds.

65%   **GERAK v QUEEN IN RIGHT OF BRITISH COLUMBIA**

(1984) 59 BCLR 273 (Canada)

G was injured when he dived off a wharf into a lake during his first visit to a park. The wharf had been built for the use of swimmers and there were no signs warning that the water was shallow or prohibiting diving. It was held that whilst the wharf was an invitation to jump and dive, G should not have dived into unknown waters. He was held to have been contributorily negligent to the extent of 65%.

2. OTHERS

66.66%   **FOWLES v BEDFORDSHIRE CC**

[1995] PIQR P380 (CA)

F, aged 21, suffered spinal injures when he attempted a forward somersault at a youth centre whilst unsupervised. One of BCC's employees had assumed responsibility for teaching F to do somersaults, but had left some gym mats unsupervised. F was an accomplished athlete and attempted a dangerous gymnastic exercise after placing the gym mats too close to the wall. He was aware of the risks and had been showing off. Contributory negligence was assessed at two thirds.

50%   **CARRIERE v BOARD OF GRAVELBOURG SCHOOL DISTRICT**

[1977] 5 WWR 517 (Canada)

C, a teacher, was required to supervise ice-skating. She fell and injured herself having not watched her step. Her contributory negligence was assessed at 50%.

25%   **FEENEY v LYALL**

1991 SLT 156 (OH)

F, a golfer, moved onto an adjacent fairway to recover a ball. He was struck by a ball hit by another golfer, L, driving off on that fairway. The opinion was expressed that even had L seen F, F would have been 25% to blame for failing to check the actions of golfers on the tee of the fairway on which he was standing.

15%   **PAWLAK v DOUCETTE & REINKS**

[1985] 2 WWR 588 (Canada)

P, a beginner, went water skiing with D and R. R accelerated the boat suddenly and P grabbed the moving towrope and was injured. P was found to have been contributorily negligent to the extent of 15%.

0%   **BUTLER v VANN**

Unreported, 1991 (CA)

B, a 15-year-old in a motorcycle race, went off the course and got some tape from a poorly erected maker post entangled in his rear wheel. He continued the race without realising that the tape was wrapped around his wheel. However, in due course he had to stop to unravel the tape and as he did so he was hit by another rider. There was no contributory negligence.

CHAPTER SEVENTEEN
TRANSPORT

1. AIRCRAFT

0%   ## GOLDMAN v THAI AIRWAYS INTERNATIONAL LTD
           (1981) 125 SJ 413 (QBD)

G was injured when he was thrown from his seat owing to severe air turbulence whilst a passenger on an international flight. G had not been contributorily negligent in not wearing his seat belt, as the pilot had not switched the "fasten seat belts" sign on. However, the trial judge's finding of common law liability against TAI was reversed on appeal.[1]

2. BUSES

100%   ## MARSHALL v LINCOLNSHIRE ROADCAR CO LTD
           Unreported, 2000 (CA)

M injured her ankle when she fell whilst attempting to alight from a slow moving bus. It was held that the bus driver had been in breach of duty by opening the doors before the bus was stationary, but that M's actions either constituted 100% contributory negligence or a *novus actus interveniens*.

---

1   [1983] 1 WLR 1186, [1983] 3 All ER 693 (CA).

50%   **GUINNEAR v LONDON PASSENGER TRANSPORT BOARD**

(1948) 92 SJ 350 (KBD)

A bus driver slowed to around 3–4 mph to allow G to board a bus and accelerated whilst he was mounting, causing him to fall off and be injured. G's contributory negligence in boarding a moving bus was assessed at 50%.

25%   **WYNGROVE'S CURATOR BONIS v SCOTTISH OMNIBUSES LTD**

1965 SLT 286 (IH)[2]

A passenger was standing on the open platform of a moving bus waiting to alight. There was no central pillar to hold onto, but there were other handholds available. He lost his balance and fell off the bus, injuring himself. His contributory negligence in failing to hold on tightly was assessed at 25%.

0%   **AZZOPARDI v STATE TRANSPORT AUTHORITY**

(1982) 30 SASR 434 (Australia)

A boarded a bus and was walking down the aisle to a seat. The bus started suddenly and A fell. There were several hand holds on the bus, but in the circumstances, A was found not to have been contributorily negligent in not firmly holding on.

---

2.   However, the decision as to liability was reversed on appeal at 1966 SLT 273.

3. TRAINS

85%   **KARAMALIS v SOUTH AUSTRALIAN RAILWAYS COMMISSIONER**

(1976) 14 SASR 432 (Australia)

K cycled across a railway line into the path of a train, which
was unable to stop in time. It was held that the railway
authority were under a duty to take steps to ensure that
people using the railway crossing looked both ways before
doing so, but K had been contributorily negligent to the
extent of 85% in crossing in front of the train.[3]

75%   **NEWBOLD v BRITISH RAILWAYS BOARD**

[1981] CLY 305 (CA)

N was a passenger on a train arriving at a well lit station.
He alighted from the train and fell into the gap between
the train and the platform, which was considerably larger
than the normal sized gap between a train and a platform.
The edge of the platform was painted white and a porter
called out "mind the gap" as the train pulled in. N failed to
establish negligence on the part of BRB, but it was said that
had the claim succeeded, contributory negligence would
have been assessed at 75%.

---

3.   Cf *Skeen* v *British Railways Board* [1976] RTR 281 (QBD), where it was said that a
      passenger in a car could not have been expected to get out and look at the railway
      line and the driver could not have been expected to telephone from 1.5 miles
      away to ascertain train movements.

75%　　　**CASEY v HUGH, JAMES, JONES & JENKINS**

[1999] Lloyd's Rep PN 115 (QBD)

C took a short cut home one night and walked through some broken fencing guarding a railway line. He was walking along the middle of the railway track, when he was struck by a train, which was travelling at 6 mph. C was subsequently convicted of an offence of trespassing on the railway. C's claim against British Railways Board was struck out for want of prosecution. In subsequent proceedings in which C alleged that his solicitors had been negligent, it was said that the claim against British Railways Board would have had virtually no chance of success at trial, but that had it been successful, contributory negligence would have been assessed at around 75%.

75%　　　**UMEK v LONDON TRANSPORT EXECUTIVE**

(134) NLJ 522, [1984] CLY 2313 (QBD)

U was killed whilst crossing a railway line. As was common at the depot, U had ignored a notice forbidding people from crossing the railway lines and advising them to use a footbridge when the subway was closed. It was held that as LTE were aware of such conduct, they should have warned their train drivers. However, U's contributory negligence was assessed at 75%.

25%   **POOLE v STATE TRANSPORT AUTHORITY (RAIL DIVISION)**

(1982) 31 SASR 74 (Australia)

P was a passenger on a train, which overshot a platform. She was injured when stepping down from the train onto a sloping ramp at the end of the platform after another passenger had opened the door for her as she was laden with parcels. P's contributory negligence was assessed at 25%.[4]

20%   **HARRISON v BRITISH RAILWAYS BOARD**

[1981] 3 All ER 679 (QBD)

H was the guard on a train, which D attempted to board whilst it was moving. In those circumstances the system was that H was required to signal the driver to stop and/or apply the emergency brakes. H gave the wrong signal to the driver and the train continued. H then tried to grab hold of D, who fell off the train injuring H. It was held that a person being rescued who has not taken reasonable care for his own safety owes a duty of care to someone whom he ought reasonably to foresee might try to assist him. However, H had not applied the emergency brakes as required and his contributory negligence in failing to reduce the danger to himself was assessed at 20%.

---

4.   See also *Sharpe* v *Southern Railway* [1925] 2 KB 311 (CA), decided at a time when contributory negligence was a complete defence.

0%   **CATERSON v COMMISSIONER FOR RAILWAYS (NSW)**

(1973) 47 ALJR 249 (Australia)

C was saying goodbye to a friend at a railway station. While he was helping his friend onto the train, it began to move without warning. The next station was 80 miles away. The train was fitted with a stop cord. However, H jumped from the train and was injured. It was held on appeal that the jury were entitled to find that CFR had been negligent. Where CFR's negligence had put C in a position whereby he could only escape inconvenience by taking a risk, the reasonableness of C's actions could only be assessed by weighing the risk against the inconvenience. The jury were not bound to find contributory negligence on C's part.

0%   **HARE v BRITISH TRANSPORT COMMISSION**

[1956] 1 WLR 250, [1956] 1 All ER 578 (QBD)

H was at a railway station seeing her husband off on a train. She remained standing on the platform facing the same direction as the train, waving to her husband as it left the platform. After the train had moved about 60 yards she was struck from behind by the open door of the guard's van. There was no contributory negligence. H was facing her husband and entitled to assume that the doors would be closed.

0%   **MURRAY v LONDON, MIDLAND AND SCOTTISH RAILWAY
COMPANY**

1948 SLT (Sh Ct) 30 (SH)

M, a girl aged 14, was standing on a railway platform when
she was injured by a carriage door, which was opened
before the train stopped. No warning had been given for
those on the platform to stand back as the train
approached, even though the railway company knew that
it was common for people to open the doors on the train
before it had come to a halt. It was held that M was not
guilty of contributory negligence. She was, at most, guilty
of inadvertence in standing too close to the platform edge.

CHAPTER EIGHTEEN
TRESPASS TO THE PERSON

80%   **TUMELTY v MINISTRY OF DEFENCE**

[1988] 3 NIJB 51 (NIQB)

T was struck by a baton round fired by a soldier whilst he
was at the front of a group of rioters attacking the soldiers.
The soldier was justified in firing the baton round, but used
unreasonable force in aiming at T's head. T's contributory
negligence was assessed at 80%.

66.66%   **REVILL v NEWBERRY**

[1996] QB 567, [1996] 2 WLR 239, [1996] 1 All ER 291 (CA)

N, aged 76, was sleeping in his garden shed in order to protect valuable items stored therein, when he was awoken by the sound of R trying to break in. N took his shotgun and without being able to see if there was anyone in front of the door, fired a shot through a hole in the door, which hit and wounded R. R was subsequently convicted of various offences committed that night and N was acquitted of a charge of wounding. R brought proceedings alleging a breach of the Occupiers' Liability Act 1984 and negligence. N counterclaimed for shock and distress. It was found that whilst N had not intended to hit R, he was negligent in firing the gun and had used greater force than was justified in lawful self defence. R's contributory negligence was assessed at two thirds. His decision and subsequent actions were taken at leisure and in full knowledge of their criminality, whereas allowance should be made for N's fears having been awoken in the middle of the night. Overall, R was twice as much to blame as N.

50%   **WASSON v CHIEF CONSTABLE OF THE ROYAL ULSTER CONSTABULARY**

[1987] 8 NIJB 34 (NIQB)

W was participating in a riot when he was struck in the head by a baton round fired by a police officer. CCRUC failed to discharge the onus on him to show that reasonable force was used, but as W's presence at and participation in the riot contributed to his injures, his contributory negligence was assessed at 50%.

33.33%   **STEELE v NORTHERN IRELAND OFFICE**

[1988] 12 NIJB 1 (NIQB)

S was remanded in custody charged with sexual offences against his daughter. On arrival in prison he was advised by a prison officer to seek protection due to the nature of his alleged offences. S said that he did not need protection, but was later assaulted by other prisoners in the exercise yard. It was found that NIO should have exercised greater care, but S's damages were reduced by one third to take account of his contributory negligence in failing to heed the advice given to him.

33.33%   **WARD v CHIEF CONSTABLE OF THE ROYAL ULSTER CONSTABULARY**

[2000] NI 543 (NIQB)

A police office pushed W over a wall when she remonstrated with him during the arrest of her son. It was found that she made some minor contact with the officer, but the police officer had used excessive force. W bore partial responsibility for the damage she suffered and her contributory negligence was assessed at one third.

MURPHY v CULHANE

[1977] QB 94, [1976] 3 WLR 458, [1976] 3 All ER 533 (CA)

M and others went to C's house with the intention of assaulting C. Upon arrival, M initiated a criminal affray in the course of which C struck him a fatal blow to the head with a plank. C subsequently pleaded guilty to M's manslaughter. It was said that M's widow's damages might be reduced to take account of his contributory negligence as M could fairly be regarded as partly responsible for the damage he suffered. However, on the facts, the claim was likely to fail on the grounds of *volenti non fit injuria* and/or *ex turpi causa*.

0%

BARNES v NAYER

(1986) *The Times*, December 19 (CA)

B's widower brought proceedings against N claiming damages arising out of his unlawful killing of B. B and N were neighbours and it was said that N and his family had been subjected to insults, abuse and minor assaults by B and her family over a period of time. On the day in question N claimed that B had provoked an assault by N by goading their respective sons to fight each other and threatening N's son with violence. N reacted by killing B with a machete, nearly severing her head completely. N was subsequently convicted of manslaughter by reason of diminished responsibility. The Court of Appeal upheld an order granting B's widower summary judgment. It was said that contributory fault on the part of the claimant could afford a defence to a claim for trespass to the person. However, on the facts of the case the disparity between B's acts and N's response was so great that no judge could hold that there was any contributory fault on the part of B or her family.

0%   ## LANE v HOLLOWAY

[1968] 1 QB 379, [1967] 3 WLR 1003, [1967] 3 All ER
129 (CA)

Relations between L and H had been strained for some time
and one evening H's wife yelled abuse at L, who replied
"shut up, you monkey-faced tart". L then challenged H to
a fight. L punched H in the shoulder and H responded by
punching L severely in the eye, hospitalising him for a
month. It was found that H went much too far and the
defence of *volenti non fit injuria* did not apply. The
argument that L's conduct and provocation constituted
contributory negligence was rejected. It was further held
that whilst provocation by a claimant victim might reduce
or extinguish any aggravated or exemplary damages, it
would not reduce the award of compensatory damages. It
was said:

> "I entirely reject the contention that because [a
> claimant] who has suffered a civil wrong has behaved
> badly, this is a matter which the court may take into
> account when awarding him compensatory damages
> for physical injuries which he has sustained as the
> result of the wrong which has been unlawfully inflicted
> on him ... I cannot see how logically or on any
> principle of law the fact that [the claimant] has
> behaved rather badly and is a cantankerous old man
> can be even material when considering what is the
> proper compensation for the physical injury which he
> has suffered."[1]

---

1.   [1968] 1 QB 379 per Salmon LJ at 390.

0%   ## MULLANEY v CHIEF CONSTABLE OF WEST MIDLANDS POLICE

Unreported, 2001 (CA)

M was a probationary police officer who was seriously injured when he was assaulted by someone he was attempting to arrest for importuning in a public lavatory. It was held that CCWMP was liable for the failure of fellow officers to respond to radio calls and come to M's assistance. Subject to public policy considerations, CCWMP was under a duty not to expose officers to an unnecessary risk of injury. This included a duty to exercise reasonable care to ensure that a safe system of work was provided. It was alleged that M was guilty of contributory negligence in: (1) entering the lavatories by himself when M and the other officers involved in the operation had been told to operate in pairs and (2) persisting in his efforts to arrest the suspect after he had become violent. It was found that M was guilty of a misjudgement in going into the lavatories alone, but was not guilty of contributory negligence. He had allowed his enthusiasm for his duty to overcome any caution that he might otherwise have had. The Court of Appeal approved the trial judge's remark that:

> "police officers should not be discouraged from doing their duty by fear of a finding of contributory negligence against them if, in consequence of a misjudgement, they sustain injury."

M was a very inexperienced officer doing his best in circumstances in which he had no reason to expect an attack of such a nature and in which he could reasonably expect back up if he called for assistance. The allegation that M should not have persevered in the arrest was also rejected. M was doing no more than he, in the heat of the moment and with some bravery, thought was his duty. Accordingly, there was no contributory negligence.

CHAPTER NINETEEN
MISCELLANEOUS

1. ANIMALS

See also page 55 above.

CUMMINGS v GRAINGER

[1976] QB 397, [1976] 3 WLR 842, [1977] 1 All ER 104
(CA)[1]

The trial judge found the claimant to have been 50% to
blame for her injuries when she trespassed at a scrap yard,
where she knew there to be a ferocious dog and was
attacked by the dog. However, the Court of Appeal found
the claimant to have voluntarily accepted the risk in
addition to finding the defendant not to have been
unreasonable in having the dog guard his scrap yard.

---

1.   The first instance decision is reported at [1975] 1 WLR 1330, [1975] 2 All ER 1129
      (QBD).

BEHRENS v BERTRAM MILLS CIRCUS LTD

[1957] 2 QB 1, [1957] 2 WLR 404, [1957] 1 All ER 583
(QBD)

B and his wife were part of an act at BM's circus. They
occupied a booth in a passageway, along which elephants
passed to get to the circus ring. B's manager brought a dog
into the booth and as the elephants passed, the dog ran out
and barked at them. This frightened the elephants, which
chased after the dog and knocked down the booth. B, who
was inside the booth, was not injured, but the shock
required him to go to bed for a week. BM alleged that B had
been contributorily negligent in permitting the dog to be
in the area, which he knew was forbidden. The defence
failed as it was found that B had not permitted the dog to
be there. It was said:

> "There are many cases in which liability has been
> successfully contested on the ground that the savage
> animal was teased or provoked by the [claimant]. I see
> no reason why the same sort of defence should not
> prevail where the fault of the [claimant] does not
> amount to recklessness of this sort, but is failure of due
> diligence to look after his own safety."[2]

0%   ## GORDON v MACKENZIE

1913 SC 109 (IH)[3]

G was bitten when he patted an unfamiliar dog in the
street. There was found to have been no contributory
negligence.

---

2.   [1957] 2 QB 1 per Devlin J at 19.
3.   Decided before the Animals Act 1971 and the LR(CN)A 1945.

2. BURNS, FUMES & SCALDS

80%   **SYKES v HARRY**

[2001] QB 1014, [2001] 3 WLR 62 (CA)

The tenant of a property suffered carbon monoxide
poisoning from fumes discharged by a defective gas heater
installed in the property by the landlord. The landlord was
found to be liable for the personal injuries caused thereby
pursuant to section 4 of the Defective Premises Act 1972.
However, the tenant was aware that the gas fire had not
been serviced for a period of eight years and that servicing
was desirable. He had also encountered some problems
with the fire, notably a yellow flame, which he was aware
signified a defect. The tenant's contributory negligence was
assessed at 80% in not arranging for the gas fire to be
serviced, which would have rectified the defect.

50%   **McBRIEN v THE ARDEN & COBDEN HOTELS LTD**

(1963) 107 SJ 791 (CA)

M was employed as a waitress at ACH's hotel. She was
provided with an electric heater in her bedroom, which
both parties knew to be defective. M switched the heater
on, and finding after a few minutes that it did not appear
to be working, deliberately touched the element and was
burned. M's contributory negligence was assessed at 50%.

25%   **LOWERY v VICKERS ARMSTRONG (ENGINEERS) LTD**

(1969) 8 KIR 603 (CA)

L, a maintenance man, was called to attend to a possible leakage of gas at VA's premises. He had been summoned by two other employees of VA, who had lit a gas fire and ring to keep themselves warm. They had noticed a smell of escaping gas, but had not turned the flames off. L arrived at the premises and was unable to smell any gas. He lit a taper to look at the pipes for the leak, but as he stamped out the taper, there was an explosion caused by a build up of gas beneath the floorboards. In the claim by VA against the gas supplier it was held that VA's employees' contributory negligence in not turning the flames off and lighting a taper amounted to 25%.

0%   **FOULDER v CANADIAN PACIFIC STEAMSHIPS LTD**

[1969] 1 All ER 283, [1968] 2 Lloyd's Rep 366 (QBD)

F was employed on CPS' vessel. Negligently and in breach of the applicable regulations, the shower provided for F discharged scalding water and did not have an anti-scalding mixing valve enabling F to select an appropriate water temperature. F, who had been drinking, entered the shower and was scalded by the very hot water. It was held that F had not been contributorily negligent in failing to test the water temperature before entering the shower.

3. FAILING TO GUARD AGAINST THEFT

25%   **PETROVITCH v CALLINGHAMS LTD**

[1969] 2 Lloyd's Rep 386 (QBD)

C were decorators carrying out work to the interior of P's house. C left the front door open and unattended, but obstructed by a stepladder. However, whilst C were in the house a thief entered and stole P's jewellery. C were held to have been negligent, but P's contributory negligence in leaving her jewellery boxes unlocked in an unlocked room was assessed at 25%.

0%   **OLLEY v MARLBOROUGH COURT**

[1949] 1 KB 532, [1949] 1 All ER 127 (CA)[4]

O was a resident at MC's hotel. She went out and left the key to her room hanging on a board in the hotel office. She returned to find that someone had entered the hotel, removed the key from the office and stolen items from her room. MC had been negligent in not keeping a watch over the open front door. O had not been contributorily negligent as she was entitled to expect that a reasonable watch would be kept on the hotel to prevent undesirable strangers from coming into the hotel.

---

4.   See also the First Instance decision at [1948] 1 All ER 955.

4. FAILING TO TURN WATER OFF IN COLD WEATHER

50%   ## R A BRAND & CO v SAMUEL BARROW & CO

(1965) 109 SJ 834, [1965] CLY 2648 (CA)

RAB were the occupiers of the basement of a building, which was where the main stopcock for the whole building was situated. SB occupied the higher floors of the building and negligently failed to turn off a stopcock controlling water flowing into a tank in their part of the building during severe weather. A pipe above SB's stopcock burst and the basement was flooded. It was held that RAB's contributory negligence in failing to turn off the main stopcock amounted to 50%.

20%   ## C B PRINTERS v P & C MANUFACTURING CO

(1968) 206 EG 311 (CA)

PCM occupied the third floor of a building under a lease from CBP. A pipe froze in PCM's part of the building and when the temperature rose again water flowed out of the pipe and flooded the basement, damaging CBP's goods. PCM were found to have been negligent, but it was held that CBP had been contributorily negligent to the extent of 20% in failing to take reasonable care of their goods, for example by cutting off the water supply or asking PCM to do so.

5. LOSS OF COMPTER DATA

50%   **LOGICAL COMPUTER SUPPLIES LTD v EURO CAR PARKS LTD**

Current Law Dec/2001 (QBD)

Unqualified employees of LCS negligently damaged the hard disk on ECP's computerised accounts system, which destroyed data and caused significant disruption to ECP's business. However, ECP's damages were reduced by 50% to take account of their contributory negligence in incorrectly operating the back up system (incorrect tapes and unqualified staff), such that it had completely failed to operate during the period in which the data was lost and for the preceding year and also in failing to check that the back up system was functioning.

APPENDIX

THE LAW REFORM

(CONTRIBUTORY NEGLIGENCE)

ACT 1945

LAW REFORM (CONTRIBUTORY NEGLIGENCE) ACT 1945

(8 & 9 Geo 6 c 28)

An Act to amend the law relating to contributory negligence and for purposes connected therewith

[15 June 1945]

1. Apportionment of liability in case of contributory negligence

(1) Where any person suffers damage as the result partly of his own fault and partly of the fault of any other person or persons, a claim in respect of that damage shall not be defeated by reason of the fault of the person suffering the damage, but the damages recoverable in respect thereof shall be reduced to such extent as the court thinks just and equitable having regard to the claimant's share in the responsibility for the damage:

Provided that –

(a) this subsection shall not operate to defeat any defence arising under a contract;

(b) where any contract or enactment providing for the limitation of liability is applicable to the claim, the amount of damages recoverable by the claimant by virtue of this subsection shall not exceed the maximum limit so applicable.

(2) Where damages are recoverable by any person by virtue of the foregoing subsection subject to such reduction as is therein mentioned, the court shall find and record the total damages which would have been recoverable if the claimant had not been at fault.

(3), (4) ...

(5) Where, in any case to which subsection (1) of this section applies, one of the persons at fault avoids liability to any other such person or his personal representative by pleading the Limitation Act 1939, or any other enactment limiting the time within which proceedings may be taken, he shall not be

entitled to recover any damages ... from that other person or representative by virtue of the said subsection.[1]

(6)   Where any case to which subsection (1) of this section applies is tried with a jury, the jury shall determine the total damages which would have been recoverable if the claimant had not been at fault and the extent to which those damages are to be reduced.

(7)   ...

2.   *(Repeated by the National Insurance (Industrial Injuries) Act 1946, s 89(1), Sch 9.)*

3.   Saving for Maritime Conventions Act 1911, and past cases

(1)   This Act shall not apply to any claim to which section one of the Maritime Conventions Act 1911 applies and that Act shall have effect as if this Act had not passed.

(2)   This Act shall not apply to any case where the acts or omissions giving rise to the claim occurred before the passing of this Act.

4.   Interpretation

The following expressions have the meanings hereby respectively assigned to them, that is to say –

"court" means, in relating to any claim, the court or arbitrator by or before whom the claim falls to be determined;

"damage" includes loss of life and personal injury;

...

"fault" means negligence, breach of statutory duty or other act or omission which gives rise to a liability in tort or would, apart from this Act, give rise to the defence of contributory negligence;

5.   Application to Scotland

In the application of this Act to Scotland:

(a)   the expression "dependant" means, in relating to any person, any person who would in the event of such first mentioned person's death through the fault of a third party be entitled to sue that third party for damages or solatium; and the expression "fault" means wrongful act, breach of statutory duty or negligent act or omission which gives rise to liability in damages, or would apart from this Act, give rise to the defence of contributory negligence;

(b)   for any reference to section six of the Law Reform (Married Women and Tortfeasors) Act, 1935, there shall be substituted a reference to section three

---

1.   Sub-section (3) and words omitted from (5) were repealed by the Civil Liability (Contribution) Act 1978, s 9(2), Sched 2. Sub-section (4) was repealed by the Fatal Accidents Act 1976, s 6(2), Sched 2, and sub-section (7) by the Carriage by Air Act 1961, s 14(3), Sched 2.

of the Law Reform (Miscellaneous Provisions) (Scotland) Act, 1940 (which relates to contribution among joint wrongdoers);

(c) for subsection 4 of section one the following subsection shall be substituted –

"(4) Where any person dies as the result partly of his own fault and partly of the fault of any other person or persons, a claim by any dependant of the first mentioned person for damages or solatium in respect of that person's death shall not be defeated by reason of his fault, but the damages or solatium recoverable shall be reduced to such extent as the court thinks just and equitable having regard to the share of the said person in the responsibility for his death."

6. Provisions as to Northern Ireland

(1) ...

(2) This Act, ... shall not extend to Northern Ireland.

7. Short title and extent

This Act may be cited as the Law Reform (Contributory Negligence) Act 1945.

INDEX